AF867179

Economic Crisis in Europe

Economic Crisis in Europe

What It Means for the EU and Russia

Edited by

Joan DeBardeleben
Professor, Institute of European, Russian and Eurasian Studies, Carleton University, Canada

and

Crina Viju
Assistant Professor, Institute of European, Russian and Eurasian Studies, Carleton University, Canada

palgrave
macmillan

Selection, Editorial Matter, Introduction and Conclusion © Joan DeBardeleben and Crina Viju 2013
Individual chapters © Respective authors 2013

All rights reserved. No reproduction, copy or transmission of this publication may be made without written permission.

No portion of this publication may be reproduced, copied or transmitted save with written permission or in accordance with the provisions of the Copyright, Designs and Patents Act 1988, or under the terms of any licence permitting limited copying issued by the Copyright Licensing Agency, Saffron House, 6–10 Kirby Street, London EC1N 8TS.

Any person who does any unauthorized act in relation to this publication may be liable to criminal prosecution and civil claims for damages.

The authors have asserted their rights to be identified as the authors of this work in accordance with the Copyright, Designs and Patents Act 1988.

First published 2013 by
PALGRAVE MACMILLAN

Palgrave Macmillan in the UK is an imprint of Macmillan Publishers Limited, registered in England, company number 785998, of Houndmills, Basingstoke, Hampshire RG21 6XS.

Palgrave Macmillan in the US is a division of St Martin's Press LLC, 175 Fifth Avenue, New York, NY 10010.

Palgrave Macmillan is the global academic imprint of the above companies and has companies and representatives throughout the world.

Palgrave® and Macmillan® are registered trademarks in the United States, the United Kingdom, Europe and other countries.

ISBN 978–1–137–00522–9

This book is printed on paper suitable for recycling and made from fully managed and sustained forest sources. Logging, pulping and manufacturing processes are expected to conform to the environmental regulations of the country of origin.

A catalogue record for this book is available from the British Library.

Library of Congress Cataloging-in-Publication Data
Economic crisis in Europe : what it means for the EU and Russia /
edited by Joan DeBardeleben, Crina Viju.
p. cm.
Summary: "This interdisciplinary volume probes the economic and political impact of both, the 2008–09 financial-economic crisis and the subsequent sovereign debt crisis in Europe. Basing their analysis on a well-researched depiction of the origins and scope of the crisis, leading experts from Europe and North America critically examine its potentially destabilizing political effects. These include questions on the capacity of the European Union to respond swiftly and effectively, challenges to key EU policy commitments (such as climate change and anti-protectionist trade policies), and the manner in which potentially discontent electorates hold their leaders to account. This volume is unique in devoting special attention to the post–communist states, both those that have joined the European Union as well as Russia, and suggests that a global crisis of this type does not respect traditional political or economic boundaries, but rather that it has effects at the regional, national and supranational level. By extending the geographic scope, the authors address important questions about why some countries have suffered more that others and what the crisis will mean for the future shape of Europe"— Provided by publisher.
ISBN 978–1–137–00522–9 (hardback)
1. Financial crises—European Union countries. 2. European Union countries—Economic policy. 3. European Union countries—Economic conditions. 4. Global Financial Crisis, 2008–2009. 5. Russia (Federation)—Economic conditions—1991– I. DeBardeleben, Joan. II. Viju, Crina.
HB3782.E25 2013
330.94—dc23 2012045205

10 9 8 7 6 5 4 3 2 1
22 21 20 19 18 17 16 15 14 13

We dedicate this volume to one of our authors, Ivanka Petrovka, who, sadly, passed away before her work could be completed for inclusion in this book. Ivanka was the founder and chairperson of the Economic Policy Institute, Sofia, Bulgaria; visiting professor at the Technical University of Sofia; former Ambassador of the Republic of Bulgaria to the Swiss Confederation at Bern (2002–04); and Deputy Chairperson of the Bulgarian Stock Exchange (1997–2001). Her main areas of research and teaching were international banking and finance, as well as the financial and macroeconomic aspects of transformation. She is greatly missed.

Contents

Illustrations

Figures

Tables

Acknowledgements

This volume is a publication of the Centre for European Studies (CES) at Carleton University in Ottawa, Canada. The Centre is grateful for financial support to enable completion of this volume from Carleton University and from the European Union, the latter based on a grant to CES, which was designated an EU Centre of Excellence by the European Commission in 2006. We also acknowledge support from the Social Sciences and Humanities Research Council (SSHRC) of Canada for supporting the research that formed the basis of some of the chapters in this volume. We are particularly grateful to our copy editor, Jane Freeland, who contributed countless hours and unwavering attention in preparing each and every chapter. We thank all of the authors for the collective effort that went into producing a coherent approach and for their attention to our many suggestions, requests, and inquiries; we are especially grateful to Jon H. Pammett for his assistance in reviewing the final version of the manuscript.

Of course, this publication reflects the views of the authors for each chapter; none of the sponsoring organizations are responsible for the content, and the contents of this publication can in no way be taken to reflect the views of the European Union.

Joan DeBardeleben and Crina Viju

Abbreviations

AAU	Assigned Amounts Unit
AD	Anti-Dumping
AIA	Abnormal Importations Act
AIG	American International Group
BP	British Petroleum
BRIC	Brazil, Russia, India and China
BZÖ	Alliance for the Future of Austria
CCL	Contingent Credit Line
CDM	Clean Development Mechanism
CDU/CSU	Christian Democratic Union/Christian Social Union of Bavaria
CEE	Central and Eastern Europe
CEECs	Central and East European countries
CER	Certified Emissions Reduction
CPRF	Communist Party of the Russian Federation
CSSD	Czech Social Democratic Party
CVD	Countervailing Duty
EBRD	European Bank for Reconstruction and Development
EC	European Commission
ECB	European Central Bank
EEC	European Economic Community
EFSF	European Financial Stability Facility
EIB	European Investment Bank
EMU	Economic and Monetary Union
EP	European Parliament
EPP	Euro Plus Pact
ESFS	European System of Financial Supervisors
ESM	European Stability Mechanism
ESRC	European Systemic Risk Council
EU	European Union
EUA	European Union Allowances
EU ETS	European Union Emissions Trading Scheme
EUROREG	Centre for European Regional and Local Studies (Warsaw)
FCL	Flexible Credit Line
FDI	Foreign Direct Investments
FOMC	Federal Reserve's Federal Open Market Committee

G8	Group of Eight
G20	Group of Twenty
GATT	General Agreement on Tariffs and Trade
GDP	Gross Domestic Product
GHG	Greenhouse Gases
IBRD	International Bank for Reconstruction and Development
IGC	Intergovernmental Conferences
IFIAC	International Financial Institutions Advisory Commission
IMF	International Monetary Fund
IPRs	Investment or Intellectual Property Rights
LDC	Less Developed Countries
LNG	Liquefied Natural Gas
LVL	Latvian Lats
MFA	Multi-Fiber Arrangements
NTBs	Non-Tariff Barriers
ODS	Czech Civic Democratic Party
OECD	Organisation for Economic Co-operation and Development
OMAs	Orderly Market Arrangements
PASOK	Panhellenic Socialist Movement
PMR	Greater Romania Party
PRGF	Poverty Reduction and Growth Facility
PvdA	Dutch Labour Party
PVV	Dutch Party for Freedom
R&D	Research and Development
RZS	Order, Law and Justice Party of Bulgaria
SBA	Stand-by Arrangement
SGP	Stability and Growth Pact
SK	The Blue Coalition Party of Bulgaria
SMER	Slovak Direction-Social Democracy Party
SPD	Social Democratic Party
SPÖ	Socialist Party of Austria
SPS	Sanitary and Phytosanitary
TBT	Technical Barriers to Trade
UK	United Kingdom
UNCTAD	United Nations Conference on Trade and Development
US	United States
VAT	Value Added Tax
VERs	Voluntary Export Restraints
VVD	Party for Freedom of the Netherlands
WEO	World Energy Outlook
WTO	World Trade Organization

Contributors

Editors

Joan DeBardeleben is Chancellor's Professor in the Institute of European, Russian, and Eurasian Studies at Carleton University in Ottawa, Canada, and holds a Jean Monnet Chair in the EU's Eastern Neighbourhood Relations. She is the founder and Director of Carleton University's EU Centre of Excellence, the university's Centre for European Studies; she is also Director of the Canada–Europe Transatlantic Dialogue (www.canada-europe-dialogue.ca), which is a major Canada–Europe research network funded by the Social Sciences and Humanities Research Council of Canada. Professor DeBardeleben has written extensively on Russian politics, the EU's relations with its eastern neighbours (including Russia), and topics related to citizen participation, federalism, and public opinion in Russia. She has edited numerous volumes relating to these subjects and to the European Union, most recently (with Achim Hurrelmann) *Transnational Europe: Promise, Paradox, Limits* (2011); *The Boundaries of EU Enlargement: Finding a Place for Neighbours* (editor and co-author, 2008); (with Jon H. Pammett) *Activating the Citizenship: Dilemmas of Citizen Participation in Europe and Canada* (2009); and (with Achim Hurrelmann) *Democratic Dilemmas of Multilevel Governance: Legitimacy, Representation and Accountability in the European Union* (2007). She has been Visiting Researcher at the Mannheim Centre for European Social Research (Germany) and at the German Institute for International Affairs (Stiftung Wissenschaft und Politik, Berlin, Germany). She is also a co-author, providing the section on the Russian Federation for the widely used university textbooks *European Politics in Transition*, 6th edition (Mark Kesselmann et al., 2009) and *Introduction to Comparative Politics*, 6th edition (Mark Kesselmann, Joel Krieger, and William A. Joseph, eds, 2013).

Crina Viju was born and raised in the southern part of Romania. After she received her BSc and MSc in Business Data Processing from the University "Babes-Bolyai" of Cluj-Napoca, Romania, she moved to the Mediterranean Agronomic Institute of Chania (MAICH), Crete, Greece, where she obtained an MSc in Economic and Management

Science. In 2008, she completed a PhD in Agricultural Economics at the University of Saskatchewan. For a period of two years, from 2007 to 2009, Dr Viju worked as Assistant Professor at Johnson-Shoyama School of Public Policy, University of Regina, Canada. In 2009, she became Assistant Professor at the Institute of European, Russian and Eurasian Studies at Carleton University in Ottawa, Canada. Dr Viju has a strong background in applied economic theory and contemporary quantitative methods. Her expertise applies to questions relating to the economic effects of different trade policies applied within the United States, Canada, and the EU; European economic integration; economies in transition; and EU enlargement.

Contributors

Patrick Conway is the Bowman and Gordon Gray Professor of Economics at the University of North Carolina (UNC) at Chapel Hill, USA. He has been in the faculty of UNC since 1983. During this time, he has taught courses in introductory economics, international economics, development economics, and macroeconomics both to undergraduate and graduate students. Dr Conway was awarded the university-wide William C. Friday Award for excellence in teaching, and has been inducted into the Order of the Golden Fleece and the Frank Porter Graham Honour Society. He received a Pew Faculty Fellowship in International Affairs from Harvard University, USA, for his innovative use of cases in instruction. Dr Conway is the author of three books and many refereed journal articles. His current research interests include the impact of the IMF lending programmes on emerging-economy welfare, the development of financial markets in transition economies, the welfare impact of exchange-rate depreciation in developing countries, and the dynamic adjustment of import-competing industries to international competition. He was named a Council on Foreign Relations fellow in 1989 for his work on the implications of the debt crisis for developing countries.

Piotr Dutkiewicz is Professor of Political Science at Carleton University in Ottawa, Canada. He was educated at Warsaw University (LLM), Poland, and the Russian Academy of Science (PhD), Moscow, Russia. Dr Dutkiewicz has been the director of four large-scale high-visibility projects in Russia funded by the Canadian International Development Agency (CIDA) (on regional development, unemployment insurance, labour market, and social policies). He was also a member of a Canadian

Official State delegation to Russia in 2003 (led by Gov. General Adrienne Clarkson). In May 2006, he received a doctorate *Honoris Causa* from the People's Friendship University, Russia, and in 2007 an honorary degree from the Russian Academy of Public Administration in Moscow, Russia, for the 'very significant contribution to the development of Canada-Russia relations and quality of research'. He is a member of the Valdai Club, a group of 40 world-renowned experts on Russia. In 2009, he received the Russian Federation's Order of Friendship from President Dmitry Medvedev. His most recent book, co-edited with Dmitri Trenin, is *Russia – The Challenges of Transformation* (2011).

Grzegorz Gorzelak is Professor of Economics, specializing in regional and local development and policies. He is the Director of the Centre for European Regional and Local Studies (EUROREG) at Warsaw University, Poland, as well as President of the Polish Section of the Regional Studies Association. Professor Gorzelak has conducted research on multivariate statistical comparisons, regional and local development in Poland and Central Europe, and post-socialist transition. He was advisor to the Polish government during the local government reform in 1990, manager of the PHARE program for local government (1991), and a consultant to several local and regional authorities on development strategies in Poland and in Ukraine. A member of several advisory councils to the Polish government and of two committees of the Polish Academy of Sciences, Dr Gorzelak has also coordinated several Polish and international (also EU-financed) research programmes on regional development, regional policy, post-socialist transition, and evaluation of the EU Cohesion Policy. He has published (as author and editor) over 50 books (several of them in English) and over 230 articles, and he is Editor-in Chief of the journal *Studia Regionalne i Lokalne.*

András Inotai is a widely published expert on the economic integration of the new Member States of Central and Eastern Europe into the European Union, on Hungarian economic policy, and on structural changes in the global economy. He was Director General of the Institute for World Economics of the Hungarian Academy of Science (Budapest, Hungary) from 1991 to 2011; the Institute studies global medium-term economic development trends and their impact on Hungary, the economic development of Europe and of Hungary, interregional economic cooperation, and successful and failed attempts at economic modernization in various countries and regions. Dr Inotai began working at the Institute in 1967 as a research fellow. In 1972, he began teaching at San Marcos University in Lima, Peru, and he also worked at the World Bank's Trade Policy Division in Washington, DC. Between 1995 and 1998 he headed the Strategic Task Force that prepared Hungary for the start of official EU accession negotiations. He recently published 'Trade Developments of New EU Member Countries: Defying Theoretical Fundamentals or Adjusting to New Realities?' in Elzbieta Kawecka-Wyrzykowska, ed., *Five Years of the EU Eastward Enlargement Effects on Visegrad Countries: Lessons for the Future* (Warsaw: Warsaw School of Economics, 2009), pp. 245–283; 'After the Crisis', *Public Finance Quarterly* no. 3 (2011), pp. 360–378; 'Remarks on the Future of the European Union: Domestic and Global Challenges Ahead', *Romanian Journal of European Affairs* 11 (4, 2011), pp. 7–11; and 'European Integration at the Crossroads', *International Issues and Slovak Foreign Policy* XX (4, 2011), pp. 53–65.

Vladislav Inozemtsev is Professor of Economics and Director of the Centre for Post-Industrial Studies in Moscow, Russia. He serves as the Presidium Member of both the Russian Council on Foreign and Defence Policy and the Russian International Affairs Council. He has authored several books, some of which have been translated into English, French, and Chinese. The most recent are *The Constitution of the Post-Economic State. Post-Industrial Theories and Post-Economic Trends in the Contemporary World* (1998) and *Catching-Up? The Limits of Rapid Economic Development* (2002). He contributes often to both the Russian daily press (*Vedomosti, Izvestiia, Moskovskii Komsomolets*) and Western journals (*The American Interest* and *Internationale Politik*).

William A. Kerr is currently University Distinguished Chair at the University of Saskatchewan, Canada. He has a BA in International Relations from the University of British Columbia, Canada, an MA in Economics (Trade and Development) from Simon Fraser University, Canada, and a PhD in Economics and Agricultural Economics from the University of British Columbia, Canada. From 1980 to 1999 Dr Kerr was at the University of Calgary, Canada (from 1989 as Professor of Economics). The focus of his research has been on international trade and international commercial policy. He has provided advice on trade policy negotiating strategies to the World Trade Organization (WTO), the North American Free Trade Agreement (NAFTA), and other regional trade associations. He has worked on trade disputes between the EU and Canada, and on those between the United States and Canada. Dr Kerr has been a consultant for numerous international organizations and also for private sector companies and organizations. He has international experience in the United Kingdom, Denmark, Poland, Slovakia, New Zealand, China, the Philippines, Mexico, Japan, Russia, the United States, and a number of other countries. He has over 250 academic publications, including ten books. Recent titles include *Handbook on International Trade Policy*; *Economic Development Through Regional Trade*; and *Conflict, Chaos and Confusion – The Crisis in the International Trading System.*

Ekaterina Kuznetsova is Senior Lecturer at the Higher School of Economics (Moscow, Russia) and the Director of European Programmes of the Centre for Post-Industrial Studies (Moscow, Russia). She is also a moderator of EU Study Weeks seminars for students and young researchers in the Russian regions (a project of the EU Delegation to Russia). Kuznetsova has contributed to a number of translation and research projects, and she is the editor of the first Russian edition of the *Bertelsmann Transformation Index 2010*. Her areas of expertise include problems of political transformation in Europe, new forms of sovereignty and citizenship (EU experience), and legal and political perspectives on European integration. She has also written extensively on Russia–EU relations for the Russian and European press. For two years she has been a columnist on EU–Russia relations in *Nezavisimaia gazeta*, one of the leading Russian newspapers; her articles have also appeared in *Handelsblad, Trouw, WeltTrends, Politique Internationale*, and *Transit*.

Patrick Leblond is Associate Professor in the Graduate School of Public and International Affairs at the University of Ottawa, Canada, as well as Research Associate at CIRANO (Montreal, Canada). He is also Affiliated Professor of International Business at HEC Montreal, Canada, and Visiting Professor at the World Trade Institute (Bern, Switzerland) and the University of Barcelona, Spain (International Economic Law and Policy [IELPO] LLM programme). Owing to his training and experience in business, economics, and international relations, Dr Leblond's expertise applies to questions related to global economic governance and international and comparative political economy, more specifically those that deal with international finance, international economic integration, as well as business–government relations. His regional expertise focuses on Europe and North America. Before moving to Ottawa, Dr Leblond taught international business at HEC Montreal and was director of the Réseau économie internationale (REI) at the Centre d'études et de recherches internationales de l'Université de Montréal (CERIUM), Canada.

Lawrence LeDuc is Professor of Political Science at the University of Toronto, Canada. His publications include *The Politics of Direct Democracy, Comparing Democracies* (with Richard G. Niemi and Pippa Norris), *Dynasties and Interludes: Past and Present in Canadian Electoral Politics* (with Jon H. Pammett, Judith I. McKenzie, and André Turcotte), and *Absent Mandate* (with Harold D. Clarke, Jane Jenson, and Jon H. Pammett), as well as articles on voting, elections, and related topics in North American and European Political Science journals. He is a member of the editorial boards of *Electoral Studies* and the *Journal of Elections, Public Opinion and Parties*. His current research deals with multilevel voting, political participation, and direct democracy.

Jon H. Pammett is Professor of Political Science at Carleton University in Ottawa, Canada. He is also Co-Director of the Carleton University Survey Centre, and Canadian delegate to the International Social Survey Programme. Dr Pammett is co-editor and contributor to *Activating the Citizen: Dilemmas of Citizen Participation in Canada and Europe* (with Joan DeBardeleben, 2010), and co-author of *Political Choice in Canada* and *Absent Mandate*, books about voting behaviour in Canadian elections. He is co-editor of and contributing author to numerous books on Canadian politics, including *The Canadian Federal Election of 2011* as well as several volumes in this series on earlier elections. Dr Pammett has published journal articles on public opinion and voting behaviour in Canada and Russia and has also worked in the field of political education. He is a co-author of *Dynasties and Interludes: Past and Present in Canadian Electoral Politics*, a book about Canadian elections through history, published in 2010.

Matthew Paterson is Professor of Political Science at the University of Ottawa, Canada. His research focuses on the political economy of global environmental change. His publications include *Global Warming and Global Politics* (1996); *Understanding Global Environmental Politics: Domination, Accumulation, Resistance* (2000); *Automobile Politics: Ecology and Cultural Political Economy* (2007); and most recently *Climate Capitalism: Global Warming and the Transformation of the Global Economy* (with Peter Newell, 2010). He is working on a series of articles on the political economy of climate change governance and has recently started a research project entitled 'Governance and Legitimacy in Carbon Markets', with Matthew Hoffmann, Steven Bernstein, and Michele Betsill. Dr Paterson was recently appointed a Lead Author by the Intergovernmental Panel on Climate Change, working on the chapter on international cooperation for the fifth assessment report.

George Ross is *ad personam* Chaire Jean Monnet and Visiting Professor of Political Science at the Université de Montréal (Canada), Hillquit Professor Emeritus at Brandeis University (USA), and Senior Associate at the Minda de Gunzburg Centre for European Studies, Harvard University (USA). He has been Chair of the European Union Studies Association, Director of the Centre for German and European Studies at Brandeis, Acting Director of the Minda de Gunzburg Centre for European Studies at Harvard University, Executive Director of the European Union Centre at Harvard, and Chair of the Council for European Studies. His honours and awards include the title of officier of the French Ordre des Palmes Academiques. Recent books include *The European Union and Its Crises: Through the Eyes of the Brussels Elite* (2011); *What Is Left of the Left?* (with James Cronin and James Shoch, 2011); *Euros and Europeans: EMU and the European Model of Society* (with Andrew Martin, 2005); *Brave New World of European Labor* (with Andrew Martin, 1999); and *Jacques Delors and European Integration* (1995).

Mikhail Zherebtsov is a PhD candidate and Lecturer at Carleton University in Ottawa, Canada. His current research projects include 'Public Administration Reform in Modern Russia', 'Russian Federalism and Regional Politics', and 'EU–Russia Transborder Partnership'. He is co-author (with Joan DeBardeleben) of 'The Transition to Managerial Patronage in Russia's Regions' in Vladimir Gel'man and Cameron Ross, eds, *The Politics of Sub-National Authoritarianism in Russia* (2010).

Introduction

Joan DeBardeleben and Crina Viju

Economic and financial crises have, in various times and places, generated major political change and spurred policy adjustments that have altered long-term trajectories. Unanticipated crises with an important exogenous or global element, such as those of 1998 and 2008–09, produce some special dynamics which introduce into the existing domestic context an external influence that the system may have few resources to cope with. Such events can sometimes pose challenges to the domestic balance of power that would not have otherwise emerged.

The Great Depression, which served as a trigger for the New Deal in the United States in the 1930s, is one of the most dramatic examples in history of the political impact of economic crisis. As Drazen and Grilli (1993) argue, economic crises may be instrumental in stimulating policy change where it otherwise would have been difficult to build an adequate constituency, an example being acceptance of increased taxation to support welfare improvement. Gourevitch (1986, pp. 32–3) explored the impact of three different periods of economic crisis (1873–96, 1929–49 and the 1970s and 1980s) in five Western countries; he concluded that, in each case, the crisis provoked changes in relationships between societal actors, sometimes associated with 'critical realignments... not only in the electoral arena but in the terms of trade among various economic actors'. Often these changes have long-lasting implications for the political system, policy approaches, and economic philosophy. While the intensity of the economic impact on a particular country or region may vary, depending on factors such as degree of export-dependence, the role of international investment and credit, debt load, and sectoral structure, the political impact may be affected by other causes such as pre-existing political tensions, patterns of elite conflict or accommodation, and institutional structures.

It is the purpose of this volume to explore the larger implications for Europe and Russia of the economic and financial crisis that began to emerge in 2007. What was initially a largely externally driven economic problem had, by 2010, spiraled into what is arguably the greatest political challenge to ever face the European Union's (EU) integration project and at the same time to spur debate within Russia about the need for economic and political modernization and the form it should take. The repercussions at the national political level, although modest at first, also took on more visible proportions as the fiscal stimulus measures required to deal with the 2008–09 financial–economic crisis battled with downturns in the real economy, and then contributed to rising sovereign debt levels that ushered in an era of austerity in many European countries that may last for years to come.

In an age of interconnected financial markets and intense trade and investment relations, national boundaries offer no protection. Accordingly, in examining the crisis in Europe, it is important not to restrict our view to the much-publicized developments that have unfolded in the EU, particularly in the Eurozone countries. While significant attention has been devoted in the press to the weak capacity of the southern Mediterranean countries and Ireland to withstand the crisis, less attention has been devoted to impacts in the new Member States of the EU and areas adjacent to the EU, such as Russia and the West Balkans. This question is significant because an economic downturn and its political repercussions in these regions could potentially have a notable effect on political stability in Europe as a whole, and economic dynamics may profoundly affect whether system liberalization occurs in countries like Russia. An overriding goal of the EU in its Eastern policy (first the enlargement policy and now the Eastern Partnership policy) is to promote deep economic ties across all of Europe, including regions beyond its own borders. Indeed the European integration experiment has been based on the premise that economic interdependence serves as the foundation for political cooperation and as a guard against violent conflict. As a neighbour, key trading partner, and critical source of energy resources, Russia is of special importance to the EU. What happens in Russian economic and political life has important implications for Europe, even if the effect may not be immediate. In addition to this factor of interaction, examining the impact of the economic crisis among a broad range of East European countries also facilitates useful comparisons. As Russia shares a common political and economic legacy with the new EU Member States of Central and Eastern Europe, its inclusion in the purview of this volume permits comparison of impacts between those post-communist countries which have entered the EU and those that remain outside.

The financial, economic, and sovereign debt crisis of 2008–12

The crisis that erupted in 2008 with the US sub-prime mortgage crisis can be divided into three important sequential stages: the global financial crisis, the global economic crisis, and the sovereign debt crisis.

At the heart of the 2008 global financial crisis was the reluctance of regulators to intervene to slow an economic boom. The crisis was preceded and caused by an overheating of the world economy. The belief that growth and prosperity could be sustained this time was based on financial innovations that allowed risks to be highly diversified (e.g., securitization, derivatives, etc.). Thus, near the end of the economic boom, in 2007, US home ownership had been extended to many who would not previously have qualified. In 2007, neither private sector bankers nor central bankers nor politicians exhibited the courage to end the economic boom and as a result eventually the boom became a bubble and then burst. The question that arose in everybody's mind was why nobody intervened to slow the economic boom. The basic answer could be the imprudence of the executives in private sector banks and related financial institutions combined with a very accommodative monetary policy by major central banks (e.g., the United States Federal Reserve and the Bank of Japan).

The imprudent behaviour of the private banks and financial institutions can be explained, first, not only by the level of their personal compensation, which was dependent on the continuation of the boom, but also by the competition between financial institutions to provide high returns to investors. This resulted in prudent behaviour by any individual bank being severely penalized. A more important element that can explain the imprudent behaviour is the failure to fully understand how the new illiquid and opaque financial innovations worked and the systemic risk that they introduced (Crotty, 2009). Through new financial innovations, the financial institutions were able to repackage debt by using various financial mechanisms (such as mortgage-backed securities and collateralized debt obligations), and thus risks appeared to be highly dispersed. The international financial regulations did not keep pace with these new approaches. At the same time, given the low level of inflation and low inflationary expectations, the prices of goods were relatively stable and, thus, central banks could keep the interest rates at very low levels. Mortgages were cheap, and through risk-spreading methods they were extended to those who previously were not qualified. The low interest rates plus the new home buyers resulted in a boom in real estate that drove up the price of housing assets. The US sub-prime mortgages worked well in a rising housing market, but, eventually, the asset prices dipped and a large number of debt holders were imprudently exposed. The housing market burst in the US in the summer of 2007, but only a few experts expected that it would affect the entire world economy. However, the incipient crisis spread quickly – first to the developed countries in the first half of 2008, and then to the emerging economies in late 2008. Several European countries suffered housing market breakdowns (Ireland, United Kingdom, Spain, Greece, the Baltic states, and Iceland). Thus, the first stage of the crisis began in the US finance sector by July 2007 and, then, it spread rapidly around the world, mostly due to the high level of financial system integration.

By mid-2007, banks and other financial institutions in the US and various European countries began hoarding cash, and as a result refinancing of debt became expensive or even impossible. Borrowing for real investment purposes dried up and consumers slowed purchases. The financial crisis had spilled over into the real economy, precipitating the second stage of the crisis.

The first response by governments in all affected countries was to provide liquidity to the financial system. This took various forms, including loans to financial institutions, governments taking large equity positions in failing banks, and outright nationalization. To take some European examples: in August 2007, the German government bailed out IKB Deutsche Industriebank; in France, BNP Paribas suspended three investment funds; and the European Central Bank (ECB) provided EUR 100 billion short-term financing to the European banking system. In February 2008, further bailouts occurred: the Northern Rock United Kingdom (UK) mortgage provider was nationalized, while other Member States rescued banks (e.g., in Germany, Hypo Real Estate; in the United Kingdom, the nationalization of the mortgage division of Bradford and Bingley and bailout of the Royal Bank of Scotland, Lloyds TSB, and HBOS; in the Benelux countries, Fortis was broken up). In Russia, there was the fear that the government would react as in the 1998 financial crisis when the banking system was partially nationalized, with five large state banks still holding 45 per cent of Russia's banking assets. A large part of the banking support during the 2008–09 crisis was directed towards selected state banks, resulting in a 'soft re-nationalisation' (Aslund, 2008).

These large infusions of liquidity prevented bank failures, but banks still did not have the financial means to lend to businesses and the refinancing of existing commercial loans was often denied. Problems in the banking sector and a decline in credit availability combined with a decrease in investor confidence produced a negative impact on the global stock market. The lack of credit led to a curtailment of business investment and drove the reduction of costs to ensure loan repayment. Payrolls were cut, workers were laid off, and spending was reduced, especially on durable goods such as automobiles; lower demand resulted in reduced employment and incomes, which further depressed the demand. The large drop in demand and international trade affected the major world economies. For countries producing raw materials and semi-manufactured goods (e.g., Russia), the effect of lower demand was felt through a large fall in prices and not necessarily an important drop in demand in physical terms. However, for countries producing manufactured goods, the effect of lower demand was transmitted through a large reduction of demand in physical terms and not through prices (Myant and Drahokoupil, 2011). The situation was worsened by the failure of the Lehman Brothers investment bank in September 2008, which, combined with further decreases in housing prices and a fall in equity values, led to reduced consumption and investment. The Lehman Brothers bankruptcy resulted in a widespread contagion effect on the world financial markets due to an increased perception of higher risk.

Governments around the world tried to use monetary policy to stimulate the economy, but as interest rates were already low, they couldn't be drawn much lower. In comparison with the United States Federal Reserve, the monetary policy of the ECB was less expansionary and, thus, the ECB increased its basic interest rate by mid-2008 when the crisis hit its first peak. However, the measures that the ECB could implement were limited by the actions of the US Federal Reserve Bank (Dabrowski, 2010). In Russia, however, the monetary policy before the crisis was based on a fixed-exchange rate regime. Due to a high current account surplus, the Russian rouble appreciated before the crisis, which, together with high inflation, high interest rates, and complete removal of capital controls, resulted in significant short-term capital inflows. After the crisis started, due to the decline in commodity prices and falling export revenues, the Russian rouble came under strong pressure from significant capital outflows, and finally the currency depreciated (Central Bank of the Russian Federation, 2011).

Governments used a fiscal stimulus to offset declines in demand, yet fiscal policy expenditures take time to organize. The effects of tax cuts on demand are more immediate but muted because consumers divert part of their tax savings into savings (or debt repayment) rather than demand-enhancing consumption.

The third stage of the crisis started at the end of 2009, when fears of a sovereign debt crisis spread among investors due to the rise in government debt levels in developed economies and the downgrading of government debt in a number of European states. Sovereign debt is a major problem for only a few Eurozone member states (Greece, Portugal, Ireland, Spain, and Italy); however, the issue has been depicted as a crisis of the euro area as a whole. Even though the causes of the sovereign debt crisis were mostly Member State-specific, there were various common factors affecting the intensification of the debt crisis in the period that followed. The literature focuses on a combination of influences. These include: globalization combined with lax regulation of the financial sector; a decrease in economic growth and a dip in international trade as a result of the financial and economic crisis of 2008; the burst of real estate bubbles; lack of competitiveness of some Eurozone member states; and fiscal policies of national governments related to the large expenditures, such as welfare programmes and bailouts of banking and financial institutions (Dabrowski, 2010; De Grauwe, 2010; Myant and Drahokoupil, 2011). Once a state enters the Eurozone, it gives up its right to implement a national monetary policy, but it retains an independent fiscal policy. Thus, when the sovereign debt crisis surfaced, Eurozone member states could not react by devaluing their currency but rather only by taking further fiscal measures that might aggravate the crisis. The sovereign debt crisis is a Eurozone crisis as the other EU Member States that are not part of Eurozone and Russia do not have high levels of public debt (except for Hungary). The ongoing European sovereign debt crisis represents a major test of the Eurozone region.

As Gourevitch (1986, p. 21) noted in his study, 'economic conditions rarely operate directly on policy disputes'; rather, the impact of economics on policy choices is mediated by a range of factors, including 'mechanisms of representation' (parties and interest groups), institutional rules, ideology, and the position of countries in the international system. In each of the three phases of the crisis described above, political decisions were made, and these (as well as prior policy choices) helped to shape economic outcomes, which themselves created new economic challenges. The shape of regulatory systems for banks and financial institutions was itself the result of earlier political choices made both in North America and Europe; these decisions created conditions that facilitated the first phase of the crisis. Once the crisis erupted, it was a political choice to implement major stimulus packages and bank bailouts. As regards the third phase of the crisis, the earlier creation of the European Monetary Union was also a political decision that laid the groundwork for the disjoining of fiscal and monetary policies in the Eurozone member countries. Once the sovereign debt crisis emerged, the tough conditions imposed on debt-ridden Eurozone countries were the result of a political negotiation. At each stage of the crisis, financial and economic conditions pressed politicians to act, but their actions shaped the manner in which each stage of the crisis unfolded. It is a premise of this volume that it is this important interaction between the political and economic forces, occurring at multiple levels, from the national to the supranational level in Europe, which profoundly affected both the short- and long-term impacts of the crisis.

From economic to political crisis

While the economic contours of the 2008 crisis and its aftermath have already been subject to extensive analysis (Carmassi, Gross and Micossi, 2009; Arghyrou and Tsoukalas, 2011; Stein, 2011; Smith and Swain, 2010), the larger political implications of the astounding sequence of events that unfolded between 2008 and 2012 will take longer to digest. The immediate political effects of the initial phase in 2008–09 appeared to be relatively modest in most affected countries, as generous fiscal stimulus packages promised to ameliorate the potentially dramatic implications for the banking sector and the real economy. Even at the crisis epicentre, the US, the economic volcano apparently did not have a decisive impact on the outcome of the November 2008 US presidential election (Johnston, Thorson, and Gooch, 2010). Across the border, the Canadian federal election of October 2008 was also not substantially affected; rather, the political fallout of the crisis began to take place in the election's aftermath (Dornan, 2009, pp. 7–9; LeDuc and Pammett, 2009, pp. 297–8). Soon, however, rising unemployment rates put the crisis more squarely in the face of large parts of the population, both in North America, the EU, and countries of Eastern Europe outside of the EU, including Russia. This was followed by additional hardship as governments faced the necessity of cutting budgets to address rising levels of accumulated debt and large deficits, themselves substantially aggravated by the stimulus programmes designed to control the first phase of the crisis. It soon became clear that incumbent governments would face major challenges in managing public concern over these developments. The effects varied greatly between countries, just as the economic impact of the crisis also differed.

The crisis may have begun in the US, but by 2010 the political effects were nowhere more strongly felt than in the EU, both at the national level in several countries and in the Union itself. The sovereign debt crisis that adversely affected vulnerable Eurozone economies soon took on clear political dimensions. On the one hand were gloomy premonitions that the Eurozone crisis might undermine the legitimacy not only of the European Monetary Union but also of the European integration project more generally. Comments from the President of the European Commission, José Manuel Barroso, were at the same time alarming and hopeful. In September 2011, he stated the goal: 'When it comes to the governance of the Euro area, I am convinced we need deeper and more results-driven integration. And let me be clear: this has to be within the Community system' (Barroso, 2011). The signing of a 'fiscal compact' by 25 EU Member States (with the United Kingdom and the Czech Republic declining) on 2 March 2012 might suggest that just such a direction is taking place.[1] Apocalyptic innuendos, however, probably did not ease market or public apprehensions. In November 2011, Barroso warned: 'in this defining moment, we either unite or face irrelevance' (Boffey and Stewart, 2011). In a much-quoted statement from the same month, Barroso warned that failure to address the crisis adequately could 'jeopardize the future prosperity of the next generation' (Waterfield, 2011). This hyped rhetoric, no doubt intended to spur Member State politicians to react, was unlikely to reassure the public.

While politicians sought policy responses, the public's confidence in both national governments and in the EU itself was noticeably declining. According to Eurobarometer results, by November 2011 only 34 per cent of respondents expressed trust in the EU, compared to 57 per cent in September 2007 and 50 per cent in September 2008, when the first phase of the financial economic crisis was picking up steam (European Commission, 2011a, p. 19). The EU's image also suffered, with only 31 per cent seeing it as 'very positive' or 'fairly positive' in November 2011, down from 48 per cent just two years earlier (European Commission, 2011a, p. 20). All of the major European institutions (the ECB, the European Parliament, the European Council, and European Commission) were marked by declining levels of trust as well (European Commission, 2011a, p. 21). If the spectre of a 'democratic deficit' haunted the EU prior to the crisis, it was intensified as

EU leaders seemed unable to fashion a response in the area of the EU's core economic competencies. Nonetheless, respondents still identified the EU as being 'the best able to take effective actions against the effects of the financial and economic crisis' (a response selected by 23 per cent of respondents in November 2011), which may in fact have been an indicator of their even more limited confidence in other actors (e.g., only 20 per cent selected Member State governments) (European Commission, 2011a, p. 17). If the EU suffered a legitimacy loss, Member State governments fared even worse, trusted by only 24 per cent of respondents in Fall 2011, down from 41 per cent four years earlier. National parliaments fared only slightly better (European Commission, 2011a, p. 19).

The public reaction varied across the EU. While the economic crisis had differential effects across the Union, as will be analysed in later chapters in this book, public attitudes had their own dynamic. A particularly interesting contrast became visible in public assessments in the new Member States of Central and Eastern Europe. While the economic vulnerability of these economies varied greatly, with the three Baltic states (Estonia, Latvia, and Lithuania) suffering economic effects (such as declines in gross domestic product [GDP]) well beyond the EU average, Poland was the success story of the EU, still maintaining a moderately positive growth rate throughout the whole period (see Table 1.1 in Chapter 1). The Baltic states were also hit by hefty increases in unemployment. Other new Member States, notably Poland, Slovenia, the Czech Republic, and Bulgaria, fared relatively better (see Table 1.3 in Chapter 1). In terms of levels of public debt, by 2010, most of the new Member States of Central and Eastern Europe (except Hungary) were among the better performers in the Union. These economic impacts, however, elicited very different public reactions. Despite the dismal economic situation in countries like the Baltic states, levels of confidence in the EU remained relatively high. As Table 0.1 indicates, in fact, in November 2011 the proportion of respondents who trusted the EU in every single one of the new Member States of Central and Eastern Europe exceeded the EU-27 average.

The opposite pattern emerged in southern Europe, notably in Greece, Portugal, and Italy. In terms of economic growth Greece, Portugal, and Spain did relatively well through 2009, but things worsened in 2010 (see Table 1.3 in Chapter 1), as unemployment also took an upward swing. Debt levels rose through the ceiling, especially in Greece and Italy. In contrast to the new Member States of Central and Eastern Europe, by 2011 countries suffering the most from the sovereign debt

Table 0.1 Levels of trust in the EU and in national governments, selected countries, 2008, 2011

Country	Trust in the EU Fall 2008	Trust in the EU Fall 2011	Trust in the national government 2011	Change Trust in EU 2008/2011	Trust in national government compared to trust in EU 2011
2004 NMS*					
Bulgaria	58	59	38	+1	−21
Estonia	67	51	49	−16	−2
Romania	63	50	10	−13	−40
Lithuania	55	50	18	−5	−32
Slovakia	70	48	21	−22	−27
Hungary	51	47	26	−4	−21
Poland	55	47	28	−8	−19
Latvia	44	40	19	−4	−21
Slovenia	60	38	12	−22	−26
Czech Republic	58	38	15	−20	−23
Average	**58**	47	24	−11	−23
EU-27	**47**	34	26	−13	−8
Eurozone crisis countries					
Italy	41	32	12	−9	−20
Portugal	50	31	24	−19	−7
Spain	55	30	16	−25	−14
Greece	58	29	8	−29	−21
Ireland	50	24	22	−36	−2
Average	**51**	29	16	−22	−13

*NMS: New Member States.
Source: European Commission, Eurobarometer 70 (2008) Question A12.4; European Commission, Eurobarometer 76 (2011b), 44–6.

crisis had levels of trust in the EU that were below the Union average (European Commission, 2011b, 46; see Table I.1). That the reaction against retrenchment measures imposed on their economies by the EU and other international agencies would be one of resentment, anger, and alienation is not surprising. Scharpf (2011, pp. 36–7) speculates that the situation could even 'create the conditions for anti-European mobilization from the extremes of the political spectrum'; he posits further that measures taken to try to deal with the Eurozone crisis 'may not only undermine democracy in EU Member States but endanger European integration itself'. Bohle (2010, p. 10) also notes that addressing issues of political legitimacy and popular democracy that have been intensified by the crisis will require a renewed public debate about 'how much [Europe] wants to allow markets to determine the fate of its citizens and countries'. Bickerton (2011, p. 416) raises an additional question of whether giving new transnational powers to the EU to deal with economic aspects of the crisis may reduce possibilities for citizens to hold national governments to account, as it becomes even less clear than previously who is responsible for decisions and actions that may have important impacts on the public.

If economics has spilled over into politics in the EU and in certain Member States more strongly than others, the situation in Russia offers an interesting contrast. Russia had already dramatically experienced the effects of one global economic crisis in 1998, an event that, arguably, produced a significant change in direction both in the country's economic and political trajectory. Following the devaluation of the rouble in 1998, Russia saw a revival of domestic production, setting the country on an upward economic path. One can debate whether Russia's renewed international self-assertion and Vladimir Putin's popular appeal to Russian national pride were also in part a reaction to Russia's successful exit from both the decline of the 1990s and the effects of that global crisis. Having regained positive growth rates only in 1999, one might expect that the 2008–09 crisis could well offer new challenges to the legitimacy of the Russian leadership. In Russia, the economic crisis hit hardest in the first phase, primarily due to the fall in the prices of fossil fuels, which are a key export commodity for Russia as well as a support for the federal budget. However, the existence of a Reserve Fund and Prosperity Fund, built up over years of high gas and oil prices, combined with the relatively short duration of the dip in commodity prices, allowed for a comparatively quick economic recovery. By Fall 2010, popular perceptions regarding the state of the Russian economy had recovered to levels preceding the shock of Fall 2008 (although they dipped again in 2011) (Fond, 2011, p. 19). We leave it to the authors of relevant chapters in this volume to try to unravel the possible political implications of the recovery for Russia's domestic political situation. In terms of the relationship with Europe, however, Russian public opinion data revealed an interesting finding; positive attitudes towards the EU improved between 2008 and 2010, a contrast with the views of the EU's own citizens.[2]

A multilevel crisis

The economic crisis had multilevel effects, at the national, EU, and broader regional/supranational levels. Given this overall perspective, this volume has several important goals. First, we explore challenges posed by the crisis to the EU. The adequacy of the EU's existing capacities for a unified response and implications about not only the fate of the European Monetary Union but also about the future of the integration project itself are discussed. We hope to provide a deep and more comprehensive analysis of this question. Second, impacts of the crisis extend beyond the most directly affected and much-discussed economic spheres (such as banking, debt levels, and so forth) and can have important secondary effects in terms of policy conflict and system legitimacy. Thus a second goal of the volume is to examine these impacts both at the national level and for the EU. A third important goal of this book is to provide a preliminary basis for assessing reasons for differential impacts of the crisis in different European countries. The economic crisis not only exposed the weakness of the current model of development in some countries and in the EU as a whole but also made painfully clear that the global financial crisis apparently produced quite different outcomes in different regions/states. Some of these outcomes are, at first glance, surprising. For example, a few years ago Ireland was identified as the economic success story of Europe (Helms, 2007); likewise, one might not have expected Poland to have emerged from the crisis as an economic leader. While it would be too early to provide a comprehensive and systematic comparison of reasons for these differential outcomes across all Member States, it is not too soon to begin identifying some of the key variables at work and to test them in terms of particular types of impacts in defined comparative contexts.

Finally, this book devotes special attention to the impact of the crisis in the post-communist countries of Central and Eastern Europe. While significant attention has been devoted to the weak capacity of the southern Mediterranean countries and Ireland to withstand the crisis, less attention has been devoted to how a crisis of this scale, occurring so soon after adoption of market economic principles, will affect the continued transitional processes in these regions. Inclusion of the Russian case permits comparison between impacts in those post-communist countries which have entered the EU and those that remain outside.

The volume

Part I of this volume focuses on the nature and scope of the crisis, as well as on its broader political and economic implications at both the

Member-State and EU levels. In Chapter 1, András Inotai sets the context with an overview of the economic parameters in various EU Member States and Russia, providing a wealth of economic data that serves as a reference for the remainder of the chapters. In Chapters 2 and 3, George Ross and Patrick Leblond draw out the political and economic implications of the crisis at the EU level. The underlying question driving both their chapters is the significance of the crisis for the underlying viability of the EU and the Eurozone. This is carried out through a detailed assessment of the EU's policy responses as well as an examination of the manner in which these policies responded to the particular difficulties in the most severely affected Member States, namely Greece, Ireland, Italy, Spain, and Portugal. Ross situates responses to the crisis in the EU's already complex and painful period of institutional and political change that was underway before the global financial meltdown of 2008. He argues that the EU and its Member States performed reasonably well in the first phase of the crisis, which involved bank bailouts, stimulus packages, and financial reregulation. However, in the third phase – the Greek/Eurozone one – the slowness of EU institutions and the reliance on intergovernmental approaches produced low common denominator results in a predictably perilous scenario. Both Leblond and Ross see responses to this phase of the crisis as the most problematic for the EU, but Leblond provides quite a different assessment from Ross. Leblond considers the extent to which international actors, including the EU, pursued an adequately customized approach to different kinds of problems facing the most vulnerable Member States.

In Chapter 4, Lawrence LeDuc and Jon Pammett turn the analysis specifically to the political effects of the crisis, focusing on electoral outcomes at the Member State-level – often the pivotal vehicle through which underlying political change is expressed, and one that can engender change. Their analysis is placed in the context of an extensive political science literature on 'economic voting', an important topic in the study of elections. Based on a rich and extensive analysis of public opinion data related to electoral contests between 2008 and 2010, including elections for the European Parliament in 2009, the authors conclude that, at least in the first two stages of the crisis, incumbent governments and those on the left end of the political spectrum suffered disproportionately at the ballot box but that the economic crisis had a lesser impact than the economic voting literature might have predicted. They conclude that electoral outcomes do not seem to provide evidence of dramatic or underlying change in political dynamics at the Member-State level, but that they do have some particular short-term effects. The analysis provided by LeDuc and Pammett suggests a mismatch between the acute crisis facing the EU and the limited ability of the public to use the mechanism of elections to provide democratic inputs on economic policy. LeDuc and Pammett conclude their chapter by providing some intriguing reflections regarding potential implications of the sovereign debt crisis for the European Parliament elections to occur in 2014.

Part II of this volume explores the impact of the crisis in three important EU policy arenas – trade relations, environmental policy related to climate change, and interaction with the International Monetary Fund (IMF). As a primarily economic phenomenon, it is not surprising that trade has been affected. While one might have expected the crisis to elicit a self-reinforcing pattern of protectionist measures introduced by individual countries to shield their productive sectors from adverse effects, Viju and Kerr argue that this in fact did not happen, and explore reasons for this outcome. They argue that an important factor lay in the relationships that had developed within Europe since the Treaty of Rome set a trajectory towards a unified commercial policy in an ever-expanding geographical region, encompassed first by the European Economic Community and now by the EU. Despite the fact that under the treaties, in practice, EU Member States still retain a large degree of autonomy in terms of external policy, Viju and Kerr demonstrate that, given the changing international environment, an assessment of the direction of EU external trade policy is important in understanding the lack of protectionism in the wake of the 2008–09 financial crisis. Viju and Kerr conclude that the completion of the EU single market brought a change in the institutional context in which external policy is made and, thus, it reduced the opportunity for Member States to use national policy tools to protect nationally sensitive sectors. They also analyse the changes in the larger international environment that can explain the relative weakness of protectionism during this latest financial and economic crisis.

In Chapter 6, Matthew Paterson explores how the economic crisis has affected EU climate change policy. The EU has promoted itself as an important global actor in the area of climate change policy. Pundits often argue that the economic crisis has put these environmental priorities on the back burner; if true, this would be a very important impact of the crisis, not only because it would signal a key shift in EU strategic priorities but also because it could have longer term impacts on the likelihood of an environmentally sustainable recovery. Paterson confronts these claims head on, leading to some surprising and provocative conclusions, which will elicit considerable interest in circles interested in the interface between economics and ecology. Paterson suggests that the design of the EU's Emissions Trading Scheme (ETS), the key plank of the EU's efforts to reduce greenhouse gas emissions, has meant that the crisis has created space for claims that the EU can and should become more ambitious in attempts to reduce greenhouse gas emissions.

The final chapter in this part considers the role that an important global institution, the IMF, has had in dealing with the effects of the crisis in Europe, alongside, and in cooperation with, the EU. Commentators have wondered why the IMF should be involved in dealing with the crisis, particularly in EU countries (including cases as diverse as Greece, Poland, Hungary, or Romania), as opposed to the EU acting alone. Patrick Conway considers the IMF's role as it manifested itself in Eastern Europe in three dimensions: forecasting the crisis, acting as lender of last resort, and providing expertise in designing and supervising macroeconomic reforms. Evidence suggests that the IMF's skill in forecasting was no greater than that of other agencies but that its 'lender of last resort' and reform expertise provided a comparative advantage in this crisis period. Conway's analysis suggests that EU action remains linked to a network of interrelated responses at multiple levels in the international system.

Finally, Part III brings a particular focus on the impact of the crisis on the post-communist countries of Central and Eastern Europe, including the new EU Member States and the Russian Federation. As countries that only recently adopted competitive market structures, this region faced special challenges. The first two chapters of this part draw attention to the impact of the crisis in Russia. DeBardeleben and Zherebtsov explore the effects of the economic crisis on political relations in Russia, with the goal of assessing the hypothesis that economic hardship produced an impetus for liberalizing reforms and for an activation of political competition. The following chapter by Ekaterina Kuznetsova and Vladislav Inozemstev engages in an analysis of the impact of the crisis on Russia's relations with the EU. The chapter highlights the sharp divide in the economic approaches of these two major players on the continent. While Europe, on the one hand, has struggled to achieve internal agreement and solidarity at the same that it has advocated economic liberalism in the international arena, Russia, on the other hand, has embarked on a path of resolute protectionism, therefore compromising the modernization strategy it adopted a few years earlier. This part of the book concludes with an examination of the differential impacts of the crisis on a range of post-communist countries; Gorzelak and Dutkiewicz explore differences in the manner in which the countries of Central and Eastern Europe were impacted and identify those factors which made some countries more vulnerable than others.

The economic and financial crisis that took on such importance in 2008, and has continued since, is not yet over in Europe at the time of writing this book, and continuing concerns about the sustainability of Russia's economic strategy are still being voiced. While the 2008–09 crisis has transformed itself from a crisis of financial institutions to one of sovereign debt, with the potential for new recessionary effects on the real economy and a challenge to the EU's project for monetary union, the three phases of the process must be understood in relation to one another. As this book goes to press, EU leaders have agreed on a framework not only to assure help to Member States that face immediate economic challenges but also to bring greater coordination in the area of state fiscal policy. However, continuing difficulties in the real economies of troubled Member States and pressures for retrenchment of state budgets will assure that an exit from the crisis will at best be gradual and by fits and starts. Furthermore, the repercussions of Europe's economic troubles may reverberate outside of the Union's borders, affecting Russia, North America, and the larger world economy. For Russia, volatility and the possibility of a decline in fossil fuel prices could reinforce current concerns about the viability of the country's resource-dependent economy.

The changing nature of the crisis over time, discussed above, creates a perplexing political landscape for citizens and voters, augmented in Europe by the multilevel nature of decision-making that characterizes the EU and in Russia by economic interdependence with Europe and susceptibility to global economic threats. Figuring out who is to blame, which policies are effective or not, and who in fact has been, and should be, held responsible for deciding on these policies is understandably difficult for citizens, as experts themselves struggle to make sense of this complex reality. We hope that this volume will provide the basis for a more systematic approach to distinguishing factors that affect the relative impact of the crisis, as it ebbs and flows across the region.

Notes

1. For the text of the Treaty on Stability, Coordination, and Governance in the Economic and Monetary Union (TSCG) see the website of the European Council (2012) http://www.european-council.europa.eu/media/639235/st00tscg26_en12.pdf, accessed on 8 April 2012.

2. See data from the website VTsIOM, 'Rossiia i evropa: sotrudnichestvo ili protivostoianie?' Press release 1550, 2 February 2010, http://wciom.ru/index.php?id=459&uid=13711, accessed on 22 November 2012.

Bibliography

Arghyrou, M.G. and Tsoukalas, J.D. (2011) 'The Greek Debt Crisis: Likely Causes, Mechanisms and Outcomes', *The World Economy* 34(2), 173–91.

Aslund, A. (2008, 24 October) 'Russia's Top Economist Needs to Face Reality', *The St. Petersburg Times*, Issue 1419, http://www.sptimes.ru/index.php?action_id=2&story_id=27448, accessed on 22 November 2012.

Barroso, J.M. (2011) *Speech by President Barroso to the European Parliament during the Debate on the Economic Crises and the Euro*, Strasbourg, 14 September, Press Release Rapid, http://europa.eu/rapid/pressReleasesAction.do?reference=SPEECH/11/572, accessed on 9 April 2012.

Bickerton, C. (2011) 'Crisis in the Eurozone: Transnational Governance and National Power in European Integration' (Editorial), *Political Geography* November 30(8), 415–16.

Boffey, D. and Stewart, H. (2011, 13 November) 'Barroso Tells Europe: We Must Advance Together or Face Decline', *The Guardian: The Observer*, http://www.guardian.co.uk/business/2011/nov/13/barroso-warns-britain-europe-closer-knit-union, accessed on 21 August 2012.

Bohle, D. (2010) *The Crisis of the Eurozone* (EUI Working Papers, RSCAS 2010/77) (Florence: European University Institute, Robert Schumann Centre for Advanced Studies – European Union Democracy Observatory), http://cadmus.eui.eu/handle/1814/14674, accessed on 8 April 2012.

Carmassi, J., Gross, D. and Micossi, S. (2009) 'The Global Financial Crisis: Causes and Cures', *Journal of Common Market Studies* 47(5), 977–96.

Central Bank of the Russian Federation (2011) 'Exchange Rate Flexibility and Russia's Monetary Policy Shift', *Bank for International Settlements Papers: Chapters*, http://econpapers.repec.org/bookchap/bisbisbpc/57-21.htm, accessed on 27 June 2012.

Crotty, J. (2009) 'Structural Causes of the Global Financial Crisis: A Critical Assessment of the "New Financial Architecture" ', *Cambridge Journal of Economics* 33, 563–80.

Dabrowski, M. (2010) 'The Global Financial Crisis: Lessons for European Integration', *Economic Systems* 34, 38–54.

De Grauwe, P. (2010) *Crisis in the Eurozone and How to Deal with It* (CEPS Policy Brief 204) (February), http://papers.ssrn.com/sol3/papers.cfm?abstract_id=1604453, accessed on 10 April 2012.

Dornan, C. (2009) 'Introduction: The Outcome in Retrospect', in J.H. Pammett and C. Dornan (eds) *The Canadian Federal Election of 2008* (Toronto: Dundurn), 7–15.

Drazen, A. and Grilli, V. (1993), 'The Benefit of Crises for Economic Reforms', *The American Economic Review* 83(3), 598–607.

European Commission (2008) *Eurobarometer, Table of Results Standard Eurobarometer 70 Public Opinion in the European Union, Fieldwork Oct-Nov*

2008, http://ec.europa.eu/public_opinion/archives/eb/eb70/eb70_full_annex.pdf, accessed on 8 April 2012.

European Commission (2011a) *Eurobarometer 76 Public Opinion in the European Union: First Results*, November (Brussels: Directorate-General for Communication, December), http://ec.europa.eu/public_opinion/archives/eb/eb76/eb76_first_en.pdf, accessed on 13 April 2012.

European Commission (2011b) *Eurobarometer, Table of Results Standard Eurobarometer 76 First Results Public Opinion in the European Union, Fieldwork November 2011*, Publication December 2011, http://ec.europa.eu/public_opinion/archives/eb/eb76/eb76_anx_en.pdf, accessed on 8 April 2012.

Fond Obshchestvennoe Mnenie (Fond) (2011) *Dominanty*, no. 15, 14 April, http://om.ru/pdf/d15sre11.pdf, accessed on 9 April 2012.

Gourevitch, P. (1986) *Politics in Hard Times: Comparative Responses to International Economic Crises* (Ithaca and London: Cornell University Press).

Helms, J. (2007, 15 May) 'Ireland an EU Success Story', *BBC News*, http://news.bbc.co.uk/2/hi/europe/6646629.stm, accessed on 10 April 2012.

Johnston, R., Thorson, E. and Gooch, A. (2010) 'The Economy and the Dynamics of the 2008 Presidential Campaign: Evidence from the National Annenberg Election Study', *Public Opinion & Parties* 20(2), 271–89.

LeDuc, L. and Pammett, J.H. (2009) 'The 2008 Election: Long-Term and Short-Term Assessments', in J.H. Pammett and C. Dornan (eds) *The Canadian Federal Election of 2008* (Toronto: Dundurn), 209–312.

Myant, M. and Drahokoupil, J. (2011) *Transition Economies: Political Economy in Russia, Eastern Europe, and Central Asia* (Hoboken: John Wiley & Sons).

Scharpf, F.W. (2011) 'Monetary Union, Fiscal Crisis, and the Preemption of Democracy' (LEQS Paper No. 37, May 2011, London School of Economics) http://papers.ssrn.com/sol3/papers.cfm?abstract_id=1852316, accessed on 8 April 2012.

Smith A. and Swain, A. (2010) 'The Global Economic Crisis, Eastern Europe, and the Former Soviet Union: Models of Development and the Contradictions of Internationalization', *Eurasian Geography and Economics* 51(1), 1–34.

Stein, J. (2011) 'The Diversity of Debt Crises in Europe', *CATO Journal* 31(2), 199–215, http://www.cato.org/pubs/journal/cj31n2/cj31n2-2.pdf, accessed on 10 April 2012.

Treaty on Stability, Coordination, and Governance in the Economic and Monetary Union (TSCG) (2012) http://www.european-council.europa.eu/media/639235/st00tscg26_en12.pdf, accessed on 8 April 2012.

VTsIOM (Russian Public Opinion Research Center) (2010) 'Rossiia i evropa: sotrudnichestvo ili protivostoianie?' Press release 1550, 2 February, http://wciom.ru/index.php?id=459&uid=13711, accessed on 21 August 2012.

Waterfield, B. (2011, 1 November) 'Eurozone Collapse "Will Send Continent into Depression"', *The Telegraph*, http://www.telegraph.co.uk/finance/financialcrisis/8882812/Eurozone-collapse-will-send-continent-into-depression.html, accessed on 8 April 2012.

Part I

The Economic Crisis in the European Union

1
Macroeconomic Impacts of the 2008–09 Crisis in Europe

András Inotai

Although the European Union (EU) was not the source of the global financial and economic crisis that commenced in 2008, that crisis had consequences that spurred the 2011 Eurozone sovereign debt problems. Europe, at the time of this writing, is still engaged in faltering efforts to stabilize its own economic and monetary situation, and it remains unclear, as of early 2012, whether those initiatives will produce a resolution or merely be one more step in a series of global economic upheavals that will require a fundamental rewriting of the international financial and economic relationships.

The 2008–09 crisis consisted of four interrelated stages that followed on from one to another with a certain time lag: financial, macroeconomic, social, and mental–ideological. Adverse social developments, taking the form of persistently high levels of unemployment, rising poverty, increasing income differentiation, and cutbacks in welfare provision, began to manifest themselves visibly in 2011, even as European countries showed unconvincing signs of recovery. Ideological and leadership crisis may be the fourth stage, and signs can already be observed in some member countries. This stage of the crisis relates to the apparently deep-rooted (protracted, still hidden) incapacity of states to remedy the impacts of the crisis and was already visible in the United States' political deadlock over how to deal with rising debts and deficits in mid-2011, showing signs of taking on a mass character in 'Occupy Wall Street' spin-offs that spread to Europe later that year. Meanwhile, European political leaders struggled to achieve a renewed or rewritten 'balance' between economic, political, social, cultural, and environmental concerns, on the one hand, and between national, EU-level, and global governance, on the other.

This chapter has a modest goal, namely to outline the macroeconomic impact of the 2008–09 crisis across the EU and in the Russian Federation, drawing on key comparative data. This data reveals the manner in which the developments of those years lay the groundwork for fundamental economic challenges that were to unfold for Europe so vividly in 2011, when sovereign debt levels in Greece (and possible contagion effects in other Eurozone countries) set the stage for the next chapter in this global economic saga, threatening to throw the global economy into a repeat tailspin. As the narrative and data that follows will demonstrate, the impact of the 2008–09 crisis varied substantially across EU Member State countries. Moreover, an examination of data provided for the Russian Federation indicates substantial differences in the effects of the world crisis on Russia and the EU. As the subsequent two chapters in this volume indicate, these impacts raised fundamental challenges not only at the national level but also for the whole European integration project.

The crisis and macroeconomic performance of EU Member States and Russia

Based on international statistical data,[1] we draw attention to six areas of macroeconomic impact: growth in gross domestic product (GDP), unemployment levels, budget deficits, public debt, international trade, and foreign direct investments.

Economic growth

In 2008–09, European growth rates experienced their sharpest declines in post-1945 history. From 2008 to 2009, global growth rates fell by just 0.5 per cent, made up of an average decline of 3.4 per cent in developed countries and average growth by 2.7 per cent in developing countries. Both the EU and Russia experienced a sharp decline in economic growth in 2009: 4.2 and 7.8 per cent, respectively (Table 1.1). For the first time since the Second World War, the crisis hit the developed countries harder, and its particular negative impact was felt in key growth-determining sectors of the economy (cars, electronics, construction). Also, the recession was accompanied by a severe downturn in international trade. In previous recessionary periods, foreign trade served as a mitigating factor, while during economic upswings it had previously proven to be a decisive driver of economic growth. Since most EU economies (not only the smaller ones but also some large ones, including Germany) are heavily reliant on international trade, the

Table 1.1 Annual growth rate in the EU-27, selected EU Member States and Russia (2006–10, in per cent)

Country	2006	2007	2008	2009	2010
EU-27	3.3	3.2	0.3	−4.2	1.1
Latvia	12.2	10.0	−4.2	−18.0	−0.3
Lithuania	7.8	9.8	2.9	−14.7	1.3
Estonia	10.6	6.9	−5.1	−13.9	3.1
Finland	4.4	5.3	0.9	−8.2	3.1
Slovenia	5.9	6.9	3.7	−8.1	1.2
Ireland	5.3	5.6	−3.5	−7.6	−1.0
Romania	7.9	6.3	7.3	−7.1	−1.3
Hungary	3.3	0.8	0.8	−6.7	1.2
Bulgaria	6.5	6.4	6.2	−5.5	0.2
Sweden	4.3	3.3	−0.6	−5.3	5.5
Denmark	3.4	1.6	−1.1	−5.2	2.1
Italy	2.0	1.5	−1.3	−5.2	1.3
United Kingdom	2.8	2.7	−0.1	−4.9	1.3
Slovakia	8.5	10.5	5.8	−4.8	4.0
Germany	3.6	2.8	0.7	−4.7	3.5
Czech Republic	6.8	6.1	2.5	−4.1	2.3
Austria	3.6	3.7	2.2	−3.9	2.0
Netherlands	3.4	3.9	1.9	−3.9	1.7
Spain	4.0	3.6	0.9	−3.7	−0.1
Belgium	2.7	2.8	0.8	−2.7	2.0
France	2.4	2.3	0.1	−2.5	1.5
Portugal	1.4	2.4	0.0	−2.5	1.4
Greece	5.2	4.3	1.0	−2.0	−4.5
Poland	6.2	6.8	5.1	1.7	3.8
Russia	8.2	8.5	5.2	−7.8	4.0

Source: IMF (2011) *World Economic Outlook April 2011* (Washington: International Monetary Fund).

collapse of trade was bound to accelerate the downturn of GDP. In addition, in some EU Member States home-made problems, due to bad or misguided policies, further exacerbated the decline.

In Table 1.1, the EU countries are classified according to their GDP decline, ordered by GDP decline in 2011. The largest GDP decline was registered in the three Baltic countries. The large drop in GDP can be explained not only by the international crisis but also by domestic mismanagement and a crucial lack of genuine transformation in the previous decade(s). The GDP decline in most of the other EU countries was a result of a combination of factors, such as mistaken economic policies, export vulnerability, and structural problems. The only EU member country with a positive growth rate was Poland, which was due to several, partly rather specific, factors that cannot be analysed here in detail.[2]

Russia, due to its heavy dependence on gas and oil exports, registered an abrupt decline of 7.8 per cent as a result of the collapse of world prices for these products. However, Russia's inability to conduct proper economic reforms as well as its reluctance to weaken government control over key economic sectors remained the major impedements on its way to overcome the recession in 2010 (Cooper, 2009).

More important than these summary figures is an examination of the trend before and after the 2008–09 slump. Striking is the fact that this unique recession followed a no less unique high-growth period experienced by the EU in general, but particularly by several Member States in the period preceding 2008. The Baltic countries, which experienced the deepest dip in 2008–09, had also reported two-digit, or almost two-digit, growth rates in 2006 and 2007. In fact, all of the Central and East European new Member States, except Hungary, excelled with surprisingly high-growth rates in the pre-crisis period. Some EU Member States entered a negative growth period already in 2008, due to substantial internal and external imbalances (Latvia and Estonia most notably) and due to the impact of the banking crisis (here mainly Ireland and partly the United Kingdom). Also, the structural and competitiveness problems of the Mediterranean members of the EU became manifest in either stagnating (Portugal), negative (Italy) or remarkably declining growth rates (Spain and Greece).

The year 2010 proved to mark the beginning of an apparent, but very slow, return to 'normality' on the EU-27 level, but by far not in all Member States. Some countries continued to register negative growth rates (Romania, Spain, Ireland, Latvia), and, for several reasons, the recession kept on deepening in Greece. Most importantly, Greece's sluggish recovery in 2010 was not strong enough to iron out the sharp fall of GDP in 2009. While the GDP of the United States returned to its 2008 level in 2010, the EU lagged behind. At least ten members will require more than three years to achieve the pre-crisis (2008) level of GDP (Inotai, 2011a). The Eurozone crisis, which followed on the 2008–09 financial and economic crisis, has complicated the recovery, making these estimates open to change. At the same time, Russia partially recovered in 2010, recording a growth rate of 4 per cent.

Table 1.2 presents two comparisons, a method to be followed in subsequent tables as well. One indicates levels for 2010, with 2007 as the base year (2007 = 100), recognizing the fact that this was the last year

Table 1.2 Depth of GDP decline as compared to pre-crisis levels in the EU, selected EU Member States and Russia (base years 2007 and 2008, respectively = 100)

Country	2010–2007*	2010–2008**
EU		
Latvia	78.3	81.8
Estonia	84.2	88.8
Ireland	88.3	91.5
Lithuania	88.9	86.4
Greece	94.5	93.6
Italy	94.8	96.0
Hungary	95.2	94.4
Finland	95.5	94.6
Denmark	95.7	96.8
United Kingdom	96.2	96.3
Slovenia	96.4	93.0
Spain	97.1	96.2
Romania	98.4	91.7
Portugal	98.9	96.1
France	99.1	99.0
Germany	99.3	98.6
Sweden	99.3	99.9
Netherlands	99.6	97.7
Belgium	100.0	99.2
Austria	100.2	98.0
Bulgaria	100.6	94.7
Czech Republic	100.6	98.1
Slovakia	104.8	99.0
Poland	110.9	105.6
Russia	114.0	89.2

*considering 2007 as the last full pre-crisis year.
**considering 2008 as the pre-crisis year.
Source: Own calculations based on IMF (2011) *World Economic Outlook April 2011* (Washington: International Monetary Fund).

without any impact of the global crisis. The second is based on a more conventional comparison, by using 2008 as the reference year, the first 'genuine' initial year of the crisis. Several conclusions can be drawn from the statistical figures. While most countries reveal a larger slump between 2008 and 2010, due to their still increasing GDP in 2007, some Member States experienced a larger gap between the GDP-measured performance in 2007 and 2010. (This difference is indicated by lower figures comparing 2010 and 2007 data than with 2008 figures.) Between 2007 and 2010, four countries suffered a growth decline of more than 10 per cent (Latvia by more than 20 per cent). Russia along with six EU countries reached, or outperformed, their 2007 level of performance by 2010. Among the six countries reaching or overcoming the 2007 GDP level in 2010 are four new Member States (Poland, Slovakia, Bulgaria, and the Czech Republic).

Unemployment

Most EU countries that were able and ready to introduce some kind of stimulus package in order to counteract the negative consequences of the crisis considered the stabilization of the labour market a key priority. In the framework of overall damage control, the remedying of short-term labour market and social consequences of the crisis enjoyed special attention. Still, as expected, in the majority of the EU Member States as well as in Russia, unemployment started to grow once the GDP decline seemed to have bottomed out and is likely to remain on the same high level even in the face of a modest recovery.

As Table 1.3 shows, for the EU-27 the average unemployment rate rose from 8.9 in 2009 to 9.8 per cent in 2010, and is expected to remain practically at the same level in 2011 (9.7 per cent). In 2010, nine countries reported two-digit unemployment figures, headed by Latvia and Spain with more or slightly less than 20 per cent. In Russia, the figures for unemployment increased by 1.4 percentage points, rising from 6.1 per cent in 2007 to 7.5 per cent in 2010, however, reaching the highest point of 8.4 per cent in 2009.

A more important aspect is the dynamic of unemployment as a consequence of the crisis. Between 2007 and 2010 the EU average unemployment rate rose by 2.7 percentage points, from 7.1 to almost 10 per cent. In some countries, the rise occurred from a relatively high level of pre-crisis unemployment, while in other countries relatively lower pre-crisis unemployment rates skyrocketed to the double-digit figures. The three Baltic countries, as well as Spain and Ireland, experienced the most dramatic increases in unemployment, with the rise registering from 9 to almost 15 per cent between 2007 and 2010. Registered unemployment figures rose almost everywhere (by 1–3 percentage points from country to country). While several member countries registered declining unemployment rates before the crisis, unemployment started to increase spectacularly as a result of the crisis between 2008 and 2010. Germany was, however, an exception that could successfully manage labour market constraints. Germany reduced its unemployment rate before the crisis (from 2007 to 2008) and instituted a massive anti-crisis

Table 1.3 Unemployment rate in selected EU-27 Member States and Russia (in per cent of registered labour force)

Country	2006	2007	2008	2009	2010	Change 2007 to 2010
EU-27	8.2	7.1	7.0	8.9	9.8	+2.7
Latvia	8.8	6.0	7.5	17.1	20.6	+14.6
Spain	8.5	8.3	11.3	18.0	19.7	+11.4
Lithuania	5.6	4.3	5.8	13.7	16.7	+12.4
Estonia	5.9	4.7	5.5	13.8	15.8	+11.1
Slovakia	13.4	11.1	9.5	12.0	14.1	+3.0
Ireland	4.5	4.6	6.3	11.9	13.8	+9.2
Greece	8.9	8.3	7.7	9.5	11.8	+3.5
Hungary	7.5	7.4	7.8	10.0	10.8	+3.4
France	9.2	8.4	7.8	9.5	10.2	+1.8
Portugal	7.8	8.1	7.7	9.6	9.9	+1.8
Finland	7.7	6.9	6.4	8.2	9.5	+2.6
Sweden	7.0	6.1	6.2	8.3	9.2	+3.1
Poland	13.9	9.6	7.1	8.2	9.2	−0.4
Belgium	8.3	7.5	7.0	7.9	8.8	+1.3
Italy	6.8	6.1	6.7	7.8	8.8	+2.7
Romania	7.3	6.4	5.8	6.9	8.5	+2.1
Czech Republic	7.2	5.3	4.4	6.7	8.3	+3.0
Bulgaria	9.0	6.9	5.6	6.8	7.9	+1.0
Germany	9.8	8.4	7.3	7.5	7.8	−0.6
United Kingdom	5.4	5.3	5.6	7.6	7.8	+2.5
Slovenia	6.0	4.9	4.4	5.9	7.0	+2.1
Denmark	3.9	3.8	3.3	6.0	6.9	+3.1
Austria	4.8	4.4	3.8	4.8	5.1	+0.7
Netherlands	3.9	3.2	2.8	3.4	4.9	+1.7
Russia	7.2	6.1	6.4	8.4	7.5	+1.4

Sources: Eurostat (2011a), IMF (2011) *World Economic Outlook April 2011* (Washington: International Monetary Fund) and own calculations (last column).

policy mainly aimed at the labour market (and at the car industry), an important component being supported by a system of part-time work.[3] By contrast, Poland substantially reduced the official unemployment rate from 2007 to 2008, in significant part due to large-scale emigration of Polish citizens (employees) to several other EU member countries. The crisis generated a rapid increase in the unemployment figure by 2010 (although not yet reaching the 2007 level) due to the back flow of workers from crisis-ridden Western European countries; these returnees could not be fully absorbed by the crisis-resistant domestic demand and growth (OECD, 2011).

Budget deficits

The development of budget deficits (see Table 1.4) is important for two reasons. First, these deficits quantify the (short-term) budgetary impact of anti-crisis measures. Second, budget deficits are one of the key Maastricht criteria that should be met by the Eurozone member countries in general and by applicant countries to the Economic and

Table 1.4 Budget deficit of selected EU Member States and Russia (in per cent of GDP)

Country	2006	2007	2008	2009	2010	Change 2007 to 2010
EU-27	−1.4	−0.8	−2.4	−6.8	−6.4	−5.6
Ireland	3.0	0.2	−7.3	−14.3	−32.4	−32.6
Greece	−3.1	−3.9	−9.8	−15.4	−10.5	−6.6
United Kingdom	−2.6	−2.6	−5.0	−11.4	−10.4	−8.6
Spain	2.0	2.2	−4.2	−11.1	−9.2	−11.4
Portugal	−3.9	−2.6	−3.5	−10.1	−9.1	−6.5
Poland	−3.9	−1.9	−3.7	−7.3	−7.9	−6.0
Slovakia	−3.5	−1.9	−2.1	−8.0	−7.9	−6.0
Latvia	−0.5	−0.4	−4.2	−9.7	−7.7	−7.3
Lithuania	−0.4	−1.0	−3.3	−9.5	−7.1	−6.1
France	−2.3	−2.7	−3.3	−7.5	−7.0	−4.3
Romania	−2.2	−2.5	−5.7	−8.5	−6.4	−3.9
Slovenia	−1.3	0.5	−1.8	−6.0	−5.6	−6.1
Netherlands	0.6	0.3	1.0	−5.5	−5.4	−5.7
Czech Republic	−2.6	−0.6	−2.7	−5.9	−4.7	−4.1
Austria	−1.7	−0.7	−0.9	−4.1	−4.6	−3.9
Italy	−3.3	−1.5	−2.7	−5.4	−4.6	−3.1
Hungary	−9.3	−4.9	−3.7	−4.5	−4.2	+0.7
Belgium	0.2	−0.3	−1.3	−5.9	−4.1	−3.8
Germany	−1.5	−0.2	0.1	−3.0	−3.3	−3.1
Bulgaria	3.0	0.1	1.7	−4.7	−3.2	−3.3
Denmark	5.0	4.5	3.2	−2.7	−2.7	−7.2
Finland	3.9	5.2	4.2	−2.6	−2.5	−7.7
Sweden	2.4	3.8	2.2	−0.7	0.0	−3.8
Estonia	2.9	2.7	−2.8	−1.7	+0.1	−2.6
Comparison						
Russia	8.3	6.8	4.9	−6.3	−3.6	−10.3
United States	−2.0	−2.7	−6.2	−11.2	−11.2	−8.5
Japan	−4.0	−2.4	−2.2	−8.7	−9.3	−6.9

Source: Eurostat (2004–08), European Economic Forecast, Spring 2011 (2009–10), IMF (2010) *World Economic Outlook April 2010* (Washington: International Monetary Fund) and own calculations (last column).

Monetary Union (EMU) in particular. In fact, in the last pre-crisis year (2007), almost all EMU members (except Greece) and almost all applicants preparing for EMU membership (except Hungary) were within the limits set by the Maastricht rules of the game (below 3 per cent of GDP). No less importantly, some EMU members reported budget surpluses (including currently crisis-ridden Spain and Ireland). Similarly, other important global players, such as the United States and Japan, had manageable (less than 3 per cent) budget deficits, while Russia had a large budget surplus.

This comfortable situation started to deteriorate in 2008, as, in the second half of the year, the first macroeconomic consequences of the unfolding crisis became manifest. More importantly, the average EU-27 figure of –2.4 per cent, still within the Maastricht limits, hid the emergence of dramatic differences among the Member States. The Greek deficit more than doubled and reached almost 10 per cent of GDP, the deficit of Great Britain (although not an EMU country) doubled, and several Eurozone member states could no longer observe the 3 per cent Maastricht criterion. Moreover, several countries' previous budgetary surpluses turned into deficits, with the most acute negative change not only in Ireland but also in Spain, Estonia, and, to a smaller extent, in Slovenia. Only three countries improved their budget deficit situation in 2008 (Hungary reducing the high deficit despite the looming crisis, the Netherlands, and Germany). Even though the Russian surplus suffered a reduction, Russia still recorded the highest surplus among the countries under study (4.9 per cent). Also, a substantial increase of the US budget deficit could be observed in 2008.

The fundamental change happened in 2009, when almost all EMU members, EU countries and Russia, registered skyrocketing budget deficits. Previously strong budget surplus positions were eroded by the crisis in countries known for their 'prudent' economic policies, such as Germany, the Netherlands, and the Scandinavian members of the EU. The German deficit in 2009 was 3.3 per cent against Finland's 2.7 per cent (see Table 1.4.) Excepting Finland, all Eurozone members surpassed the 3 per cent red-line and became violators of the Maastricht criteria and of the Stability and Growth Pact (SGP). The overall budget deficit of the EU jumped from 0.8 per cent in 2007 and 2.4 per cent in 2008 to 6.8 per cent in 2009. However, the initial conditions of high/increasing budget deficits were various. While some countries accumulated high deficits even before the crisis (particularly Greece and Hungary), in most cases the underlying factors were linked to the crisis, either in passive form (falling government revenues) or in active form (large-scale stimulus packages financed by the central budget). Budget deficits reached double-digit levels in Greece, Ireland, Great Britain, Spain, and Portugal (similar to the United States, with serious global economic and financial implications that, unfortunately, are, at the time of this writing, only being addressed).

In 2010, budget deficits remained high despite the easing of the financial and macroeconomic crisis and relevant policy measures to curb them. Although the EU-27 average was somewhat reduced, it was still at a very high level. At the same time, some countries reported further increasing budget deficits (Ireland being a unique case). All Eurozone members (except Finland) remained in the 'red area'.

Following a consistent decrease in budget surpluses throughout 2006–08, Russia experienced its first high budget deficit in 2009, registering a sharp decline of 11.2 per cent compared to 2008.

The last column of Table 1.4 summarizes the change that took place in the budget position of the EU-27 member countries and Russia between 2007 and 2010. It is obvious that the budgetary position of all member countries, except Hungary (which had had to accept an austerity programme just in the period of the global crisis), experienced a radical deterioration. Similar processes characterized developments in Russia, the United States, and Japan.

The story of rapidly increasing budget deficits, or, in a less pessimistic case, the stagnation of deficit levels, is far from finished. While stimulus packages are relatively easy to implement, it is much more cumbersome and risky to discontinue them, with special regard to the sequencing, the speed, and the timing of withdrawing such support. There are two opposing opinions under discussion regarding this issue. One position argues that, as recovery has already started in some countries (see Germany), no further financial injection is necessary, since growing domestic demand (and the restarting of the export engine) will provide the necessary conditions for self-sustained growth. In addition, any prolongation of anti-crisis measures would further deepen budget deficits and contribute to ever less sustainable public debt levels.

The other view considers the abandoning of fiscal stimulus packages as premature, due to the not yet clear (let alone fully fledged) recovery. Even in Germany, surprisingly high growth rates have been generated mainly by growing exports and not by higher domestic demand. It is uncertain whether exports alone can provide the engine for sustainable growth and, no less importantly, when (or even if) export-fueled growth will ignite the engine of domestic demand. This is a particularly important question for the new Member States, where, according to medium-term forecasts, growth will be based on exports and not on the sluggish, stagnating, or even further declining domestic demand (Inotai, 2011a). It should not be forgotten that the first stage of European recovery (if observable) has been connected with very low interest rates, depreciation of the euro vis-á-vis the US dollar (in the first half of 2010), and still expansive fiscal policies. If one or more of these factors are removed, there could be a fall back into a W-type crisis or, in a less pessimistic scenario, Europe could become the hostage of a 'low-growth equilibrium' (Münchau, 2010), similar to Japan, for a longer period. It is interesting to note that it was the negative growth rates, accompanied by a rapid fall of domestic demand (and of foreign trade), that has kept inflation very low. As a result, the inflation rate proved to be the only one of the Maastricht criteria that could be fulfilled by practically all EU member countries in 2010 (except Hungary, Romania, Greece, and the United Kingdom, three of which are not Eurozone countries).

Public debt

This is probably the most serious development with longer-term consequences for the EU in general and for the Eurozone, in particular. According to the Maastricht criteria, the public debt of a member country (let alone that of an applicant country) is not allowed to surpass the 60 per cent (GDP related) limit. However, this rule was already breached at the birth of the EMU as several countries, with much higher levels of public debt at the time of admission, were nonetheless admitted to the club (Italy, Belgium, and later Greece). Partly due to this 'original sin', the public debt of the Eurozone was already at 66 per cent of GDP in the pre-crisis year of 2007, while the non-members (except Hungary) had an average clearly below the 60 per cent mark.

Table 1.5 classifies EU member countries in three groups based on their public debt figures for 2010. Two EMU member countries, namely Italy and Greece, have a public debt higher than 100 per cent of GDP. Another group consisting of ten countries (including eight Eurozone members plus the United Kingdom and Hungary) violates the rule by reporting GDP-related public debt between 61 and 97 per cent. Finally, the third group complies with the Maastricht criteria, including nine new members of 2004 and 2007, without taking into account Cyprus and Malta. In this group, we only can find four Eurozone countries, and out of them three are the new members that joined (Slovenia, Slovakia, and Estonia)[4] the EMU after accession in 2004.

Even more disturbing than the high level of debt is the very rapid increase in public indebtedness in recent years. Moreover, this trend

Table 1.5 Public debt of selected EU Member States and Russia (in per cent of GDP)

Country	2006	2007	2008	2009	2010	Change 2007 to 2010
EU-27	61.5	59.0	62.3	74.4	80.2	21.2
Eurozone-17*	68.4	66.2	69.9	79.3	85.4	19.2
Greece	106.1	105.4	110.7	127.1	142.8	37.4
Italy	106.6	103.6	106.3	116.1	119.0	15.4
Belgium	88.1	84.2	89.6	96.2	96.8	12.6
Ireland	24.8	25.0	44.4	65.6	96.2	71.2
Portugal	63.9	68.3	71.6	83.0	93.0	24.7
Germany	67.6	64.9	66.3	73.5	83.2	18.3
France	63.7	63.9	67.7	78.3	81.7	17.8
Hungary	65.7	66.1	72.3	78.4	80.2	14.1
United Kingdom	43.4	44.5	54.4	69.6	80.0	35.5
Austria	62.1	60.7	63.8	69.6	72.3	11.6
Netherlands	47.4	45.3	58.2	60.8	62.7	17.4
Spain	39.6	36.1	39.8	53.3	60.1	24.0
Poland	47.7	45.0	47.1	50.9	55.0	10.0
Finland	39.7	35.2	34.1	43.8	48.4	13.2
Latvia	10.7	9.0	19.7	36.7	44.7	35.7
Denmark	32.1	27.5	34.5	41.8	43.6	16.1
Slovakia	30.5	29.6	27.8	35.4	41.0	11.4
Sweden	45.0	40.2	38.8	42.8	39.8	−0.4
Czech Republic	29.4	29.0	30.0	35.3	38.5	9.5
Lithuania	18.0	16.9	15.6	29.5	38.2	21.3
Slovenia	26.4	23.1	21.9	35.2	38.0	14.9
Romania	12.4	12.6	13.4	23.6	30.8	18.2
Bulgaria	21.6	17.2	13.7	14.6	16.2	−1.0
Estonia	4.4	3.7	4.6	7.2	6.6	2.9
Comparison						
Russia	9.1	8.5	7.9	11.0	9.9	1.4
United States	61.4	62.4	71.5	84.7	92.0	29.6
Japan	191.3	187.7	195.0	217.6	223.1	35.4

*including Estonia (member of Eurozone as of January 2011).
Source: IMF (2010) *World Economic Outlook April 2010* (Washington: International Monetary Fund) (2006–07), Eurostat (2011a) and own calculations (last column).

cannot be suddenly halted, even if Member States were ready to stop stimulus packages immediately. The already achieved budget deficits will keep on spilling over into public debt, which for Eurozone countries has reached 85.4 per cent in 2010 (as compared to 79.3 per cent in 2009). Despite the outstanding priority given to fiscal consolidation in almost all EU countries, public debt is anticipated to keep on rising until 2012 (from 80.2 to 83.3 per cent for the EU-27 and from 85.3. to 91.1 per cent for the Eurozone, respectively). Similar trends are forecast for the United States (from 98.5 to 107.6 per cent) and Japan (from 219 to 241 per cent) as well. By contrast, Russia has received more positive prognoses with the general government public debt slowly decreasing up until 2012 (from 9.9 to 9.5 per cent) (IMF, 2012).

Between 2007 and 2010 the increase in public debt reveals two-digit figures in almost all EU countries (except Bulgaria and Sweden, both at the lowest end of public debt/GDP indicator). Particularly worrisome are the indicators for Ireland (a three-year increase from a comfortable 25 to 96 per cent), Greece (by 37 percentage points), and for the United Kingdom (from 45 to 80 per cent). Russia, on the other hand, demonstrates relatively low and steady indicators with the greatest increase of 3.1 percentage points in 2009 compared to 2008.

It should be stressed that the importance of reducing public debt is not primarily in order to meet the (somewhat artificial) Maastricht criteria but rather in the interest of keeping or regaining the confidence of global capital markets. Without that confidence, the necessary amount of refinancing may not be available or could be obtained only at very high interest rates, further aggravating the debt situation.

Several dilemmas underlie the difficulty in finding a way to manage the current situation. In principle, the policy options are well known; each one presents its own advantages and risks. Furthermore, their implementation may generate reluctance or even open opposition due to the expected economic and social costs. The first and the best version would be if the stimulus programmes had been applied with the priority of establishing favourable conditions for long-term and sustainable growth, higher productivity, and competitiveness. Unfortunately, with very few exceptions, all national programmes were aimed at bailing out banks (without the necessary restructuring), saving ailing industries, such as car manufacturing and construction, as well as maintaining the employment level (again, without the necessary restructuring/flexibilization of the labour market). As a result, the optimistic scenario can be forgotten.

There are other approaches which could be implemented in various combinations. Two policy options are strictly linked to the reshaping of the budget. The first option is that budgetary revenues could be increased by higher taxes (in some countries by more efficient tax collection). However, this approach would immediately strangle the process of recovery at its initial and rather uncertain stage. A second budgetary option is the (fundamental) restructuring of the expenditure side of the budget, with sensitive cuts in social welfare benefits and a potentially even more important reduction in the role and influence of the state in redistributing a (large) part of the GDP. Resistance can be predicted by large segments of society, including public administration (and other vested interests linked to financial sources from the central or even regional/local budgets). Most probably this option cannot be avoided, but it will not be able to achieve sizeable cuts within a short time. Implementing this option is also made difficult because of the long duration needed to realize this approach and the growing gap between political and economic rationalities. In a democratic system, political rationality is strictly linked to the electoral cycle (in Europe generally four-year terms of the government formed by coalitions of several parties). Therefore, politicians are obviously led by short-term (in the best case four year) considerations of re-election. By contrast, economic rationality at times of radical transformation requires a much longer time horizon in key sectors, such as public administration, healthcare, pensions, education, research, and development. No basic reform can be successfully (and sustainably) carried out within a four-year political cycle. It is a key open question to what extent democratic systems of the developed countries will be able to adjust themselves to these new economic challenges (they are far more important than annual budget deficits or public debt figures) and reconcile short-term political and longer term economic interests without undermining the foundations of the current democratic system.

This leads to the final, perhaps unavoidable, option – the social (certainly not equitable) redistribution of the accumulated debt. It should happen in two (parallel) ways. First, a large part of the debt will need to be inflated within a relatively short period (with relatively high inflation). Second, in the framework of an intergenerational redistribution, part of the debt will be transferred to the next generation, be redistributed across countries, accompanied (if possible) by some kind of social dialogue and consensus, or between the public and private sector (as is occurring at the moment). However, a fully fledged fiscal transfer union could make cross-country redistribution likely.

Impact of the crisis on EU and Russian trade

An outstanding feature of the current global crisis has been the collapse of international trade. As one of the key engines of sustainable and high economic growth in the past decades, trade has generally grown two to three times more quickly than GDP. This pattern was generally maintained even in periods of (modest) economic recession. By contrast, the global crisis of 2008–09 had a devastating impact on international trade in general, and on economies that had been building their development strategy on the export-oriented pattern, in particular. From 2008 to 2009, global output fell by 2.4 per cent, at the same time that international trade shrunk by more than 12 per cent. Similar, but even stronger trends, can be identified for the EU. While its GDP fell by 4.2 per cent in 2009, exports decreased by 17.9 and imports by 20.4 per cent as compared to 2008. The somewhat less sharp decline of exports than imports can mainly be attributed to the relevant fall of the international price of raw materials and energy commodities, of which the EU is one of the largest importers.

However, international trade saw an unexpectedly quick recovery. While GDP growth is likely to need several years to reach the pre-crisis level (2007 or 2008), international trade has shown a more rapid upswing, or 'return to normality'. EU exports in 2010 reached the level of 2007 (the last full year without crisis). The same process, although at a slower pace, can be seen in import figures as well (Table 1.6).

Interestingly, intra- and extra-EU trade indicate contradictory developments. While intra-EU exports fell by 19.1 per cent from 2008 to 2009, extra-EU exports suffered a loss of 'only' 16.1 per cent. By contrast, intra-EU imports declined less (by 19.0 per cent) than extra-EU imports (by 22.9 per cent), mainly due to lower commodity prices imported from outside the EU. As a consequence, the share of extra-EU exports increased, while that of extra-EU imports shrunk. This trend became reinvigorated during the first year of recovery. In 2010, as compared to the crisis level of 2008, extra-EU exports experienced growth of 3.3 per cent. The explanation is that most EU member countries facing the serious downturn of domestic and intra-EU demand tried to discover new and potentially dynamic markets outside the EU (particularly in Asia, mainly in China).

Tables 1.7 and 1.8 contain detailed data on the development of total, intra- and extra-EU exports and total exports for Russia in the period of the global crisis. None of the EU Member States could avoid the shrinking of total exports in 2009 (as compared to 2008). The main victims of the export collapse were some old and partly competitive countries, first of all Finland and also Sweden, Italy, Austria, and Great Britain. The relatively best performance was produced by crisis-ridden Ireland. New member countries performed about or slightly above the EU average (Romania, Slovakia, Poland, and the Czech Republic).

At the same time, export developments of all members between 2009 and 2010 have felt the positive impact of recovery. In fact, exports

Table 1.6 Impact of the global crisis on trade relations of the European Union

Exports (in euro billion)							
Exports to	**2006**	**2007**	**2008**	**2009**	**2010**	**2010 (2007 = 100)**	**2010 (2008 = 100)**
World	3.656	3.880	4.011	3.294	3.888	100.2	96.9
Intra-EU	2.497	2.705	2.715	2.197	2.539	96.1	93.9
Extra-EU	1.160	1.241	1.307	1.097	1.349	108.7	103.3
Imports (in euro billion)							
Imports from	**2006**	**2007**	**2008**	**2009**	**2010**	**2010 (2007 = 100)**	**2010 (2008 = 100)**
World	3.770	3.999	4.189	3.335	3.966	99.2	94.7
Intra-EU	2.417	2.564	2.624	2.128	2.463	96.1	93.9
Extra-EU	1.353	1.435	1.565	1.207	1.503	104.7	96.0

Source: Eurostat (2011b).

Table 1.7 Impact of the global crisis on total (intra+extra-EU) exports of selected EU Member States and Russia (in euro billion)

Country	2006	2007	2008	2009	2010	2010 (2007 = 100)	2010 (2008 = 100)
EU-27	3.656	3.880	4.011	3.294	3.888	100.2	96.9
Germany	882.5	967.8	983.3	803.0	957.1	98.9	97.3
Netherlands	369.3	401.6	433.7	357.0	432.5	107.7	99.7
France	394.9	403.4	408.8	347.6	393.3	97.5	96.2
Italy	332.0	358.6	365.8	291.7	337.4	94.1	92.2
Belgium	292.2	314.3	320.8	265.2	311.0	99.0	96.9
United Kingdom	357.3	319.5	312.5	253.0	306.0	95.8	97.9
Spain	170.2	175.9	191.4	163.0	185.3	105.3	96.8
Austria	108.9	118.9	123.3	98.2	115.1	96.8	93.3
Poland	88.2	101.3	115.9	97.9	117.5	116.0	101.4
Sweden	117.7	123.3	124.7	93.9	119.4	96.8	95.7
Ireland	86.7	88.4	85.5	83.1	88.0	99.5	102.9
Czech Republic	75.6	89.1	99.8	81.0	100.2	112.5	100.4
Denmark	73.7	75.4	79.3	67.3	73.7	97.7	92.9
Hungary	59.9	69.0	73.8	59.5	72.0	104.3	97.6
Finland	61.4	65.5	65.6	45.1	52.8	80.6	80.5
Slovakia	33.4	42.4	48.3	40.2	49.3	116.3	102.1
Portugal	34.5	37.4	38.0	31.7	36.8	98.4	96.8
Romania	25.9	29.4	33.7	29.1	37.3	126.9	110.7
Slovenia	18.5	21.9	23.2	18.8	22.0	100.5	94.8
Greece	16.5	17.2	17.2	14.7	16.3	94.8	94.8
Russia	–	257.0	318.0	216.4	301.3	117.2	94.7

Source: Eurostat (2011b), International Trade Statistics: http://www.trademap.org/tradestat/index/ and own calculations.

became, once again, the key pillar of economic growth. In 2010, the pre-crisis level, measured by figures of 2007, was restored by the EU-27. Moreover, eight Member States outperformed the 2007 figures, some of them by spectacular growth (Romania, Slovakia, Poland, and the Czech Republic, all new and increasingly competitive members of the EU). As compared to the crisis year of 2008, five members could report a complete recovery of exports in 2010 (four new members, plus crisis-ridden, but continuously competitive, Ireland). Most other countries were around the EU average of 97 per cent and with justified hopes to reach the pre-crisis export level in 2011. Interestingly, the exceptions are represented not only by weak competitors, such as Greece and Italy, but also by high competitors of the past, such as Finland, Denmark, Austria,

Table 1.8 Comparative impact of the global crisis on intra- and extra-EU exports of selected Member States (change between 2007/2008 and 2010)

Country	Intra-EU exports		Extra-EU exports	
	2010 (2007 = 100)	2010 (2008 = 100)	2010 (2007 = 100)	2010 (2008 = 100)
EU-27	96.1	93.9	108.7	103.3
Germany	92.2	92.9	111.3	105.1
Netherlands	106.3	97.3	112.6	108.8
France	91.2	92.2	109.2	103.1
Italy	89.7	90.4	100.7	94.9
Belgium	94.4	92.2	113.8	112.5
United Kingdom	88.8	92.6	105.5	105.0
Spain	102.1	94.3	112.9	102.6
Austria	95.1	92.1	101.2	96.7
Poland	115.8	102.4	116.7	98.0
Sweden	90.6	91.3	106.7	102.5
Ireland	91.1	95.4	114.3	115.8
Czech Republic	110.8	99.3	121.2	106.4
Denmark	91.7	87.9	112.6	104.7
Hungary	102.2	96.2	112.2	102.5
Finland	77.7	78.8	84.5	82.7
Slovakia	113.3	101.3	135.3	107.2
Portugal	96.2	98.5	105.3	92.6
Romania	127.5	113.2	125.4	104.8
Slovenia	103.3	99.4	94.5	86.5
Greece	92.7	93.1	98.2	97.9

Source: Eurostat (2011b) and own calculations.

and Sweden. The latter phenomenon needs a more detailed survey that is not part of this chapter.

Table 1.7 demonstrates a rise in Russian exports in 2010 compared to the pre-crisis year 2007, registering a slight decrease compared to the first year of the crisis, 2008. The relative stability in terms of Russian exports can primarily be explained by the most important sources of Russia's hard currency revenues, namely, exports of energy resources. Throughout 2007–10, profits from exports of oil, natural gas, and coal constituted on average 60 per cent of Russia's total export revenues (Economist Intelligence Unit).

The growing discrepancy between intra- and extra-EU exports can be clearly identified on the country level as well (see Table 1.8). While the intra-EU exports of only three Member States could reach the 2008 level (all of them new members, namely Romania, Poland, and

Slovakia), 13 members reported higher extra-EU exports than in 2008, and most of them (except Greece, Slovenia, and Finland) higher values than in 2007. Without questioning the fundamental importance of the EU market (representing 55 to 80 per cent of total exports), several Member States not only turned more attention to rapidly developing (emerging) markets but also their economic policy and production structures were able to carry out the necessary adjustments required for a (partial) geographic reorientation. Maybe surprisingly in this context, not only almost all new Member States (except Slovenia, suffering from its one-sided Western Balkan links) but also some small economies of the 'old EU' (Ireland, Belgium, Netherlands) played an above-average role.

In this process, as well as in the crisis management of the EU in general, China requires special attention.[5] Among all major extra-EU partners, China was the only one to which EU exports kept on growing, even during the crisis year of 2009. In contrast to an export collapse by 17.9 per cent (in total exports) and by 16.2 per cent (in extra-EU exports), EU exports to China grew by 4.1 per cent. It should be noted that imports from China fell by 13.4 per cent, but still much less than total extra-EU imports (by 23 per cent). As a result, China not only could consolidate its role as the leading extra-EU supplier of the EU (16.7 per cent of total extra-EU imports in 2010) but also became the second-largest extra-EU export market for the EU (8.8 per cent, ahead of Russia) (Eurostat, 2011b). Another important feature is that most EU member countries, particularly the new members, could substantially expand their exports to China in 2009. Romanian exports jumped by 33 per cent, while the respective figures were 32 per cent for Slovakia, 21 per cent for Poland, and 18 per cent for Hungary. Among the EU-15, similar growth rates were reported only for Belgium (26 per cent) and low-volume exporter Portugal (21 per cent). However, the most striking development is that, by 2009, China became the second-largest export market for Germany and the United Kingdom, and the third most important one for a number of other countries (Belgium, Denmark, France, Italy, Netherlands, Slovakia, Finland, Sweden, and the EU-27). Simultaneously, the leading Chinese role in extra-EU imports continued to be strengthened. In 2009, China was not only the largest supplier of the EU (from outside the EU-27, a position held since 2005) but also the largest exporter to no less than ten Member States (Germany, Greece, Italy, Spain, Luxembourg, Malta, the Netherlands, and the Czech Republic, Hungary and Romania among new members). To continue, in 2010 China replaced the United

States as the leading extra-EU supplier of France and the United Kingdom. However, the 'top surprise' was delivered by Germany, because in 2010 China became the leading supplier of this country not only among extra-EU exporters but also ahead of Germany's two traditional trading partners, the Netherlands and France. In other words, Chinese exports to Germany ranked first even considering intra-EU figures.

Impact of the crisis on foreign direct investment flows of the EU and Russia[6]

Tables 1.9, 1.10, and 1.11 present some basic figures on the behaviour of foreign direct investment during the first period of the crisis. Developments have been surveyed on three levels: inflow, outflow, and changes in the capital exporter versus importer position.

Global direct capital inflows and outflows were seriously hit by the financial and macroeconomic crisis. Inflows fell by almost half, while outflows by more than 50 per cent between 2007 and 2009. Both as capital importer and exporter, the relative weight of the EU in global

Table 1.9 Impact of the global crisis on direct capital inflows[a]

Target country	2007 US$bn	2008 US$bn	2009 US$bn	Change[b] (2009/2007)	Share 2008	Share 2009
World	2100.0	1770.9	1114.2	53.1	100.0	100.0
EU-27	923.8	536.9	361.9	39.2	30.3	32.5
France	96.2	62.3	59.6	62.0	3.5	5.3
UK	186.4	91.5	45.7	24.5	5.2	4.1
Germany	76.5	24.4	35.6	46.5	1.4	3.2
Belgium	118.4	110,0	33.8	28.5	6.2	3.0
Italy	40.2	17.0	30.5	75.9	1.0	2.7
Netherlands	115.4	-7.6	26.9	23.3	(−0.4)	2.4
United States	266.0	324.6	129.9	48.8	18.3	11.7
Canada	108.4	55.3	18.7	17.3	3.1	1.7
Japan	22.6	24.4	11.9	52.7	1.4	1.1
LDCs	564.9	630.0	478.3	84.7	35.6	42.9
Russia	55.1	75.5	38.7	70.2	4.3	3.5
China	83.5	108.3	95.0	113.8	6.1	8.5
HK	54.3	59.6	48.4	89.1	3.4	4.3

[a]According to the definition of UNCTAD foreign direct investment (FDI) includes equity investment, intra-company loans and reinvested earnings.
[b]Figures for 2007 are always 100.
Source: UNCTAD (2010).

Table 1.10 Impact of the global crisis on direct capital outflows[a]

Capital exporting country	2007 US$bn	2008 US$bn	2009 US$bn	Change[b] (2009/2007)	Share 2008	Share 2009
World	2267.5	1928.8	1101.0	48.6	100.0	100.0
EU-27	1287.3	915.8	388.5	30.2	47.5	35.3
France	164.3	161.0	147.2	89.6	8.3	13.4
German	162.5	134.6	62.7	38.6	7.0	5.7
Italy	90.8	43.8	43.9	48.3	2.3	4.0
UK	318.4	161.1	18.5	5.8	8.4	1.7
Netherlands	28.4	20.1	17.8	88.6	1.0	1.6
Belgium	105.9	130.0	−15.1	62.7	6.7	(−1.4)
United States	393.5	330.5	248.1	63.0	17.1	22.5
Canada	59.6	80.8	38.8	65.1	4.2	3.5
Japan	73.5	128.0	74.7	101.6	6.6	6.8
LDCs	292.1	296.3	229.2	78.5	15.4	20.8
Russia	45.9	56.1	46.1	100.4	2.9	4.2
China	22.5	52.2	48.0	213.3	2.7	4.4
HK	61.1	50.6	52.3	85.6	2.6	4.8

[a]see Table 1.9.
[b]see Table 1.9.
Source: UNCTAD (2010).

capital inflows and outflows was substantially reduced, not least due to the dramatic decline of mergers and acquisitions among the EU Member State businesses (and, to some extent, as a consequence of still existing barriers to free capital flows in the internal market). Previous large capital importers, such as the United Kingdom, Belgium, and the Netherlands (all with figures above US$ 100 billion in 2007), became modest players by 2009. China alone has imported more direct capital than any EU Member State, and even Hong Kong obtained more capital than EU countries (except France). Some consolidation took place between 2008 and 2009 due to the sharp decline of capital inflows to the United States. Still, the share of the EU in global direct capital inflows remains a bit less than one-third (as compared to 44 per cent in 2007, the last pre-crisis year). In 2007, the EU registered capital inflows that were more than 60 per cent higher than those reported by all less developed countries (LDCs) together. By contrast, in 2009 the latter group imported one-third more capital than the EU. These contrasting patterns are not only a sign of differential macroeconomic impacts of the crisis but provide clear evidence of shifting trends in global economic growth.

Table 1.11 The global crisis and the balance of FDI inflow and outflow (in US$ billion)

Regions and countries	2007	2008	2009
EU-27	−363.5	−378.9	−26.6
France	−68.1	−98.7	−87.6
Germany	−86.0	−110.2	−27.1
Italy	−50.6	−26.8	−13.4
Netherlands	+87.0	−27.7	+9.1
UK	−132.0	−69.6	+27.2
Belgium	+12.5	−20.0	+48.9
United States	−127.5	−5.9	−118.2
Canada	+48.8	−25.5	−20.1
Japan	−50.9	−103.6	−62.8
LDCs	+272.8	+333.7	+249.1
Russia	+9.2	+19.4	−7.4
China	+61.0	+56.1	+47.0
Hongkong	−6.8	+9.0	−3.9

[a]see Table 1.9.
Source: UNCTAD (2010).

While Russia's share of global direct capital inflows was 4.3 and 3.5 per cent in 2008 and 2009, respectively, putting the country far behind the EU-27, it nevertheless exceeded the shares of some individual Member States (such as Germany, France, and Italy in 2008 and Belgium and the Netherlands in 2009). Generally, the period of 2007–09 is charaterized by a sharp decrease in global direct capital inflows (by 70.2 per cent).

Traditionally, together with the United States and Japan, the EU has been the largest direct capital exporter and, thus, the driver of growth both in the EU, in transatlantic relations and also in economic contacts with a number of LDCs. In 2007, almost 57 per cent of global direct capital outflow originated in the EU. As a result of the crisis, mainly felt in some of the largest capital exporting countries of the European Union (such as the United Kingdom), potential capital exporting sources dried up. Consequently, the EU's share fell to 35 per cent of global direct capital outflow. Still, it remains the largest source of global direct capital, ahead of the United States and the rapidly catching up developing countries (35.3, 22.5, and 20.8 per cent, respectively, in 2009) (UNCTAD, 2011).

Despite its relatively small share in direct capital exports (only 2.9 and 4.2 per cent in 2008 and 2009, respectively), Russia experienced a general increase in direct capital outflows in 2009, exceeding the indicators for 2007. In contrast to the general decline in direct capital outflows that befell such major players as the EU and the United States in 2008, Russia reached its highest point of US$56.1 billion, greatly exceeding its 2007 level.

The impact of the crisis can best be observed in the balance between direct capital inflow and outflow. Both the EU and all major developed countries used to be strong net capital exporters. This position experienced a dramatic meltdown in 2009, when the net balance of US$ 363.5 and US$ 378.9 billion (for 2007 and 2008, respectively) shrunk to an almost negligible US$ 26.6 billion. By contrast, Russia went from being a net capital importer in 2007 and 2008 to a net capital exporter in 2009.

While, traditionally, the EU capital outflow (export) surplus was able to fully cover the net capital inflow (import) needs of the LDCs (coverage of 133 per cent in 2007 and 113 per cent in 2008), in 2009, strikingly, only a bit less than 10 per cent of this demand could be satisfied by the available EU capital export surplus. The dramatic change is fundamentally due to the fact that as a consequence of the economic crisis, the United Kingdom turned from a large net capital exporter to a net capital importer (the same trend could be observed for Belgium and the Netherlands), while the previously similarly large capital export surplus of Germany and Italy decreased to one-third to one-quarter of their levels in the last pre-crisis year.

Conclusion

The financial and macroeconomic crisis has fundamentally affected the architecture of European integration in general and the decade long construction of the Eurozone in particular. Similarly, it had a significant impact on Russia's economy. On the one hand, a number of radical institutional, economic, and financial steps were taken in the period between 2008 and 2011. In fact, the three-year trajectory or crisis management can best be described as a 'path from the impossible to the inevitable'. On the other hand, most of the instruments agreed on were the result of lengthy and sometimes thorny negotiations that tried to overcome or reconcile different member country interests, partly due to the uneven impact of the crisis on individual countries. In addition, radical decisions sometimes required a lengthy and contradictory period of implementation and overwhelmingly remained reactive to the repeated challenges produced by ever new stages of the crisis. The common EU currency, suffering from construction failures from the very beginning and lacking a strategy for bad weather periods, has been particularly hit. While in several countries economic growth and external trade could recover in a relatively short period, serious problems have been accumulated in the budgetary area and, even more, in the field of public debt. Both need a longer-term strategy and the creation of a new quality of European integration to be remedied. These tasks represent a unique challenge, since very different and mostly conflicting goals must be reconciled, such as the (re)balancing of sustainable growth under conditions of budgetary constraints, persuasive public debt reduction, and the management of labour market and social issues in a slow (or zero) growth period. Even more importantly, the cohesion of the EU can be seriously jeopardized as Member States reveal rather different economic fundamentals, as well as widely differing degrees of financial stability and international competitiveness. These problems manifest themselves with unique vigour in the permanent crisis of the Eurozone.

The world economic crisis of 2008–09 caused a downturn in Russia's economy as well. The country's steady GDP growth observed during the period prior to 2008 came to an abrupt halt when the indicators reached their lowest point, having dropped by 7.8 per cent in 2009 from 2008. As had been predicted, Russia managed to recover its modest annual growth rate in 2010; however, its GDP remains lower than the pre-crisis level. Russia's heavy dependence on revenues from natural resource exports made it vulnerable to any change in world gas and oil prices resulting in the rapid decline in the Russian economy when the latter crashed in 2008. An overall decrease in the country's oil revenues precipitated a major budget deficit in 2009, followed by a slight recovery in 2010. The country's slow response to the world crisis as well as high government control over the economy are among other reasons for Russia's economic downturn.

Although the initial phase of crisis of 2008–09 seems to be over, the current period, characterized as 'the management of the costs of crisis management', hides several sources of future conflicts, ranging from slow or negative growth, through rising unemployment and increasing income polarization, to various open and potential cleavages among different groups of member countries or even between individual members. In sum, the crisis generated several threats for the EU that can stop or even decompose part of the integration project carefully established over more than half a century and mostly in an international (and European) framework very different from that of today. At the same time, the crisis has opened up new opportunities as well that include a dynamic deepening of European integration in practically all fields of activities, with a clear direction towards fiscal and political union and renewed competitiveness in the 21st century. At the moment, the majority of challenges and open questions are well known and wait for adequate responses, on which the future of the EU will crucially depend in the second decade of the 21st century.

Notes

1. Data are drawn from Eurostat, the International Monetary Fund (IMF) and the Organisation for Economic Co-operation and Development (OECD), according to sources indicated in the associated tables.
2. See Chapter 10 for a discussion of the Polish case.
3. The advantage of this system can be manifold. On the one hand, it continues employing people and paying them (a reduced amount of) salary. As long as the reduced salary is higher than the unemployment benefit, it has a positive impact on (potential) private consumption. On the other hand, the budget is not further burdened by unemployment benefit payments. Last, but not least, part-time workers can easily be re-employed as full-time employees, once the recovery restarts (as was the case in Germany in 2010). However, it has to be added that the part-time scheme resulting in lower unemployment does not solve the fundamental problem, namely it does not raise the total volume of the labour market (calculated in total hours worked, it may even reduce it).
4. Estonia became part of the Eurozone in January 2011, so it was not a member during the crisis years.
5. For a detailed statistical analysis, see Inotai (2010, 2011a and 2011b).
6. Although most recent figures are beyond the timeframe of this study, it has to be noted that, similar to the rapid recovery of trade flows, the international direct capital flows also experienced the return to high growth in 2010. Also the EU's global position could be strengthened, mainly due to the large capital exports from Germany and France. By contrast, capital inflows to the Central European member countries of the EU reveal a rather mixed picture. While FDI inflow in 2010 to the Czech Republic and Hungary was higher than in 2009 (and turned to be positive for Slovakia), respective figures remained below the 2009 mark for Poland and Romania (UNCTAD, 2011).

Bibliography

Cooper, W.H. (2009) 'Russia's Economic Performance and Policies and Their Implications for the United States', CRS Report for Congress, http://www.fas.org/sgp/crs/row/RL34512.pdf, accessed on 10 July 2012.

Economist Intelligence Unit 'Country Profile Russia', http://www.eiu.com/index.asp?layout=country&geography_id=1750000175, accessed on 16 July 2012.

Eurostat (2011a) 'European Economic Forecast, Spring', *European Economy 1* (Brussels: Directorate General for Economic and Financial Affairs of the European Commission).

Eurostat (2011b) 'External and Intra-European Union Trade, Monthly Statistics', 02/2011 (Brussels: European Commission).
Inotai, A. (2010) 'Impact of the Global Crisis on Trade Relations between the European Union and China', *Hungarian Statistical Review*, 14, 46–68.
Inotai, A. (2011a) 'After the Crisis?' *Public Finance Quarterly*, 56 (3), 360–378.
Inotai, A. (2011b) 'Impact of the Global Crisis on EU-China Relations: Facts, Chances and Potential Risks', in T. Matura (ed.), *Asian Studies* (Budapest: Hungarian Institute of International Affairs), 80–102.
International Monetary Fund (IMF) (2012) *Fiscal Monitor Update*, January 24 (Washington: International Monetary Fund).
Münchau, W. (2010, July 12) 'Even Eurozone Optimists Are Not Optimistic', *The Financial Times*.
Solbes, P. and R. Youngs (2010) 'Europe Is Failing to Shape the Global Governance Debate', *Europe's World*, Summer, 8–13.
Organisation for Economic Co-operation and Development (OECD) (2011) *International Migration Outlook* (Paris: Organisation for Economic Co-operation and Development).
United Nations Conference on Trade and Development (UNCTAD) (2010) *World Investment Report 2010* (New York: United Nations).
United Nations Conference on Trade and Development (UNCTAD) (2011) *World Investment Report 2011* (New York: United Nations).

2

EU Institutions Face the Great Recession: How Has the Machinery Worked?

George Ross

The European Union's (EU) mode of operating has changed significantly since the Maastricht Treaty. Citizens are now more sceptical and Member States are more reluctant to cede power to the EU. Enlargement to 27 members has made high-level dealings more cumbersome, and new treaty arrangements – the Lisbon Treaty in particular – have enhanced the importance of intergovernmental decision-making. Because of all this, the EU is likely to be slow in making important choices and its decisions are more likely to reflect the lowest common denominator of diverse Member State positions.

The global crisis that began in 2007–08 came in three moments and sorely tested EU institutions. During the first moment, after 2008, the EU had to save its financial industries, stimulate its economies to stop a downward spiral of activity, and re-regulate its financial sector. In the second moment, which began in later 2009, the EU then had to try and save the Eurozone, which came close to exploding because of sovereign debt problems. The third moment began even before the second had finished, as EU governments had to reduce the large debts and deficits contracted in the crisis at the cost of domestic distress caused by harsh austerity. This chapter will survey how the EU's institutions have performed in these very different moments, which have presented the most dramatic economic and political challenges in the EU's history.

Phase 1: Bailouts, stimuli, regulation

The economic storm began in the United States. US governments had long encouraged Americans, particularly lower income ones, to buy homes. This led to new and looser types of housing financing and a housing bubble after the end of the dot.com boom in 2000–01. Risky new financial techniques plus banking deregulation complicated the bubble situation. Financial sector risk-management models were inadequate and credit rating agencies were too closely tied to the institutions whose products they rated. Extraordinary bonuses gave financial operators incentives to trade and deal as much as possible, whatever the consequences. Finally, the academic economics profession, very important to the intellectual climate around business, had convinced itself that financial markets were infallibly self-regulating.

The bubble began to burst when the US Federal Reserve pushed up interest rates, housing prices fell, and the financial sector panicked. Credit tightened and the overleveraged American financial sector needed outside help to avoid collapse. By 2008, the US government was reorganizing and refinancing large government-sponsored mortgage financing organizations (Fannie Mae and Freddie Mac), while Wall Street investment houses, the biggest commercial banks, and the mortgage sector faced mortal dangers. In September 2008, Lehman Brothers went bankrupt, there were very large stock market losses and the global financial sector suffered a massive credit squeeze. The 'Great Recession' had begun (Kelley and Love, 2010; Eichengreen, 2011, Chapter 5; Madrick, 2011).

Many Europeans initially believed that Europe would escape the worst. It seemed better regulated, more prudent, and better endowed with automatic stabilizers. This was, however, to underestimate financial internationalization. There were housing bubbles in the United Kingdom, Spain, Ireland, and elsewhere, as Wall Street's risky financial practices had found their way into the heart of Europe's financial sectors. In the terms of a European Commission analysis, '...cross border transmission was...extremely rapid, due to the tight connections within the financial system...and also the strongly integrated supply chains in global product markets...' (European Commission, 2009a).

The first stage of the Great Recession would prove to be a huge test of the EU's capacities for responding to emergencies. As American housing, credit, and derivatives markets sank, European banks faced daunting solvency problems. The European Central Bank (ECB) quickly injected new liquidity to keep the Eurozone credit flowing and coordinated with the American Federal Reserve Board and other central banks (Trichet, 2010; Quaglia, Easterwood and Holmes, 2009, pp. 74–75). Serial banking disasters across Europe elicited specific national responses, which were initially hastily improvised bailouts. The collapse of the Icelandic banking system and an Irish governmental guarantee of bank deposits precipitated a broader approach, however, because both raised the spectre of uncoordinated beggar-thy-neighbour national actions (Wade and Sigurgeirsdóttir, 2010).[1]

The turning point was a British decision in early October 2008 to provide massive liquidity to the UK financial system, recapitalizing and partially nationalizing its biggest banks and guaranteeing their new debt issuances (Quaglia, 2009). The British had 'first mover' gifts because of the flexible Westminster system and Gordon Brown's long experience as Chancellor of the Exchequer. With this decision, the energy level of European coordination went up, mainly because French President Nicolas Sarkozy, leading the French Presidency of the Council of the EU, pushed for new European responses modelled on the British initiative. The Barroso Commission, barely present to this point, then proposed an action plan, which, approved by the European Council on 15–16 October, called for ECB intervention to boost liquidity and for Eurozone governments to underwrite bank debt to prevent the collapse of core financial institutions.

What followed had to be *ad hoc* because of EU intergovernmentalism. In the Commission's words, national governments proposed national plans, 'more or less following these (Commission) guidelines' (Quaglia, Easterwood and Holmes, 2009, pp. 76–77). Sometimes banks were recapitalized and semi-nationalized, sometimes deposits were guaranteed by governments; sometimes private banks reconfigured their operations by consolidation and mergers. At the end of the day, however, the precise terms of what was done were left to Member State governments.

Intergovernmental coordination did not stop at the EU's borders. Simultaneous efforts on a more global scale began when European G4 leaders (the heads of the British, French, German, and Italian governments) met together in early October 2008 to plan for the G7. Sarkozy and Barroso then flew to Washington to persuade President Bush to convene the G20 in November, a decisive step enlarging discussion beyond the rich North.[2] The International Monetary Fund's (IMF) $29 billion loan to Hungary, negotiated in part by the EU, made clear as well that the stability of the Central and East European countries (CEECs) was not solely EU business.

The November 2008 G20 meeting in Washington concluded that members should use fiscal stimulation to avoid massive collapse in the 'real economy'. The European Commission had projected EU growth in 2009 at –4 per cent. Deep recession meant rapidly rising unemployment (nearly 10 per cent EU-wide in 2009), more spending on social programmes and fewer tax revenues, worsening the budgetary situations of Member States.[3] Stimulus packages were then devised, with differing notions about how much to spend and for what purposes. Most Member

States listened to Commission proposals in November for a coordinated European recovery plan that suggested a stimulus of €200 billion totalling 1.5 per cent of EU gross domestic product (GDP) – spread over 2009 and 2010, which would come primarily from Member State budgets (European Commission, 2008).[4]

Americans were critical about the relative modesty of European stimulus plans (Watt, 2009). One reason for this modesty was that the Stability and Growth Pact was still in effect, even if its criteria were relaxed in the crisis. The budgetary situations in the Member States also varied greatly, with some, like Finland, Denmark, Sweden, Luxembourg, and Poland, in good shape and others with much greater deficit and debt issues. The deeper reasons for modesty were that the EU was not the United States, a huge single jurisdiction with vast stimulus needs magnified by a feeble welfare state, while most EU members had much more substantial safety nets. In addition, the EU's own budget was small, around 1 per cent of GDP. Finally, there were big divisions among Member States. The United Kingdom, like the United States, wanted as much stimulation as rapidly as possible to save its financial sector, even if this meant huge new deficits. Other EU Member States either preferred more targeted plans, could not afford more than they proposed or did not agree with the neo-Keynesian orthodoxy of American critics.[5]

Prior to the crisis, almost everyone believed that the new Central and East European Member States were on a fast track to catch up economically with the EU-15. However, the CEE area was among the regions hardest hit by the crisis, with projections of a 15.8 per cent GDP decline through 2009 (Darvas, 2009). The CEECs differed greatly from one another. Poland, the Czech Republic, Slovakia, and Slovenia were in reasonable shape, even if recession meant declining foreign investments and demand for exports. Latvia and Lithuania, small new Baltic members, plus Bulgaria and Romania, the least developed CEECs, had much larger deficits, debts, dangerous ties to Western banks, and less successful economies.[6] Hungary, where complicated politics combined with economic mismanagement, had such high debts and deficits that bankruptcy loomed. Finally, many CEECs had threatening, large euro-denominated, EU-15 originated, consumer debts (often mortgages) that were dangerous in a context of collapsing credit. These different effects also varied by exchange rate regimes – Slovenia and Slovakia belonged to the Economic and Monetary Union (EMU), others had floating rates (Poland, the Czech Republic, Hungary, and Romania), while still others had currency boards pegged to the euro (Latvia, Bulgaria, Estonia, Lithuania).

EU responses to the CEECs' troubles were mixed. The Commission sped up structural funding and loosened rules. The Union greatly increased medium-term financial assistance, made conditional loans to Hungary, Latvia, and Romania, and agreed to invest more in Trans-European Network projects. The European Investment Bank (EIB) expanded activities in the region by 30 per cent in 2008–09 and the European Bank for Reconstruction and Development (EBRD) chipped in with a joint action plan for the CEECs' banking sectors. The danger that Western European banks with CEECs' portfolios might pass their liquidity problems eastward was limited by commitments from the ECB, Sweden, and the EU itself. Finally, the IMF made large loans to Hungary, Latvia, and Romania.[7]

Remodelling financial sector regulatory systems was the next big task. The EU's main approach to the financial sector prior to the crisis had been deregulatory.[8] This meant that despite substantial new cross-border financial operations, EU financial institutions remained regulated and supervised nationally and there was a diversity of approaches (Pisani-Ferry and Sapir, 2009). Given the political power of financial actors, promoting regulatory change at European level was bound to be difficult. In addition, because new EU reforms would have global significance, the EU had to gauge its proposals towards international cooperation through the G20 and other international organizations.

The Commission took the lead by naming a 'high level group on financial supervision', chaired by Jacques de la Rosière, which in February 2009 recommended strengthening capital requirements for banks, reforming and better supervising credit-rating agencies and changing asset valuation and other accounting techniques. Its larger conclusions were that every part of the financial system of systemic importance needed to be regulated and supervised. Derivative products should be standardized and simplified and there should be a new EU clearing house to make credit default swaps transparent. New policies on corporate governance and remuneration should control bonuses, beef up risk management, and oblige prefunding of deposit insurance programmes. There should also be a single set of core regulatory and supervisory standards to iron out national differences within a new EU crisis management and resolution framework. Finally, the rules that governed investment funds needed to be strengthened (European Commission, 2009b).

The Commission quickly committed to legislating these recommendations, and most of them became law in Fall 2010 (European Commission, 2009c). There would be a new European Systemic Risk

Council (ESRC) under the ECB's roof to produce risk warnings and recommendations, with legal access to all information. National supervision would continue, given the variety across the Union, but the ESRC could constrain national supervisors and coordinate with other international risk supervision bodies, including the Financial Stability Board recommended by the G20. There would also be a new micro-prudential European System of Financial Supervisors (ESFS), plus three new 'European Authorities' on banking, insurance and pensions, and securities' regulation (Véron, 2010).

In this first crisis moment, EU responses helped stem the collapse of the financial sector and limit damage to the real economy. By Fall 2010, European output, growth, and GDP per capita were again expanding, if only very slowly (*Financial Times*, 2010a). The primary actors in this were governments who, through intergovernmental coordination, patched together crisis policies that had worked for the most part. The main constitutional reasons for such an intergovernmental approach were that EU Member States retained sovereignty in those financial and economic policy areas that needed to be coordinated. The EU's supranational institutions played secondary, but not insignificant, roles. The Commission tended to act only when it knew what key Member States wanted to do. When it did act, however, its proposals were timely, clear, workable, politically astute, and usually well received. The European Council worked more erratically, depending upon who held the rotating presidency. French President Sarkozy brought great energy to the task in the Fall of 2008; the Czech Presidency that followed was a dismal failure (in part because the Czech government collapsed early in its term); while the Swedish Presidency of later 2009 was quiet but efficient.

Without the EU, national governments might well have taken their individual paths. But EU single market and competition policies placed limits on such dangerous centrifugal forces, particularly protectionism. The EMU was equally important. The ECB was the central actor for the Eurozone, supplying liquidity, following an accommodative monetary policy, meshing well with the global network of central banks upon which the maintenance of trade and stability depended and demonstrating surprising flexibility. That the EMU existed in the first place may have been even more important. Without the euro, separate EU Member State currencies would have floated wildly, some would have been devalued, and a few countries would have faced default.

In the final analysis, intergovernmental coordination helped stop the downward spiral of crisis primarily because the EU existed as the most compelling arena for such coordination. EU Member States worked in many different arenas of governance, and their financial sectors and economies were embedded in national, European, and global networks. But on economic and financial matters it was the EU networks that counted the most, mainly because building such networks and the arenas within which they were regulated was what the EU was mainly about. Intergovernmentalism may have been growing, but when EU governments had to sort out serious economic matters, no matter how much they differed on substance, they sought to do so within the EU.

Phase 2: The Eurozone under siege: crisis in the crisis

There had been evidence of a widening in sovereign bond yield rates between the weaker and stronger EU economies early in the crisis, but concern about it was sidelined in the face of more urgent matters. These differences widened rapidly in late 2009; however, when it became clear that Greece might be unable to meet its sovereign debt obligations. Greece had an extraordinarily bad history financially and it had at first been denied entrance to the Eurozone in 1998. Its annual deficit then miraculously dropped to 1 per cent and even though its debt level was above 100 per cent (lower than that of the Italians and Belgians, already in the EMU) it was admitted in 2001. The miracle was in part accomplished by book cooking and inaccurate statistics (Lynn, 2011, Chapters 2 and 3).

The Greek economy grew rapidly in the early 2000s, helped greatly by foreign investment and the very low Eurozone interest rates. This growth hid underlying problems of low competitiveness, high private and public deficits, and growing debt, and when the global crisis hit, it collapsed. Shipping and tourism, among the few sectors where Greece had a comparative advantage, went into a coma. Tax revenues also declined, as Greek citizens never have been eager taxpayers. The fundamental problem, however, was that financial markets had focused on the possibility that the Greeks would be unable to pay their debts. Widening bond yield spreads between the two Eurozone extremes, Greece and Germany, forced Greece to come clean (Lynn, 2011, Chapters 7 and 8). The new Greek socialist government elected in Fall 2009 first announced that the advertised 6 per cent annual deficit was really 12.7 per cent, which, after recalculation, rose to above 14 per cent.

When European leaders like Frederick Reinfeldt, the Swedish Prime Minister (at that time also representing the rotating Swedish Presidency of the EU Council of Ministers), announced in December 2009 that there would be no bailouts for Greece, bond market assumptions that the EU would stand behind Eurozone members' problems were shattered. Such statements also fed talk about the EMU collapsing and led to a drop on global stock markets. Repeated downgrading of Greek debt by rating agencies made it possible that Greece would turn out to be the EU's Lehman Brothers. In addition, other Eurozone countries with serious crisis-related debt problems fed bond market contagion and threatened the EMU. The way the story subsequently unfolded was complicated, but highly revelatory about the state of today's EU.

From the outset, German Chancellor Angela Merkel stressed that Germany would not allow a bailout and would refuse to allow the Eurozone and the EU to make one collectively. The Greeks had created their own problems, she said, and should fix them themselves. In general, Germany believed that the Greek crisis was not a matter of EU 'solidarity' and that the EMU was not a 'transfer union', a coded reference to the no bailout clause in the Maastricht EMU Treaty.

Germany had always insisted that monetary union be based on strong rules constraining Eurozone members to adopt a culture of financial stability, following traditional German *Ordnungspolitik*. The Eurozone crisis demonstrated that this culture, if it had ever really existed within the EMU, had broken down. However, the German government, backed strongly by German public opinion, was initially unwilling to allow the original EMU architecture to be changed.[9] By contrast, French leaders, echoing the concerns of other Latin Eurozone members, wanted a rapid bailout out of fear that the entire Eurozone might be imperilled and proposed an 'economic government' with stronger European-level supervision and legal constraints on national fiscal and budgetary practices, a position that French President Mitterrand and Commission President Delors had earlier argued at Maastricht.

The February 2010 European Council nonetheless concluded that the Greeks might be helped in some ways if the Eurozone were really in danger, provided they undertook strong enough measures to reduce their deficit levels to 3 per cent by 2012 – an impossible demand (Ludlow, 2010; European Council, 2010a). Greek Prime Minister Papandreou then duly produced harsh cutback plans, which briefly calmed market speculation and produced massive protests in Athens.[10] The European Council's February communiqué solemnly promised to take action, if needed, to protect the Eurozone. Angela Merkel, on the other hand, was adamant that EU intervention could only happen as a last resort – a term that media, other EU Member States, and financial operators found unclear. Such declarations left open what these actions might involve and when they would be decided. The bond markets concluded that Greece would have difficulty imposing austerity and that a bailout solution would take time, if it happened at all. Greece's bond costs rose to twice those of Germany.

Intergovernmental bickering went on through March 2010 as Eurozone member states, excepting Germany, debated extending bilateral loans to Greece at subsidized interest rates. The Greek government tried to precipitate events by threatening to seek an IMF loan if Eurozone partners did not soon act.[11] The Spring European Council then responded in very vague terms. The ECB was more precise, however, when it announced that it would accept Eurozone members' bonds as collateral even if the rating agencies had downgraded them.

Concrete action depended upon the Greeks formally asking for help, which they did not do until late April of 2010.[12] In the meantime, Standard and Poor's had lowered Greece's bond rating by three more grades and the global stock market took another large hit. It took two more weeks before Eurozone heads of state reacted, in panic, in an emergency Eurogroup meeting beginning on 7 May 2010 (Lynn, 2011, Chapter 8).[13] By this point it was clear that the euro crisis was on the verge of becoming a new Lehman Brothers.

The European Commission put a paper on the table proposing a large programme of bailout loans (without the IMF) with the money to be raised by creating European bonds, close to what the French wanted (European Commission, 2010a). But the thought of this appalled the Germans, who feared that the German Constitutional Court would rule the Eurobonds unconstitutional. Under huge pressure from the opening of global stock markets, however, Eurogroup leaders then compromised in the German direction. There would be a new bailout body with deeper financial pockets that could provide loans to the menaced Eurozone countries: the European Financial Stability Facility (EFSF) with €440 billion in loans from EU countries, €60 billion from the EU budget, and a further €250 million from the IMF, a total of €750 billion.[14] The first use of the new EFSF was a loan of €110 million to Greece, in exchange for a fourth Greek austerity programme.[15] Merkel and other German leaders intimated that these huge sums would only buy time, unless everyone shifted quickly into a harsh austerity mode.[16] Their scepticism was correct. The euro exchange rate went down like a stone (rising later in the year as the US dollar declined), temporarily boosting European, mainly German, exporters, but in late Summer 2010 the troubles returned.

Ireland was the next victim. The Irish problems had begun in the private banking sector, rather than, as in Greece, in the public budget. The backdrop was the 1990s Celtic Tiger moment of high growth rates due to Ireland's favourable location in globalization, plus seductive tax policies – a very low 12.5 per cent corporate tax rate, among other incentives – that welcomed foreign companies. With intelligent labour relations and a well-qualified workforce, Ireland, which had very recently been one of Europe's most backward small countries, then became a booming centre for American foreign direct investment (FDI). Alas, in the later 1990s, Irish banks, like Greece, taking advantage of low EMU interest rates and deregulation, launched an extraordinary real-estate bubble that saw Irish house prices rise 172 per cent in a dozen years. The Irish spree of flipping real estate, borrowing against housing equity, government subsidies for housing developments for which there were no buyers, and an explosion of personal credit fed declining competitiveness. When the Great Recession pushed Ireland into downturn, in Fall 2008, the government imprudently guaranteed the debts and deposits of the country's six largest banks for two years, a blunder that put the state on the hook for $650 billion and transformed a private sector problem into one of sovereign debt (Lynch, 2010, Chapters 8 and 9; *The Economist*, 2010).

Bond market worries and downgrades from the American rating agencies about Irish default brought the Eurozone and the EU back to full alert, but this time there was a solution ready at hand. The Irish could borrow from the EFSF, and the bond markets would then quickly calm down. The Irish did not really want to borrow, however, because they had enough money to pay debt interest for several months and preferred not to impose the austerity on Irish citizens that borrowing would oblige. No matter, the EU and the Eurozone heavyweights, including the ECB, forced them to take €85 billion anyway. An Irish blogger characterized what happened as '...political hardball: Brian Lenihan... [Irish Finance Minister]...from Castleknock versus the heirs of Bismarck and Cardinal Richelieu' (*Financial Times*, 2010b).

The Eurozone crisis then continued its perplexing way, propelled forward by trigger-happy bond markets. Portugal was targeted next and forced to borrow €78 Billion from the EFSF in April 2011. The Portuguese lending operation was similar to the earlier Irish one, with considerable pressure coming from Brussels, Berlin, and Paris to move rapidly. Unlike Greece and Ireland, where policy blunders and dubious behaviour abounded, Portugal was more of a hard luck story. It had joined the EMU despite a relatively backward state of economic development and had never been able to catch up. Beyond this, its problems followed from the effects of the EMU's low interest rate after 1998, which encouraged new debt to sustain consumption and the dramatic shift in its budgetary situation in 2008–09 (Torres, 2009).

A lasting pattern of EU intergovernmental dithering and relative political power had emerged. At each step of the way, and often in between, there was conspicuous quarrelling about how to respond. The feuding then most often ended in an inadequate compromise, almost always struck on German terms that eventually stimulated renewed bond market anxiety about sovereign debt. As the October 2010 European Council approached, for example, Germany proposed new emergency crisis mechanisms, including harsh sanctions for national deficits and debts, even urging that EU voting rights be suspended for exaggerated fiscal profligacy.[17] Germany got the French to agree to much of this by watering down the automaticity of proposed sanctions in exchange for French support for a surgical treaty change (the insertion of one sentence into the Treaty on the EU) to accommodate a long-term European Stability Mechanism (ESM) that would replace the temporary EFSF (European Council, 2010b).[18] The bond markets, however, were not convinced.

The political processes of crisis decision-making in both the Eurogroup and the European Council, where answers had to be found, were by now clearer. The 'Franco-German' couple were at the core of EMU and the processes of both institutions. When the two disagreed, however, Germany almost always carried the day. For example, the Germans held their line against the Eurozone as a 'transfer union'. Germany was also reluctant to accept constraining new bailout commitments: as Merkel announced early on, such commitments might have to be made, but 'only as a last resort', and then only on Germany's terms. A later example came in the 'Eurobond' episode that began in 2010, part of the broader debate on setting up the ESM. Eurobonds were pushed hard by the French and would have 'federalized' or 'mutualized' the Eurozone bond market, with Eurozone members collectively issuing bonds. The change would have made richer EMU members responsible for the less successful and possibly raised their borrowing costs and credit risks. Germany, with other rich country allies (Austria, the Netherlands, and Finland), would have none of this. The new ESM would be built from grouped national loans, like the EFSF before it.

The 2010 loan to Greece did not resolve Greece's debt problems and by Springtime 2011 there had to be new discussions about loaning Greece even more to stave off default – eventually another €110 billion. The country's indebtedness had shot up to well over 150 per cent of GDP, even as new austerity policies had eliminated growth and provoked more public anger. Germany again played hardball about restructuring existing loans. Finance Minister Schäuble, the most avid 'European' in Angela Merkel's inner circle, insisted that bondholders should accept 'haircuts' and share the costs of bailouts with taxpayers. This brought the German leadership into conflict with the ECB, which feared Greek default (*Financial Times*, 2011a, 2011b, 2011c; Boone and Johnson, 2011). Germany again won. Beyond lower Greek interest rates, the July 21 deal included a substantial rollover on older loans and much longer maturity dates for new ones, implying technical defaults on some Greek debt. Germany's original insistence that restructuring be obligatory (which could have produced a large 'credit event') scared the ECB, leading the French to broker 'voluntary' acceptance. Once again, Greece was obliged to implement austerity more assiduously.

Conditions in the bond market eased following this summit, but bond buyers changed their minds when again faced with 'haircuts', which, once the markets began to suspect that they might extend beyond Greek debt, turned out to be a tactical mistake on Germany's part. The coincidence of the new Greek deal with American political confrontation over the legal debt ceiling, plus evidence that wealthy country economic growth was stalling did not help. The consequences of new bond market unrest and threats of contagion to the much larger economies of Spain and Italy were frightening.

Nicolas Sarkozy and Angela Merkel then held another Franco-German summit on 8 August 2011 to make new policy proposals and also to have a big public show that might help calm the troubled political waters both leaders faced at home. Merkel had to cope with difficult regional elections, growing voter Euro-scepticism and criticism of her leadership from her own party and coalition partners. Sarkozy, a year away from a decisive re-election campaign, was way down in the polls. Their proposals for addressing the Eurozone's problems included a 'real economic government', a new instance where heads of state and government would meet twice a year presided over by the President of the European Council. Next, all EMU members should adopt a constitutional 'golden role' (the French translation of the German *Schuldenbremse*, or 'debt brake', which had been added to the German Basic Law in 2009) obliging balanced budgets. However, few other EMU members seemed interested. Sarkozy's government had proposed it to the French parliament, however, mainly to trap the opposition socialists into coming out against it, in the hope of costing the socialists opinion poll points in the upcoming presidential campaign for refusing to cooperate in saving the EMU. The third proposal was for a Tobin Tax (a transnational financial transaction tax) on EU financial transactions. Here there was no enthusiasm at all beyond Sarkozy. Finally, Merkel and Sarkozy pledged to develop identical corporate tax systems as a pilot project for the Eurozone, something that was even implausible between Germany and France and fiercely opposed elsewhere. The bond markets could see through all this and were unimpressed. Nonetheless, the episode indicated yet another shift in German positions after their earlier turnaround on bailouts. They were also admitting that traditional German ordo-liberal insistence on an EMU rules culture was needed to keep Eurozone members from dangerous fiscal and budgetary imprudence.

The Eurozone quagmire had worsened again by early Fall 2011. The second payout to Greece slowed down because bankers balked at accepting 'haircuts' while the EU, the ECB, and the IMF had a difficult time persuading the Greek government to stop dragging its feet on austerity plans. Italy, with high debts and a government that obstinately avoided doing much about them, had become the markets' next target, with bond interest rates reaching a danger point. The Italian economy was very large, however, as was its financial mess, and, in the worst case, the EFSF would have insufficient funding to bail Italy out. The new threat was doubly ominous because French and German banks held much of the Italian and Spanish debt.

Yet another Eurozone summit on 26 October 2011 – depending on how and what one counted, the 15th since the Greek difficulties had emerged – produced solemn pledges for a 50 per cent haircut on Greek debt, a fourfold multiplication of EFSF funding to serve as a 'firewall' to stop bond market contagion in Italy and Spain, a mandatory 9 per cent bank capitalization within the EU to block systemic bank problems and new pledges from Berlusconi to cut Italy's debt. New calm in the markets lasted only for a few days, however, since even a cursory reading of the meeting's vague communiqué showed that the discrepancies between the pledges made and actual programmes were very great. Many commentators then began talking about the need for the ECB to become the Eurozone's lender of last resort, even if they all knew that Germany would never allow this to happen.[19]

Any remaining optimism that the bond markets would calm was then shattered by George Papandreou's proposal to have a referendum on his government's policies. Following this, the 'Merkozy' gloves came off, leading to the almost immediate removal of Papandreou in Greece and Berlusconi in Italy, both quickly replaced by skilled technocrats, in ways that looked very much as if France, Germany, and Brussels had put the two countries under direct trusteeship.

During these two years of bewildering and often inconclusive intergovernmental fire fighting there was nonetheless a great deal of incremental EMU repair work begun towards building 'new EU economic governance' to remedy the obvious problems with the Maastricht

Treaty arrangements (European Commission, 2011). Whether a single currency area could succeed without more serious constraints on national fiscal autonomy had been a long-running argument, and these repairs pointed towards greater Eurozone and EU prerogatives over national budgetary and financial practices. The first large changes were the new ESFS from the de la Rosière report. Next, in Fall 2010, the European Commission proposed a package of six directives to strengthen EU and Eurozone oversight over national fiscal frameworks and practices that started working in December 2011 (European Commission, 2010b) with the goal of speeding up excessive deficit procedures, scrutinizing the sustainability of public debt, using the EU budget as a monitoring/sanctioning device (e.g., by holding back structural funds payments) and seeking better control of national macro-financial and structural imbalances. Eurozone members had also agreed to establish an ESM to take over from the temporary EFSF from the middle of 2013. Beginning in 2011, the EU also implemented its first 'European Semester', an annual exercise during which national budget peer reviews and the development of the EU's Broad Economic Policy Guidelines were done in sequence. The March 2011 European Council adopted a 'Euro Plus Pact', whose signatories (Eurozone countries, plus six others) committed to new procedures to foster competitiveness, employment, sustainable public finances, and financial stability. Finally, EU Member States (minus the UK, which refused to cooperate and the Czech Republic, which refused to make its position clear) drafted a new 'fiscal compact' treaty in 2012 that would oblige Member States to constitutionalize balanced budget 'golden rules' and to add new monitoring and enforcement mechanisms to oblige compliance, partly in the hope that this might persuade the ECB to take larger steps towards becoming a Eurozone lender of last resort.

This may look like a long list of virtuous changes. But, as close observers know, the EU is constantly making declarations, writing detailed analytical papers, legislating new procedures, and establishing new institutions. Whether such things turn out to do what they advertise is often another story. In the case of the Eurozone crisis, strong incentives exist to make them work, but forces that could lead them to fall short are strong as well. It is also the case that almost everything that has been done is designed to work in the medium and longer term. Processes of shorter-term first-aid measures have nonetheless been repeatedly fraught with problems and, more often than not, failed to stem the bond market agitation at the heart of the crisis. Indeed, it has often looked as if Member States could agree on the new general architecture for the EMU, perhaps in the hope of buying time, rather than on the kinds of shorter-term measures that might have ended the crisis outright, an approach that has turned out to be very costly.

The biggest problems revealed in the Eurozone crisis have been the deficiencies of EU intergovernmentalism as a way of reaching decisions. The EU worked surprisingly well in the first phase of the financial meltdown because of the fit between its intergovernmentalism and the immediate situation after Lehman Brothers in 2008. However, it has worked badly indeed during the second phase. There have been several reasons for this. The absence of crisis provisions in EMU law obliged Eurozone member states and the EU to devise responses from scratch under intense pressure. These responses could only be reached intergovernmentally, because this was how the Eurozone was governed. Alas, the exercise of making decisions turned out to be about as far from a win–win bargaining situation as one could have imagined among friendly neighbours. Virtually all possible outcomes were costly both philosophically and economically, but for some more than for others. In such a situation, urgency, relative bargaining power, and the interplay of national preferences determine outcomes. This meant that strong German opinions about the EMU and disagreements within the powerful Franco-German 'couple' handicapped the search for timely and coherent responses that could actually have stopped the market frenzy. This handicap also meant that it was easier to make commitments about longer-run rather than shorter-run matters, in the hope that they would buy time that would minimize the costs of short-term fire fighting. In part, the substance of this was a repetition of the arguments about the basic EMU architecture that had already been won at Maastricht by the Germans, where greater weight was placed on longer-term economic-cultural changes, rather than shorter-term vigilance over Member State behaviour. In the circumstances of the Eurozone crisis, however, these arguments contributed to confusing rhetoric, half measures, and slow decision-making. The bond markets then repeatedly responded by demanding greater risk premiums for investing in the EMU members most under threat. As a result, intergovernmental bickering and the slow processes of negotiation consistently made the crisis more threatening and raised the costs of fixing it.

The Eurozone and the broader EU have rarely been able to avoid the most predictable dilemmas of multilateral bargaining, like slow decision-making and the likelihood of less than optimal solutions. Following Maastricht, some had held out hope that greater political union might follow from the EMU and help transcend these dilemmas.

Instead there was a retreat towards more selfish intergovernmentalism, partly encouraged by growing citizen scepticism about the EU. However, some of the underlying structures of intergovernmentalism had also changed. German obduracy in the Eurozone crisis has been widely interpreted as representing a new, more assertive, expression of German national interests. Joschka Fischer, the former Social Democratic Foreign Minister, asserted about Angela Merkel that 'Mrs Europe has become Frau Germany' (*Nouvel Observateur*, 2010, p. 30). No less an observer than Jürgen Habermas added that '...the current German elites are enjoying the return to normality as a nation state. Having reached the end of a "long path to the West", they are certified democrats and can once again be "just like the others"...' (Habermas, 2010; Patterson, 2011).[20] This may help explain changes to the 'Franco-German couple', whose efficient cooperation was the *sine qua non* of confronting the Eurozone crisis. France had long used German 'semi-sovereignty' to advance its own preferences. However, after 1989, and then reunification, German semi-sovereignty was no longer available for such French purposes. On top of this, the meaning of the French proposals for the EMU 'economic government' have never been very clear, beyond some form of policing national fiscal policies that was likely to be weak, given other French preferences for intergovernmental decision-making in such matters.

Therefore, changes in German outlooks were far from the only story. In the demanding conditions of the Eurozone crisis, divergence in national economic strategies, which had grown larger over the first decade of the EMU, made productive compromise between national preferences much more difficult in general. Solving the crisis looked to be costly and many Member States either could not afford the costs or would not accept them because of their domestic political situations. This may become less important if and when the current crisis eases, but it might also be that differences in economic strategies between key Member States will push future political disagreements nearer to a breaking point.

Phase 3: How to grow in the midst of austerity?

The Eurozone crisis thrived at the same time as most EU members scrambled towards a third crisis moment involving the imposition of harsh austerity programmes to reduce the deficits and debts that bailouts and stimulus plans had earlier caused to explode. The outcome of these austerity efforts will depend in large part both on the performance of the global economy and on what ultimately happens in the Eurozone. With bad economic luck, cutbacks and reforms in most EU Member States could well mean lower European growth over an indefinite period, even if a few Member States came out of the Great Recession in reasonable shape. The present political predominance of centre-right national governments and the neo-liberalism of the European Commission probably mean that these austerity policies will have severe consequences. Recent history tells us that it is difficult to reform pensions, rebuild educational systems, control healthcare costs, and reconfigure labour markets in the absence of fruits of growth to reward potential losers. Such fruits could be very difficult to find in most EU countries in the next period. Resistance, protest, and more volatile electoral politics have already played important roles in reversing governments in the EMU's worst hit peripheral countries like Greece, Portugal, Ireland, and Spain, and in others like the UK and Denmark. The situation may also feed Europe's rapidly growing far-right xenophobic populisms. All of these processes, depending on their severity, could produce greater scepticism about the EU and lead to more difficult intergovernmental dealings even than those just discussed. The EU is not about to disappear, but its credibility and ability to confront future problems could suffer.

Notes

1. The Irish move, a clear act of 'fiscal dumping', induced a run from other European, particularly British, banks. However, there was nothing illegal in EU terms about what the Irish did. The EU had regulations about minimum levels of deposit insurance but none about maximum ones.
2. Commission officials close to Barroso claimed credit for the emergency meeting in Washington that led to the G20 event. But Jean-Pierre Jouyet and Sophie Coignard (2009, p. 62) recount a conversation in late September, in which Barroso responds to Jouyet's concerns, with Jean-Pierre: 'you are mistaken ... we shouldn't scare people. It is above all an American crisis ...' (author's translation). In other words, the Commission was behind the Sarkozy curve.
3. The recession was long and deep: The aggregate EU GDP began to decline in the second quarter of 2008, hit its deepest point in the first two quarters of 2009 (at which point only Poland and Slovakia were not officially in recession), and did not break zero again until the third quarter of 2009.
4. The Commission would later estimate that the total of stimulus packages, including the workings of automatic stabilizers, was between 3.3 and 4 per cent of GDP.
5. Those more dependent on industrial success, like Germany, preferred to re-launch exports and keep valuable workers employed part-time rather than pumping up consumer demand. Smaller, more corporatist, countries like the Nordic countries and Austria had experience with targeting quick economic stimulation, while many others had none. Finally, some, particularly most of the CEECs, were too poor to stimulate much at all.

6. These ties were as threatening to the Western banks as to their CEE creditors. Austrian banks, for example, were exposed at 55 per cent of Austrian national GDP. Swedish banks were also heavily exposed in the Baltic region.
7. At the April 2009 G20 meeting in London, European governments committed €125 Billion to the IMF, a part of which would go to the CEECs' needs.
8. Before the crisis began, the EU's main concern about financial markets had been opening them under the single market programme through an ambitious Financial Services Action Plan, which invoked competition policy concerns to facilitate cross-border transactions, mergers, and acquisitions. The first aim of this approach was to seduce financial actors into supporting European financial market-building. In the medium term, new Euro-level regulatory practices would come following the tried-and-true EU single market spillover tactics.
9. Electoral constraints were important. There were crucial regional election campaigns going on at the time, the Christian Democrat-Free Democrat coalition was unpopular and influential parts of the German media – *Bild*, for example – were adamant against helping the Greeks.
10. The Greek government increased Value Added Tax, cut public sector wages and benefits, froze pension levels, blocked new public sector hiring, slowed infrastructure spending, and talked about attacking corruption and tax evasion.
11. This was then followed by a high-level EU discussion about whether help from the IMF would be a humiliation, with the ECB clearly believing it would be.
12. The Greeks were clearly playing the last card remaining in their hand that if they did not get the right conditions they would put the euro itself in jeopardy.
13. Obama, then IMF Director-General Dominique Strauss-Kahn and ECB President Jean-Claude Trichet lobbied furiously in the meantime for a weightier Eurozone action, and Nicolas Sarkozy allegedly threatened to pull France out of the EMU if nothing more was done.
14. The EFSF money would come from bonds backed by Eurozone countries raised by the three-year 'Special Purpose Vehicle' under Luxembourg law. The British and Danes refused to participate because they were not part of the Eurozone. This prompted various threats from Eurozone leaders that should the pound get into trouble the United Kingdom could not count on getting help from Eurozone countries.
15. Greece pledged, among other things, tax reform and increases, cutbacks and wage cuts in public employment, and pension reforms.
16. Bundesbank leaders grumbled about this and argued that the ECB's emergency purchase of bonds was a violation of Maastricht. The German popular press continued to campaign against subsidizing incompetent and cheating countries.
17. The French wanted a new Eurozone Council with summits, a secretariat, and new powers but knew they would not get it. Germany wanted a new and more stringent structure of rules and obligations for all 27 EU Member States, and they had more power.

18. Treaty changes were to fend off the German Constitutional Court's likely refusal to allow new bailout mechanisms because of Maastricht's no bailout clause.
19. In fact, after Mario Draghi replaced Jean-Claude Trichet in Fall 2011 the ECB began quietly buying €1 trillion of debt, particularly from banks, doing a creditable imitation of last resort lending, leading to market calming until Spanish debt fell under new siege in early 2012.
20. The argument was that prior to reunification, the Bonn Republic had used European integration to re-enter the good graces of neighbours, to prove German civility and reliability, and to overcome memories of the Nazi era. The Berlin Republic then came to feel less need to hide behind European integration.

Bibliography

Boone, P. and S. Johnson (2011) *Europe on the Brink* (Washington: Peterson Institute for International Economics Policy Brief).

Copsey, N. and T. Haughton (eds) (2009) *The JCMS Annual Review of the European Union in 2008* (Oxford: Wiley-Blackwell).

Copsey, N. and T. Haughton (eds) (2010) *The JCMS Annual Review of the European Union in 2009* (Oxford: Wiley-Blackwell).

Copsey, N. and T. Haughton (eds) (2011) *The JCMS Annual Review of the European Union in 2010* (Oxford: Wiley-Blackwell).

Darvas, Z. (2009) *The EU's Role in Supporting Crisis-Hit Countries in Central and Eastern Europe* (Brussels: Bruegel Policy Contribution).

Eichengreen, B. (2011) *Exhorbitant Privilege: The Rise and Fall of the Dollar and the Future of the International Monetary System* (New York: Oxford University Press).

European Commission (2008) *Communication from the Commission to the European Council, a European Recovery Plan* (Brussels: European Commission).

European Commission (2009a) 'Economic Crisis in Europe: Causes, Consequences and Responses', *European Economy* 7 (Brussels: European Commission).

European Commission (2009b) *Report of the High Level Group on Financial Supervision, chaired by Jacques de la Rosière* (Brussels: European Commission).

European Commission (2009c) 'Communication for the Spring European Council: Driving European Recovery', COM (2009) 114 final (Brussels: European Commission).

European Commission (2010a) 'Communication from the Commission to the European Parliament, The European Council, The Council, The European Central Bank, The Economic and Social Committee and the Committee of the Regions: Reinforcing Economic Policy Coordination', COM (2010) 250 final (Brussels: European Commission).

European Commission (2010b) 'Communication from the Commission... Reinforcing Economic Policy Coordination', COM (2010) 250 final (Brussels: European Commission).

European Commission (2011) 'The EU's Comprehensive Policy Response to the Crisis', Directorate-General for Economic and Financial Affairs, *Quarterly Report on the Euro Area*, 10(2) (Brussels: European Commission).

European Council (2010a) http://www.consilium.europa.eu/uedocs/cms_data/docs/pressdata/en/ec/112856.pdf (Brussels: European Council).
European Council (2010b) *EUCO 25/10, Co EUR 18 Concl 4* (Brussels, October 28).
Financial Times (2010a, 2 August), 'European Growth'.
Financial Times (2010b, 19 November) 'Ireland: A Punt Too Far'.
Financial Times (2011a, 16 May) 'Dogmatists Raise the Costs of the Euro-zone Crisis'.
Financial Times (2011b, 24 May) 'Euro-zone: Frankfurt's Dilemma'.
Financial Times (2011c, 11 August) 'Europe: Four Steps to Fiscal Union'.
Habermas, J. (2010, 9 June) 'Germany and the Euro-Crisis', *The Nation*.
Jouyet, P. and S. Coignard (2009) *Une Présidence Des Crises* (Paris: Albin Michel).
Kelley, B. and P. Love (2010) *From Crisis to Recovery: The Causes, Course and Consequences of the Great Recession* (Paris: Organization for Economic Co-Operation and Development).
Ludlow, P. (2010) 'A View on Brussels, In the Last Resort: The European Council and the Euro Crisis', *Eurocomment*, 7.7 and 8 Brussels.
Lynch, D. (2010) *When the Luck of the Irish Ran Out* (Basingstoke: Palgrave Macmillan).
Lynn, M. (2011) *Bust: Greece, the Euro, and the Sovereign Debt Crisis* (New York: Bloomberg Press).
Madrick, J. (2011) *The Age of Greed* (New York: Knopf).
Nouvel Observateur (2010) 20–26 May.
Patterson, W. (2011) 'The Reluctant Hegemon: Germany Moves Centre Stage in the European Union', in N. Copsey and T. Haughton (eds) *The JCMS Annual Review of the European Union in 2010* (Oxford: Wiley-Blackwell), 57–75.
Pisani-Ferry, J. and A. Sapir (2009) *Banking Crisis Management in the EU: An Interim Assessment* (Brussels: Bruegel Working Paper).
Quaglia, L. (2009) 'The British Plan as a Pace-Setter: The Europeanization of Banking Rescue Plans in the EU', *Journal of Common Market Studies*, 47(5), 1063–1083.
Quaglia, L., R. Easterwood and P. Holmes (2009) 'The Financial Turmoil and EU Policy Co-operation in 2008', in N. Copsey and T. Haughton (eds) *The JCMS Annual Review of the European Union in 2008* (Oxford: Wiley-Blackwell), 63–88.
The Economist (2010, November 20) 'Briefing: Ireland's Economy', 79–81.
Torres, F. (2009) 'Back to External Pressure: Policy Responses to the Financial Crisis in Portugal', *South European Society and Politics*, 14(1), 55–70.
Trichet, J. (2010) 'State of the Union: The Financial Crisis and the ECB's Response, 2007–2009', in N. Copsey and T. Haughton (eds) *The JCMS Annual Review of the European Union in 2009* (Oxford: Wiley-Blackwell), 7–19.
Véron, N. (2010) *EU Financial Regulatory Reform: A Status Report* (Brussels: Bruegel Policy Contributions).
Wade, R. and S. Sigurgeirsdóttir (2010) 'Lessons from Iceland', *New Left Review*, 65, September–October, 5–29.
Watt, A. (2009) *A Quantum of Solace? An Assessment of Fiscal Stimulus Packages in Response to the Economic Crisis* (European Trade Union Institute Working Paper 5) (Brussels: European Trade Union Institute).

3

Fiscal Crises in the Eurozone: Assessing the Austerity Imposed by the Bailouts

Patrick Leblond

Introduction

In the aftermath of the 2008–09 global financial crisis, the European Union (EU), most especially its Eurozone member states, was hit by a number of fiscal (or debt) crises, which began in Greece in December 2009, before moving on to Ireland and Portugal in 2010 and 2011, respectively. For their part, Spain, Italy, Belgium, and even France also ended up facing more or less strong headwinds from sovereign bond market investors as contagion, in the form of market and political uncertainty, spread throughout the Eurozone. The EU, with the help of the International Monetary Fund (IMF), worked hard to contain the debt crisis (or crises) and prevent it from propagating itself, but with limited success given the political difficulties involved in providing financial assistance to crisis-hit governments and banks (for details, see Chapter 2 by Ross in this volume). In the end, direct financial assistance (i.e., bailouts) had to be provided to Greece, Ireland, and Portugal. In Greece's case, a second bailout package had to be put together a year and half after the first one, this time involving a restructuring of Greece's public debt in order to avoid an outright (i.e., official) default.

These bailouts and the economic adjustment programmes that have accompanied them have been highly controversial politically as well as economically. For instance, there are those who claim that no bailouts should have been forthcoming and that Greece and company should have been left to fend for themselves. Then there are those who argue that the austerity packages imposed on Greece and others as a result of the bailouts are too harsh and will only make things worse. In the light of these controversies, it is worth asking ourselves whether the EU's (and IMF's) response to the fiscal crises in Europe (i.e., the bailouts and the accompanying adjustment programmes) has been appropriate under the circumstances at hand.

In order to answer this question, this chapter is structured as follows. First, the chapter provides a review of the literature on debt crises in order to tease out the lessons that have been learned from past fiscal consolidation and economic restructuring efforts. Second, applying these lessons, it analyses the EU's response to the fiscal crises in order to determine whether or not bailouts and their associated economic adjustment programmes have been appropriate to the situations at hand. What we find is that, in fact, the EU's response to the fiscal crises has been the right one and that the conditions that it imposed on Greece, Ireland, and Portugal, in exchange for financial assistance, are in line with the lessons offered by successful fiscal consolidations in the past. However, there is an important issue that plagues the Eurozone debt crisis, and it is one that the literature does not really address. This is the fact that there have been not one but many debt crises, with many countries in the same region adopting austerity measures at the same time, including those countries that did not receive bailouts. This has had the effect of making the fiscal consolidation process even more difficult, both economically and politically. Finally, the chapter concludes with the implications for the EU and the euro of the fiscal crises in Europe and the way that they have been managed.

Lessons from past fiscal consolidations

If the bailouts of Greece, Ireland, and Portugal have prevented these countries from defaulting on their debts, they must nevertheless cut down their fiscal deficits drastically and do so for a long period of time. Only once public finances are credibly back on a sustainable path will private investors be ready to buy these countries' sovereign bonds at acceptable rates of interest. The need for fiscal consolidation also applies to countries like Italy and Spain, which face serious threats to their public finances. In the end, the goal is to regain, or maintain, sovereign bond investors' confidence that their investments are safe and, as such, will be paid back in full with interest. The issue of concern here for policy makers is to know what the key elements of a successful fiscal consolidation process are, in order to design a proper response to the fiscal crises.

According to studies of past fiscal consolidation efforts, reductions in current government spending are more likely to lead to sustained adjustments than increases in tax revenues or cuts in investment expenditures (Alesina and Ardagna, 2010; European Commission, 2007, p. 196; Guichard et al., 2007, p. 7). The reason is that cutting government consumption and transfers is more difficult to achieve politically than raising taxes and cutting investment expenditures. As such, they are less likely to be reversed. Moreover, it sends a credible signal to investors that the government is committed to a lasting fiscal consolidation exercise, which will likely lead to a reduction in the yields demanded by investors. If the fiscal consolidation exercise is primarily based on increasing tax revenues, then government spending has a tendency to grow along with the additional revenues that are generated, thereby preventing the desired fiscal adjustment from being achieved (Guichard et al., 2007, p. 16). On the other hand, in a recent study, Paolo Mauro and his IMF colleagues find that intended or planned revenue-based adjustments grounded in reforms can also sometimes be effective alongside spending cuts (Mauro, 2011).

It is not just the size of the reductions in government spending that matters; their composition is also very important. According to Alesina and Perotti (1997), reductions in social welfare spending, as well as in government wages and employment, not only lead to more permanent fiscal consolidations, but also are beneficial for economic growth, since unit labour costs decrease. This is because cuts in government wages and employment influence wage setting in the private sector. For example, if the public sector is shedding workers or freezing new hirings, then it means that there is more competition for jobs in the private sector, which drives down the price of labour. Moreover, cuts in social welfare spending are likely to force more people to seek or remain in employment, which also contributes to the labour supply in the private sector, thereby pushing wages downward.[1] Such a decrease in average unit labour costs makes an economy more competitive, which leads to higher exports and investment and, ultimately, overall economic expansion. Combining government spending adjustments with structural economic reforms significantly enhances the chances of a successful consolidation, according to the European Commission (2007) and Mauro (2011). Since structural reforms entail liberalizing markets for labour, products, and services in such a way as to improve competition, lower costs, and increase innovation and investment, they further contribute to improving competitiveness and growth in the medium to long run, which in turn helps make the fiscal consolidation exercise durable.

If the right mix of government spending reduction is good for economic growth in the medium to long term, tax increases and reduced investment expenditures tend to have a negative impact on growth

(Alesina and Perotti, 1997; Ardagna, 2004). This is because they usually hurt an economy's competitiveness, which, as argued previously, is bad for exports and investment.[2] For instance, higher taxes are likely to lead to higher prices for goods and services. This is especially true for direct taxes on income (for both individuals and corporations) and social welfare contributions paid by businesses, whereby workers will ask for higher wages to compensate their loss of purchasing power, and businesses will pass on their increased costs to their customers in order to maintain profitability. As for investment expenditures by government, they are also important for competitiveness since they help maintain, if not improve, an economy's infrastructure (e.g., roads, ports, railways, etc.). Thus, if lowering public investment leads to a continued degradation of a country's productive public infrastructure, then the cost of doing business for firms will only increase, thereby hurting an economy's competitiveness and growth prospects. Lower economic growth also means lower revenues in the government's coffers, as well as higher social welfare expenditures.

With regard to improving an economy's competitiveness, the devaluation of the currency is often considered an easy way to make exports cheaper internationally and thereby stimulate growth. According to Alesina and Perotti (1997), many instances of past fiscal consolidation have been preceded by exchange rate depreciations. In fact, Lambertini and Tavares (2005) find that a depreciation of the nominal exchange rate increases the probability of a successful fiscal adjustment. This is why they conclude that countries that have adopted the euro may find it more difficult to achieve a sustainable fiscal consolidation, because they cannot effect any currency depreciation unless they abandon the euro and reintroduce a national currency, which as we will see below is no panacea. Fortunately, for Eurozone member states, Ardagna (2004, p. 1049) finds that exchange rate devaluations are not a necessary condition for 'successful and expansionary fiscal contractions'. Hence, a sustainable fiscal consolidation is not impossible for Eurozone countries; it may just be a little harder.

In their study of past fiscal consolidations, Paolo Mauro and his colleagues from the IMF argue that it is not so much whether fiscal consolidation is expenditure-based or revenue-based that really matters; the adjustment must be 'reform-based' with a clearly established plan that includes contingencies for the fact that things will not turn out as planned (e.g., lower than expected rates of economic growth or unforeseen political developments) (Mauro, 2011). This is why the authors argue that consolidation plans should have medium-term objectives, rather than simply short-term ones (i.e., three to five years rather than one year). This would provide policy makers with enough flexibility in the short term to adjust the plan in accordance with changed economic and/or political situations while maintaining the focus on achieving the stated objectives.

> The experience of the past few decades [...] shows that plans face sizable risks and often encounter substantial implementation difficulties along the way. Unexpected declines in economic growth, upward revisions in the initial fiscal deficit, changing priorities, lack of support among the general public, poor plan design, all have the potential to derail fiscal adjustment plans. Conversely, when favorable economic and political conditions emerge, objectives are often met or exceeded, even when plans envisage ambitious reductions in deficits and debts.
>
> (Mauro, 2011, p. 178)

The final issue concerning fiscal adjustment programmes is whether they should be short and sharp – akin to the shock therapy treatment applied to a number of Central and Eastern European countries after the demise of the Soviet bloc – or more gradual in nature. There are two views on this matter. One the one hand, the political window of opportunity to instil fiscal and structural reforms in the context of a crisis is narrow before reform fatigue sets in and opposition to reforms mounts to such an extent as to make them politically infeasible. That is why it is often recommended to adopt painful measures soon after a new government has been elected. On the other hand, precisely because of the politically sensitive nature of the adjustments and reforms to be put into place, they need to be done gradually over time in order to make them palpable to the electorate and their representatives. According to the European Commission (2007, p. 196), the gradual approach seems to be a better fit with a successful fiscal consolidation exercise, most especially when politically sensitive government expenditures have to be heavily cut and/or the economy is in particularly bad shape at the beginning of the process. Although this may be so, the general evidence in support of fiscal consolidation exercises leading to government unpopularity and ensuing collapse is weak. For instance, Alesina, Perotti, and Tavares (1998) find that pursuing fiscal adjustment programmes does not negatively affect a government's popularity or increase the probability that it will collapse. In a more recent study, Alesina and other colleagues obtain similar results, whereby governments are no more likely than usual to be voted out of office if they quickly decrease budget deficits (Alesina, Carloni, and Lecce, 2011). These findings are also corroborated by those of Mauro (2011) (see also Chapter 4 of this volume). Even when governments lose power during a consolidation process, the adjustment programme's implementation usually remains unaffected. This is because what truly matters is the degree of support for the reduction of the deficit and debt among the general population (Mauro, 2011). It does not mean, however, that austerity measures are not generally associated with social unrest (Ponticelli and Voth, 2011), but the latter does not necessarily translate into electoral behaviour against the incumbent government, as unrest tends to be more associated with particular lobbies such as labour unions (Alesina, Carloni, and Lecce, 2011). Therefore, although it seems reasonable to conclude that adopting a gradual approach might be more effective at ultimately reducing fiscal deficits and set public finances on a sustainable path, the evidence does cast a shadow on the political cost of 'cold shower' consolidations, as the European Commission calls them. After all, Alesina, Carloni, and Lecce (2011) do not find that governments are more likely to lose power if they undertake 'large' fiscal consolidations (i.e., those leading to a reduction in the budget deficit of 1.5 per cent of gross domestic product [GDP] in a given year).

Assessing the EU's response to the fiscal crises

From the above, it is clear that any attempt to consolidate public finances among Eurozone member states affected by a debt crisis should begin with significant (but probably gradual) cuts in current government spending, most especially wages and employment, as well as social welfare entitlements. In addition, structural reforms to make the economy more productive and competitive should accompany fiscal adjustment efforts. Whether the EU and the IMF have adopted such a framework in the conditionality programmes that they have negotiated with Greece, Ireland, and Portugal in exchange for financial assistance is what this section sets out to assess. Before doing so, however, it is important to assess whether the provision of bailouts themselves made sense for the EU.

Were the bailouts a good idea?

The fact that three Eurozone countries have received financial assistance with their sovereign debt is something that will be debated for years to come, and we will only broach the surface of this debate herein, as it goes beyond the scope of the present chapter. Opinions are certainly divided on whether bailouts are the appropriate way to deal with fiscal crises inside the Eurozone.

On the one hand, there are arguments in support of the core Eurozone member states (e.g., Austria, Belgium, France, Germany, Luxembourg, and the Netherlands) abandoning those on the periphery – like Greece, Ireland, and Portugal – that are experiencing fiscal difficulties. Without financial assistance, the countries on the periphery would eventually be forced to default and, as a result, give up the euro and reintroduce their national currencies (or form their own monetary union). Proponents of this viewpoint argue that only then would true optimal currency areas exist in the EU,[3] because periphery economies are not synchronized with those of the core and, therefore, should not share a common currency and monetary policy (e.g., Feldstein, 2012).

On the other hand, there are those who argue that EU institutions and Eurozone leaders did the right thing in providing bailout funds to Greece, Ireland, and Portugal and in setting up the European Financial Stability Facility (EFSF) and European Stability Mechanism (ESM).[4] Otherwise, the Eurozone banking system would have experienced a serious crisis, because Eurozone banks hold the majority of the sovereign bonds issued by Eurozone member states. Defaults by Greece, Ireland, and Portugal would have caused serious losses to the Eurozone banking system, creating a panic and credit freeze, such as the one that occurred in the Fall of 2008, when the global financial crisis reached its apex. Investor panic would also spread to Spanish and Italian sovereign bonds, as a result of a contagion effect, which would only compound the crisis. The entire financial system would be jeopardized, and the EU would face another deep recession, just when Member States' economies were beginning to recover from the previous crisis. As in that crisis, EU governments would then have to intervene again by providing financial assistance to their banking systems, while the European Central Bank (ECB) would have to provide massive amounts of liquidity to the financial system. Given the existing weakness among both financial institutions and governments' fiscal capacities, it would not be at all clear that governments and the ECB would have the means to manage the crisis and to prevent a great European depression from happening. As a result, the Eurozone and the EU would be at great risk of completely imploding, whereby every EU government would run for the exits and try to save its economy and financial system. History would repeat itself, as such behaviour would be akin to what happened during and, following the Great Depression, in the 1930s (e.g., see Eichengreen, 1992).

Given these dire prospects, it seems fair to conclude that providing financial assistance to only a few Eurozone member states, in order to prevent an economic meltdown, was a less risky and less costly option. Furthermore, this approach offered the opportunity to use the bailouts to finally bring about much needed reforms in countries like Greece and Portugal, by imposing strict conditions for the assistance. Let's now examine whether the conditionality programmes for Greece, Ireland, and Portugal are appropriate under their particular circumstances.

Are the conditionality programmes appropriate?

Several Eurozone member states (Portugal, Ireland, Italy, Greece, and Spain) faced difficult fiscal situations, even if they were in fact not identical (see Figures 3.1 and 3.2). For instance, Spain's public debt has remained well below the Eurozone's average and was still within the Stability and Growth Pact's limit of 60 per cent of GDP in 2010; however, its fiscal deficit jumped substantially in 2008 and 2009. As for Italy, although its public debt is the second highest after Greece's, its fiscal deficit is the lowest among the 'PIIGS' and has remained below the Eurozone's average since 2008. Consequently, its public debt has increased less rapidly than in other member countries. But, looking at debts and deficits is not enough to understand the fiscal crises.

There are two other factors that need to be considered, in tandem with debts and deficits, in order to fully appreciate the extent to which each member of the affected Eurozone countries was in trouble and,

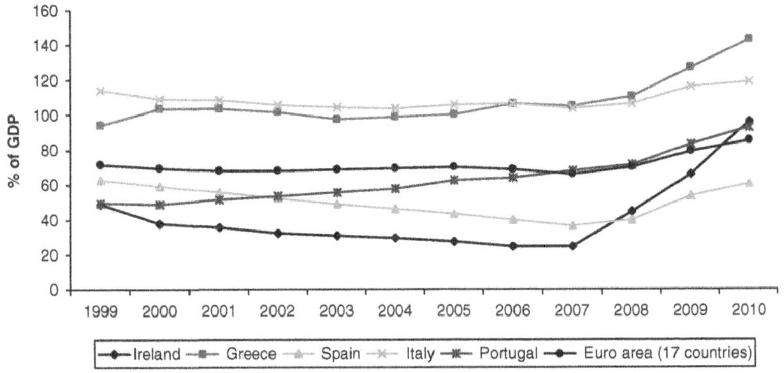

Figure 3.1 General government gross debt (% of GDP)
Source: Eurostat (2012a) *General Government Gross Debt – Percentage of GDP* http://epp.eurostat.ec.europa.eu/tgm/table.do?tab=table&init=1&plugin=1&language=en&pcode=teina225, accessed on 15 March 2012.

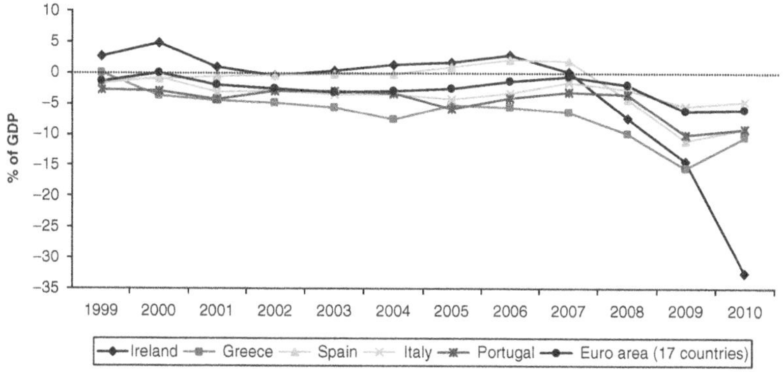

Figure 3.2 General government deficit/surplus (% of GDP)
Source: Eurostat (2012b) *General Government Deficit/Surplus* http://epp.eurostat.ec.europa.eu/tgm/table.do?tab=table&init=1&plugin=1&language=en&pcode=tsieb080, accessed on 15 March 2012.

consequently, what economic remedies needed to be applied. These two factors are the economy's overall competitiveness and the degree to which domestic banks made loans to the private sector as a function of the size of the economy. According to Figure 3.3, as the global financial crisis erupted, Greece and Italy had the least competitive economies among the states most affected by the sovereign debt crisis, but their banks were also less exposed to the national economy's performance. On the other hand, Ireland had the most competitive economy but its banks were 2.5 times more exposed to the economy's performance than those of Greece and Italy. As for Spain and Portugal, they stood in between Ireland on the one hand and Greece and Italy on the other. Thus, each country's economic situation at the beginning of the financial crisis, when combined with its level of public debt and the trend in its fiscal performance, explains in good part the outcomes described earlier.

In the case of Greece, a high public debt with a growing fiscal deficit, owing to uncontrolled spending, tax evasion, and low competitiveness, made investors panic and refuse to buy Greek sovereign debt at a sustainable rate of interest. This is why the solution to Greece's problems was to drastically cut government spending, significantly lower tax evasion, and introduce reforms that would allow the economy to become more competitive. In Italy's case, the deficit has remained relatively low and the public debt stable; consequently, investors have not forced a bailout by asking for very high yields. Nonetheless, investors have

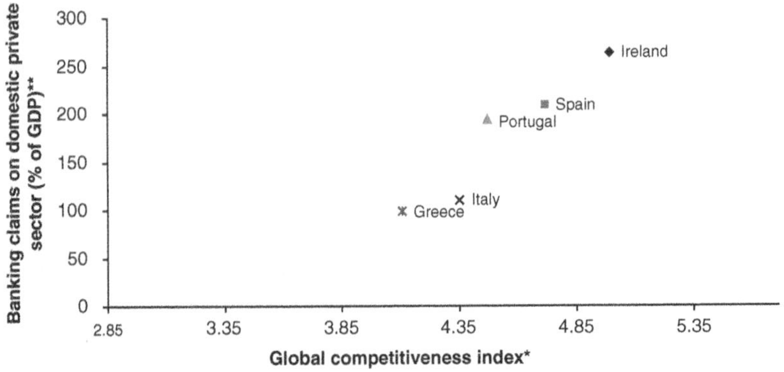

Figure 3.3 Economic situation of Greece, Ireland, Italy, Portugal, and Spain at the beginning of the financial crisis
*2008–09.
**2008 (end of year).
Source: World Economic Forum (2008) *Global Competitiveness Report 2008–2009* (Geneva: World Economic Forum), https://members.weforum.org/pdf/GCR08/GCR08.pdf, accessed on 15 March 2012, p. 10; Banking Claims on Domestic Private Sector: International Monetary Fund, International Financial Statistics (Claims on other Sector/GDP, Line 22s.u/Line99b).

signalled concern about the low competitiveness of the Italian economy and the associated lack of economic growth by requiring higher yields to buy Italian sovereign debt. Without a decent rate of growth, it has been difficult for the government to see fiscal revenues increase, while justifying cuts in welfare spending to balance the budget. This is why Italy's public debt has remained stable throughout the first decade of the 21st century (see Figure 3.1), and why it is likely to remain so without appropriate structural reforms, which are needed to make the economy once again competitive.

With regard to Ireland, the problem has not been competitiveness or the government's fiscal performance; it has been a banking crisis caused by the bursting of a major real estate bubble. In Figure 3.3, we observe that Irish banks had the highest level of exposure to the domestic economy. In addition, their lending had served to fuel a housing boom. According to Hibers et al. (2008, p. 13), real house prices in Ireland experienced the second-largest increase in Europe since 1985 after Spain, with the majority of the increase occurring after 1995. So when the banks went bust, the Irish government had to bail them out to save the financial system, which added close to 50 per cent of GDP to the public debt. This means that the formula for Ireland to bring public finances back to health has been, first, to get the banking system on its feet as quickly as possible, so that it no longer needs the government's help, and, second, to reduce the deficit by cutting government spending and, where possible, increasing tax revenues. These measures are meant to help stabilize the public debt so that it can begin to decrease again once economic growth returns. In the Irish case, only minor structural reforms should be necessary to make the economy even more competitive.

For Portugal and Spain, as already mentioned, their situation is in between that of Ireland on the one hand and Greece and Italy on the other. As opposed to Portugal, the only reason why Spain has not been forced (yet) to request a bailout from the EU and the IMF is because its public debt has remained much lower. The main shadow hanging over Spain has been the continuing weakness of regional and local savings banks, as a result of the bursting of a housing bubble, and the extent to which the government must offer them additional financial assistance and, therefore, add to the public debt. Although Portugal did not have a housing bubble as in Spain (Hibers et al., 2008), its banks were similarly exposed to the national economy, and the latter's weakness could force the government to intervene. Since the public debt is about 20 percentage points of GDP higher than in Spain, such intervention could be problematic. Moreover, since the Portuguese economy is less competitive than that of Spain, the fiscal consolidation effort must be greater. Therefore, in the absence of a political consensus on fiscal austerity measures and structural reforms, sovereign bond investors simply panicked – by demanding very high yields for buying Portuguese debt – as they could not see how Portugal's government would achieve fiscal sustainability. The EU–IMF bailout put the necessary pressure on Portuguese politicians to achieve a political consensus on necessary economic adjustments.

Let's now examine the conditions imposed by the EU and the IMF on Greece, Ireland, and Portugal in exchange for receiving bailout funds and assess whether the content of these economic adjustment programmes has in fact been appropriate, given each country's circumstances. The Greek programme has both short-term and medium-term commitments to restore fiscal sustainability (European Commission, 2010a). In the short run, the programme's aim involves a number of fiscal measures to shrink the country's fiscal deficit, in order to stabilize public indebtedness and restore confidence in financial markets. On the expenditure side, the Greek government has committed itself to cutting government expenditures by 7 per cent of GDP over the rescue package's duration (i.e., between 2010 and 2013).[5] This reduction in (over)spending is to occur mainly through cuts in public sector wages, employment, and pensions. Social programmes are also to be reviewed in terms of their appropriateness. On the revenue side, the most important measures adopted by the Greek government were immediate increases of the Value Added Tax (VAT) rate from 21 to 23 per cent, and of excise taxes on fuel, alcohol, and cigarettes by 10 per cent. Moreover, the government undertook to aggressively tackle tax evasion, which is notorious in Greece.[6]

The adjustment programme also includes several structural reforms to the Greek economy, in order to render the latter more competitive in the medium term. These reforms focus on the labour and services markets. For instance, regulations are to be made more flexible so that high unemployment groups, like the young and women, may more easily enter and stay in the formal labour market. In terms of services (e.g., tourism, education, retail, transportation, energy, and professions), regulations are also to be made more flexible through liberalization, in order to increase competition and to lower prices. For example, Greece was the only country in the EU that restricted entry into the national trucking transportation market and fixed freight rates (Barnard, 2010). The adjustment programme also envisages cutting government red tape, in order to reduce the administrative burden that Greek businesses face as they go about their operations and investments.[7]

According to reviews conducted jointly by the European Commission, the IMF, and the ECB, the Greek government generally complied with its Economic Adjustment Program in the year that followed the bailout agreement (European Commission, 2010b, 2010c, 2011a). This good performance allowed Greece to receive a total of €65 billion in financial assistance as of July 2011. Nevertheless, in spite of the significant progress achieved by the Greek government, the latter has been pressured to do more in terms of fiscal consolidation, since fiscal deficits were higher than expected in 2009, 2010, and 2011 because of deeper recessions than originally anticipated. As a result, the government had to agree to additional fiscal measures of 2.5 per cent of GDP for 2011, over and above those already agreed in May 2010. For the period 2012–14, it had to find an extra 6 per cent of GDP in new revenues, and/or lower spending in order to meet the May 2010 adjustment programme's targets for fiscal deficits. This new wave of austerity, in a context of growing unemployment and continued negative economic growth, has only served to enhance an already deep sense of resentment among the Greek population, which makes the implementation of reforms even more difficult. Consequently, sovereign bond investors became increasingly convinced that Greece would not be able to stabilize its fiscal situation and that a restructuring of its debt (or outright default) was the only option. In June 2011, Greece's credit rating was again downgraded, making it the lowest sovereign rating in the world (Oakley and Spiegel, 2011), with a negative outlook towards default (which is the lowest possible rating: D). In response, the Eurozone member states and the IMF agreed on a new rescue package that would add more than €100 billion to the existing one, which would allow Greece to meet its public debt commitments until 2015, if not beyond. This package eventually came to be associated with a restructuring of Greece's sovereign debt, whereby private-sector investors were asked (with incentives) to voluntarily accept to extend the maturities of their Greek bond holdings, as well as decrease the nominal rates of interest on those bonds. This restructuring of Greece's sovereign debt amounted to about a 50 per cent loss in the value of the holdings of Greek bonds by private-sector investors. In spite of this agreement with private-sector investors, there remained, at the time of this writing (January 2012), much uncertainty surrounding the ability of the Greek government, now led by former central banker Lucas Papademos, to stabilize Greece's fiscal situation given the depth of the ongoing recession and the heavy political opposition by labour unions and other industry groups to fiscal and structural reforms. In spite of significant accomplishments in terms of fiscal and structural reforms, progress remained insufficient and it was evident that Greece would not be able to meet the medium-term objectives set in its adjustment programme. The adjustment process and the bailout period were likely to be extended beyond the current 2015 deadline.

In Ireland's case, in exchange for receiving financial assistance from the EU and the IMF in November 2010, the government unveiled a new four-year fiscal consolidation plan,[8] which aimed to reduce the fiscal deficit by €15 billion by 2014, in order to bring it back to a more sustainable 3 per cent of GDP (Ireland, 2010). The largest part of this deficit-reduction exercise was to come in the form of cuts to public spending. This is because government revenues were already hurting, not only owing to the general slowdown of the economy but also due to the particular difficulties experienced by the financial and construction sectors.[9] For 2011 and 2012, the government planned to cut spending by €6 billion, through reductions in social welfare payments, public service employment and pensions, general purchases of goods and services, and lower capital expenditures. In addition, the Irish government undertook to continue reforming its financial sector, as well as introducing structural reforms to its labour market and domestic services sector (e.g., legal and pharmacy professions). For instance, the national minimum wage was set to be cut by €1 per hour, in order to facilitate hiring by firms. Unemployment and social assistance benefits were also expected to be restricted in order to create stronger incentives for people to seek paid work, while decreasing pressure on the public purse. In a sense, the idea behind the cuts seemed to be that the Irish welfare state should go back to what it was before it became unduly generous along with the real estate bubble (Alderman, 2010). Overall, the Irish adjustment programme appears to have been successful, since economic growth returned in 2011, aided by strong exports. In addition, in spite of lower tax revenues, the Irish government managed to bring its budget deficit for 2011 below the target set by the programme. Although Ireland's economic growth forecast was lowered for 2012, as a result of an expected global economic slowdown, most especially in Europe, the European Commission and the IMF remained confident that the Irish government would reach its fiscal deficit target of 3 per cent of GDP by 2015 (European Commission, 2011b). There were even expectations that the Irish government would return to the financial markets to raise funds by the first half of 2013.

As with Greece and Ireland, the Portuguese bailout package included a series of undertakings that the government had to commit to in order to receive the promised funds at various intervals over the programme's three-year duration. These 'conditions' were based on the same general approach (or strategy) as the one applied to Ireland: fiscal consolidation, economic competitiveness, financial sector stabilization; however, in Portugal's case, the relative emphasis was on competitiveness rather than on financial sector stabilization, with fiscal consolidation playing the same role as in Greece and Ireland (Portugal, 2011). Just as in Greece, Portugal's economy had been suffering from a lack of competitiveness for quite some time, making for sluggish economic growth, which in turn led to repeated fiscal deficits and a growing public debt (see Figures 3.1 and 3.2).

In terms of fiscal policy, the goals were to reduce the deficit to 3 per cent of GDP in 2013, from 9.1 per cent in 2010 (see Figure 3.2). Such a deficit reduction was to be achieved through both spending cuts and revenue increases. On the expenditure side of the ledger, savings were to come from a freeze in public employee wages, improvements in the effectiveness and efficiency of the public administration (including the healthcare system and state-owned enterprises), as well as reductions in government services, transfers to public bodies and local/regional authorities, subsidies to private producers, public service employment and benefits (including pensions), and capital investments. On the revenue side, gains were to come from reductions in corporate tax deductions and special regimes, as well as personal income tax benefits and deductions. Additional revenues were also to be generated by increases in the VAT, as well as excise taxes on cars and tobacco.

In terms of structural reforms to make the Portuguese economy more competitive, the conditionality programme envisaged reforms to the labour market, as well as to the goods and services markets. With respect to improving the competitiveness of Portuguese labour, the government committed itself to, for instance, revising unemployment benefits, so as to cap their duration at no more than 18 months, while their value would decline over time, except for certain categories of self-employed workers. The government also planned to make it easier for firms to hire and fire employees, while ensuring that severance payments were in line with the EU average. In addition, the government was required to improve the quality of its secondary and vocational education system, as well as its training and support schemes for the unemployed. As for goods and services markets, the Portuguese government was tasked with, *inter alia*, liberalizing its energy (gas and electricity), telecommunications, transport, postal and professional sectors, in accordance with existing EU legislation. Finally, it was deemed necessary for the government to improve the overall business environment, namely making public administration more efficient and effective and removing any special protection from competition accorded to certain sectors or (public and private) enterprises.

According to the European Commission (2011c), the Portuguese adjustment programme was generally going well, although significant challenges remained. The main challenge pertained to achieving the targeted fiscal deficits in 2011 and 2012, as it was proving more difficult than expected to rein in government spending. Moreover, it was expected that the Portuguese economy would fall into recession as a result of a slowdown in global economic activity, which would hurt exports. However, the arrival in June 2011 of a new centre-right government strongly committed to fiscal and structural reforms was expected to make it easier to achieve the programme's medium-term objectives. Based on the new government's budget, the Commission expected that Portugal would meet its targeted deficit of 4.5 per cent of GDP in 2012, in spite of a recession projected to be more pronounced than originally forecast by the programme.

Conclusion

The economic adjustment programmes imposed on Greece, Ireland, and Portugal by the EU and the IMF are generally in line with the lessons offered by past fiscal consolidations, where deep cuts in current government expenditures and structural reforms to make the economy more competitive are deemed essential to a successful outcome. These are certainly the main elements contained in the Greek and the Portuguese programmes, although tax evasion is a major issue for the Greek government on the revenue side. In the Irish case, deep cuts in public spending are at the core of the adjustment programme; however, structural reforms are less predominant than in Greece and Portugal, since the economy is already quite competitive. Cleaning up the financial system to make it self-reliant again is much more important. It is important to note that, although they set yearly targets for fiscal deficits, the programmes in fact aim to achieve medium-term objectives, which are the expected results to be achieved once the programme is completed. Furthermore, assumptions about forecasted economic growth and external demand for exports are also revised on a biannual basis. Hence, in line with Mauro's (2011) conclusions, the adjustment programmes have flexibility built into them.

The main issue that the adjustment programmes are facing is not so much popular opposition to the required fiscal and structural reforms – after all, new governments were elected in Ireland and Portugal on the basis of their commitment to implementing the programmes – but deeper than anticipated recessions, which then make achieving the fiscal deficit targets more difficult and, as a result, create a demand for greater austerity, potentially pushing growth further downward. One of the main reasons for this state of affairs is the fact that many EU governments have adopted austerity measures at the same time, something that the literature on fiscal consolidation does not address. As a result, there is less opportunity for governments to get out of their fiscal mess through strong external demand for exports, which is what has happened in many successful consolidations in the past (Mauro, 2011).

This is why some analysts of the euro crisis have argued that the German government should do more to stimulate its economy so that it can act as a locomotive for other Eurozone countries that have to stabilize their debts and reduce their deficits (e.g., Matthijs and Blyth, 2011). The problem, however, is that it is politically difficult to convince German voters that they should not only provide financial assistance to governments of countries facing fiscal crises but should also spend more and, in a way, indebt themselves collectively to stimulate economic growth in the Eurozone. The alternative for Germany, on the other hand, is to provide financial assistance to these countries for longer than originally anticipated as they take more time to reduce their deficits, given that overall economic growth in the euro area is slower to revive.

This is why an intergovernmental approach, as described by Ross in this volume, is ultimately counterproductive. What is needed is a more integrated or supranational approach to fiscal policy in the Eurozone, if not the EU. Such an approach includes not only coordinating national fiscal policies (e.g., through approval of budgets by the Council of Ministers on a recommendation of the Commission) but also creating commonly issued eurobonds. In the latter case, to be effective at keeping interest rates low for all, the eurobonds would have to be issued by a supranational agency that would only issue them for a member country if fiscal sustainability of the public debt had been ascertained. This is the only way to deal with the moral hazard problem of jointly guaranteed bonds by all member countries; Eurozone member states would thus be prevented from free riding on the system by issuing too many bonds (similarly to the 'tragedy-of-the commons' problem as originally identified by Garrett Hardin [1968]).

Although important steps were taken in this direction at the December 2011 meeting of the European Council, namely in terms of greater fiscal policy coordination, more needs to be done, especially with respect to eurobonds. In spite of Ross's (this volume) scepticism that the EU can move positively in such a direction, we can expect that sovereign bond investors will continue to put pressure on EU/Eurozone governments to achieve a greater degree of fiscal integration at the EU or the Eurozone level. The bailouts may have been successful in preventing outright sovereign defaults and keeping the euro intact, but at the time of this writing the most affected countries (Greece, Ireland, Italy, Portugal, and Spain) were still facing major fiscal and economic challenges that financial markets were bound to react to for the foreseeable future. The euro's 'fat lady' has yet to sing.

Notes

1. It is true that cutting social welfare benefits is likely to have a negative impact on economic growth as individuals' consumption is reduced; however, if unit labour costs decrease and it leads to greater employment in the private sector, then the negative impact on consumption will be nullified. Moreover, lower labour costs are likely to stimulate investment in the national economy, which

will be beneficial to growth. The real issue is one of timing, in terms of the time lag between the removal of social welfare benefits and the positive private sector employment impact following reduced labour costs.

2. There are instances where taxes can actually improve competitiveness, especially if they replace more inefficient taxes. According to a study by Widmalm (2001), some taxes have a negative impact on economic growth while others can have positive effects.
3. For details on the theory of optimal currency areas, see Kenen and Meade (2008, Chapter 2). In a nutshell, the theory aims to identify the conditions that would mitigate the limited degree of synchronicity between economies should they adopt a common currency. An optimal currency area is one where either the economies are synchronized in terms of their boom-bust cycle or they possess the necessary conditions that mitigate the absence of synchronicity.
4. For details on the EFSF and ESM, see Leblond and Paudyn (2011).
5. In late June 2011, the Greek rescue package was extended to 2015 and beyond, if necessary.
6. Greece's informal economy is estimated to range between 20 and 25 per cent of GDP (Katsios, 2006).
7. According to the World Bank, Greece ranked 109th out of 183 countries in terms of the ease of doing business in 2010 (http://www.doingbusiness.org/rankings).
8. The Irish government had already adopted €14.5 billion worth of spending cuts and tax rises in order to quell the mounting deficit. In spite of these measures, the deficit was still slated to reach 12 per cent of GDP in 2010, not including bailout funds to the banking sector (*The Economist*, 2010, p. 79).
9. Tax revenues dropped by €14 billion between 2007 and 2009 (*The Economist*, 2010, p. 81).

Bibliography

Alderman, L. (2010, 24 November) 'Ireland Unveils Austerity Plan to Help Secure Bailout', *The New York Times*.

Alesina, A. and S. Ardagna (2010) 'Large Changes in Fiscal Policy: Taxes versus Spending', *Tax Policy and the Economy*, 24, 35–68.

Alesina, A., D. Carloni, and G. Lecce (2011) *The Electoral Consequences of Large Fiscal Adjustments* (NBER Working Paper No. 17655) (Cambridge: National Bureau of Economic Research).

Alesina, A. and R. Perotti (1997) 'Fiscal Adjustments in OECD Countries: Composition and Macroeconomic Effects', *IMF Staff Papers*, 44(2), 210–248.

Alesina, A., R. Perotti, and J. Tavares (1998) 'The Political Economy of Fiscal Adjustments', *Brookings Papers on Economic Activity*, 1, 197–266.

Ardagna, S. (2004) 'Fiscal Stabilizations: When Do They Work and Why', *European Economic Review*, 48(5), 1047–1074.

Barnard, B. (2010) 'Greece Passes Truck Reform', *Journal of Commerce*, September 22, http://www.joc.com/government-regulation/greece-passes-truck-reform.

Eichengreen, B. (1992) *Golden Fetters: The Gold Standard and the Great Depression, 1919–1939* (New York: Oxford University Press).

European Commission (2007) 'Part IV: Lessons from Successful Fiscal Consolidations', in 'Public Finances in EMU – 2007', *European Economy*, 3 (Brussels: Directorate-General for Economic and Financial Affairs), 193–238.

European Commission (2010a) 'The Economic Adjustment Programme for Greece', *European Economy*, Occasional Papers, 61, May (Brussels: Directorate-General for Economic and Financial Affairs).

European Commission (2010b) 'The Economic Adjustment Programme for Greece, First Review – Summer 2010', *European Economy*, Occasional Papers, 68, August (Brussels: Directorate-General for Economic and Financial Affairs).

European Commission (2010c) 'The Economic Adjustment Programme for Greece, Second Review – Autumn 2010', *European Economy*, Occasional Papers, 72, December (Brussels: Directorate-General for Economic and Financial Affairs).

European Commission (2011a) 'The Economic Adjustment Programme for Greece, Third Review – Winter 2011', *European Economy*, Occasional Papers, 77, February (Brussels: Directorate-General for Economic and Financial Affairs).

European Commission (2011b) 'The Economic Adjustment Programme for Ireland, Fourth Review – Autumn 2011', *European Economy*, Occasional Papers, 88, December (Brussels: Directorate-General for Economic and Financial Affairs).

European Commission (2011c) 'The Economic Adjustment Programme for Portugal, Second Review – Autumn 2011', *European Economy*, Occasional Papers, 89, December (Brussels: Directorate-General for Economic and Financial Affairs).

Feldstein, M. (2012) 'The Failure of the Euro', *Foreign Affairs*, 91(1), 105–116.

Guichard, S., M. Kennedy, E. Wurzel, and C. André (2007) *What Promotes Fiscal Consolidation: OECD Country Experiences* (Economics Department Working Papers No. 553) (Paris: Organisation for Economic Co-operation and Development).

Hardin, G. (1968) 'The Tragedy of the Commons', *Science*, 162(3859), 1243–1248.

Hibers, P., A.W. Hoffsmaister, A. Banerji, and H. Shi (2008) *House Price Developments in Europe: A Comparison*, (IMF Working Paper 08/211) (Washington: International Monetary Fund).

Ireland (2010) *Memorandum of Understanding on Specific Economic Policy Conditionality*, 7 December, http://ec.europa.eu/economy_finance/articles/eu_economic_situation/pdf/2010-12-07-mou_en.pdf, accessed on 20 June 2011.

Katsios, S. (2006) 'The Shadow Economy and Corruption in Greece', *South-Eastern Europe Journal of Economics*, 4(1), 61–80.

Kenen, P.B. and E.E. Meade (2008) *Regional Monetary Integration* (New York: Cambridge University Press).

Lambertini, L. and J. Tavares (2005) 'Exchange Rates and Fiscal Adjustments: Evidence from the OECD and Implications for the EMU', *Contributions to Macroeconomics* [now *The B.E. Journal of Macroeconomics*], 5(1), Article 11.

Leblond, P. and B. Paudyn (2011) 'One for All and All for One? The Eurozone's Bail-Out Arrangements', *EU Political Economy Bulletin*, 15, Winter, 5–10.

Matthijs, M. and M. Blyth (2011, November 17) 'Why Only Germany Can Fix the Euro', *Foreign Affairs*, online, http://www.foreignaffairs.com/articles/136685/matthias-matthijs-and-mark-blyth/why-only-germany-can-fix-the-euro?page=show, accessed on 6 January 2012.

Mauro, P. (ed.) (2011) *Chipping Away at Public Debt: Sources of Failure and Keys to Success in Fiscal Adjustment* (Hoboken: John Wiley & Sons).

Oakley, D. and P. Spiegel (2011, 13 June) 'Greek Rating Now Worst in the world', *Financial Times.*

Ponticelli, J. and H.-J. Voth (2011) *Austerity and Anarchy: Budget Cuts and Social Unrest in Europe, 1919–2009* (CEPR Discussion Paper No. 8513) (London: Centre for Economic Policy Research).

Portugal (2011) *Memorandum of Understanding on Specific Economic Policy Conditionality,* 17 May, http://ec.europa.eu/economy_finance/eu_borrower/mou/2011-05-18-mou-portugal_en.pdf, last accessed on 21 June 2011.

The Economist (2010, 20 November) 'Briefing: Ireland's Economy', 79–81.

Widmalm, F. (2001) 'Tax Structure and Growth: Are Some Taxes Better than Others?', *Public Choice,* 107(3/4), 199–219.

World Bank (2011) 'Economy Rankings', http://www.doingbusiness.org/rankings.

4

The Electoral Impact of the 2008 Economic Crisis in Europe

Lawrence LeDuc and Jon H. Pammett

The severe economic crisis that unfolded in Western economies in 2008 could be expected to have had political consequences as well as economic ones. As European economies slipped into recession in the latter part of 2008, the focus of attention in both European Union and national politics turned increasingly to economic matters. The immediate cause of the recession was widely attributed to external shocks, particularly the financial crisis in the United States, which was precipitated by events such as the collapse of the Lehman Brothers investment bank, the bailout of the insurance conglomerate AIG, and the ripple effects throughout the economy of those events. For most European economies, the low point was reached in the second quarter of 2009, with the average net growth in gross domestic product (GDP) for the EU27 at that time registering –4.2 per cent (Table 4.1). Only Poland escaped recession conditions, showing weak growth at an annualized rate of +1.7 per cent in this period. By the first quarter of 2010, all European countries had begun at least a modest recovery from the recession. However, this recovery began to stall as a second economic crisis took shape in Europe, involving sovereign debt markets in Greece, Spain, Ireland, and some other countries, generating pressures on European banks and other institutions and even raising anxieties about the potential survival of the Euro. The term 'economic crisis', therefore, is inadequate to capture both the complexity and the interrelated nature of the many pressures on European economies, which arose during this period. For purposes of this analysis, we consider only the first stage of the crisis, beginning in late 2008 and continuing through the end of 2010. This is the period that conforms most readily to traditional definitions of economic recession. The events of the second crisis, which began to take hold subsequently with the collapse of sovereign

Table 4.1 Economic conditions and net gain/loss of governing parties in EP and national elections

	Economic conditions				Governing party		
	GDP	Unemployment (%)	'A lot worse'		EP net Loss	Nat net Loss	Defeated
			Now	Future			
Austria	−3.5	5.0	39	9	−5.5	−6.1	
Belgium	−3	7.8	33	7	−4.1	−7.6	■
Bulgaria	−5.0	6.5	34	25	−15.5	−16.3	■
Cyprus	−1.7	5.3	22	23	3.8		
Czech Republic	−4.1	6.8	31	19	*	*	
Denmark	−4.9	6.3	32	3	−6.6		
Estonia	−14.1	13.5	65	23	−12.5		
Finland	−7.8	8.4	45	8	−4.1		
France	−2.6	9.5	55	18	−11.7		
Germany	−4.9	7.7	48	11	−4.5	−1.4	
Greece	−2.0	9.2	44	32	−9.5	−8.3	■
Hungary	−6.3	9.9	60	23	−30.8	−28.9	■
Ireland	−7.1	12.1	77	23	−17.5		
Italy	−5.0	7.7	27	9	−2.1		

Latvia	−18.0	17.2	82	45	*		
Lithuania	−14.8	13.5	69	31	7.2	−8.9	■
Luxembourg	−3.4	5.4	28	9	−6.7	1.9	
Malta	−1.5	7.1	29	10	−8.8		
Netherlands	−4.0	3.4	36	10	−6.4	−12.9	■
Poland	1.7	8.1	21	9	2.9		
Portugal	−2.6	9.7	35	10	−18.4	−8.4	
Romania	−7.1	6.4	52	31	−2.7	−13.2	■
Slovakia	−4.7	11.6	39	10	2.9	5.7	
Slovenia	−7.8	6.1	55	11	−12.0	−0.6	■
Spain	−3.6	18.1	41	13	−5.4		
Sweden	−5.1	8.3	44	5	−7.4		
UK	−4.9	7.8	52	11	−19.9	−6.2	■
EU-27	−4.2	8.9	44	18	−7.8	−7.9	

*Czech Republic and Latvia not included in net gain/loss calculations. In both countries, the government was defeated in a parliamentary vote prior to the EP election. A non-party caretaker government was in place in Czech Republic up until the May 2010 national election.

Sources: Economic statistics, Eurostat (European Commission), http://epp.eurostat.ec.europa.eu, Election results: Europa, www.europarl.europa.eu/parliament/.../elections2009, accessed on 17 June, 2010.

debt markets, particularly in Greece, raised the threat of a more prolonged and more severe recession throughout Europe. The potential consequences of these events, both in Europe and elsewhere, remain unknown and are in many respects of a different nature than temporary economic decline, since they involve fundamental underpinnings of the economy.

While the possible political effects of the second crisis are still uncertain, the expected consequences of the first, and more conventional, period of economic crisis in Europe can be clearly delineated. The most direct result, suggested by the extensive literature on 'economic voting', is that voters would likely punish governments for poor economic performance, even in circumstances when many of the forces affecting the national economies might have been well beyond their control. It was therefore predictable that many incumbent governments would have difficulty achieving re-election if they had the misfortune to face the electorate during the course of, or in the immediate aftermath of, the economic crisis. Outright defeat might be expected for governing parties or coalitions or, at the very least, a drastic reduction in the number of legislative members returned.

A 'punishment model' that operated in a mechanical manner would not discriminate according to the partisan or ideological cast of governments but would rather sweep them away willy-nilly if they were seen as ineffective in dealing with economic problems. Furthermore, the avenging electorate might be expected to take the seriousness of the situation into account in a straightforward way – the worse the crisis, the more severe the punishment. If the 'punishment fits the crime', we should expect to find a substantial correlation between a decline in major economic indicators for a country and the number of votes received by governing parties and their candidates.

The fallout from the previous worldwide economic crisis that dominated the time period between 1973 and the mid-1980s may give some additional clues as to what to expect in the 2008–10 crisis. At that time, the persistent high rate of inflation produced by drastic price rises in oil was joined by an increase in unemployment and drops in growth rates, a condition called 'stagflation' by many analysts (Solomon, 1999). During that period, incumbent governments were indeed defeated in many countries. However, there was in addition a 'turn to the right' observed in many (but not all) Western industrial states. Most prominent in this trend were the United States (Reagan), United Kingdom (Thatcher), and West Germany (Kohl). A countertrend existed in France (Mitterand) (see Hall, 1986) and Spain (Gonzalez). But in general, the principles advocated by the apostles of economic neo-conservatism were accepted, as the money supply was tightened, interest rates were raised to try to slow down inflation, and austerity measures and cutbacks were introduced to try to hold down the burgeoning debt. Monetarism became the consensus economic policy (Thomas, 1989) as Keynesianism was seen by many as having failed. Retrenchment of the welfare capacities of the state became the consensus social policy (Krieger, 1986), accompanied by a lowering of concern for the fate of lower strata of society.

The prolonged and seemingly intractable nature of the crisis of the 1970s and 1980s had a number of effects on public opinion in most countries. First, 'lack of understanding of what was going on in the economy made for uncertainty and thus for volatility in attitudes and behavior' (Katona and Strumpel, 1978, p. 2). Public hesitancy to act decisively in their own buying habits when information was scarce meant that consumer confidence waned and there was a drastic tempering of expectations regarding jobs, employment, and economic growth in general. As the crisis continued, public expectations got lower and lower. Second, because of the external nature of the putative causes of the crisis, there was only muted policy debate about possible solutions. Because national governments blamed the problems on a 'worldwide phenomenon' in order to escape responsibility for them, their universal message was that there was little they could do domestically to solve them in any proactive way. In electoral terms, the economic dimension was treated as a classic 'valence issue' (Butler and Stokes, 1969; Clarke et al., 1979; Clarke et al., 2004). Inflation and unemployment were general problems threatening the well-being of the state, and all parties and politicians promised to attack the problem with vigour. The struggle was not over which side of a particular policy presented the right approach, but who could be trusted to lead the common attack on the problem.

A focus on the European Union

This chapter focuses on the 27 countries of the EU and considers a time frame of two years, from June 2008 to June 2010, thus capturing most clearly the period of the first economic crisis. Fifteen of the EU member countries held national elections during this period, and the European Parliament (EP) elections, in which all 27 Member States voted, occurred in June 2009 at the mid-point of this period. We thus capture a number of different electoral contexts, ranging from cases such as Austria or Slovenia, which held elections in September 2008 just as the crisis was beginning to unfold, to those of the United Kingdom or The

Netherlands, where national elections were held in mid-2010, well after stimulus measures were in place. The EP elections took place at the point in this cycle (June 2009) when economic indicators in most countries had reached their most negative readings, as did those national elections occurring a short time later in Bulgaria, Germany, Portugal, and Greece. Luxembourg was the only country in this cycle that scheduled its national elections to take place simultaneously with those for seats in the EP. We can thus examine three distinct clusters of elections occurring over this cycle, with the EP elections and several national cases at or near the centre of the distribution and the others clustered either earlier or later in the cycle.

European economies, together with those in much of the rest of the developed world, began to slow down in the second half of 2007. The decline over the course of the next year was modest, although widespread. By mid-2008, growth rates in most countries had slowed but had not yet turned negative. In Romania, Bulgaria, and Slovakia, they were still a robust 6–7 per cent, while Portugal and the United Kingdom displayed little or no economic growth in the same period. With the onset of the dramatic economic events in the second half of 2008, however, European economies fell quickly into recession. By the time of the EP elections in June 2009, all of the EU member countries except Poland displayed negative growth. As might be expected, this steep drop in economic activity was accompanied by rising unemployment. By the time of the 2009 EP elections, unemployment in the EU member countries had risen to 8.9 per cent, albeit with considerable variation in this statistic from one country to another (Table 4.1).

Economic adversity was reflected in public opinion. In the surveys conducted following the June 2009 EP elections, as many as four out of every five respondents in most countries found economic conditions to be 'worse' than they had been a year earlier, and almost half of the respondents rated them 'a lot worse' (Table 4.1). Many were also pessimistic about the future. In some of the hardest hit countries, a considerable number of the respondents to the 2009 European Election Study expected conditions to continue to worsen over the next year. Residents of the former communist countries were generally the most negative in their expectations. For the EU as a whole, 38 per cent of those surveyed were pessimistic about the near future. About one respondent in four expected that conditions would, at best, stay about the same. In only a few countries (Germany, The Netherlands, the UK), were there substantial numbers of respondents who felt that over the next year economic conditions might get at least 'a little better'.

Economic voting

The relationship between the economy, public opinion, and voting in elections has generated a substantial political science literature. Many studies examine voting choice in elections as well as public opinion more generally, in response to varying economic conditions. In particular, incumbent governments are hypothesized to be vulnerable to declining economic conditions and also (but less conclusively) able to benefit politically from an improving economy. Furthermore, the ideological cast of governments is postulated to make a difference on the accountability dimension, with governments of the left being more vulnerable to rising unemployment, while right-wing governments are subject to public backlash when inflation rises (Evans, 2004, p. 130). The economic voting literature proceeds on both the individual and aggregate levels to consider these and other relationships.[1] On the individual level, voters are seen as evaluating the retrospective or prospective economic performance of political parties to render judgments about the most beneficial choice to make (Duch and Stevenson, 2008). More recently, a wide variety of 'contextual effects' have been proposed as affecting the basic relationship between the economy and the vote; these have been tested and often found to be relevant (Hellwig, 2010). Aside from the ideological complexion of political actors, already mentioned, examples of contextual effects are the length of time a government has been in office and the credibility of the opposition. If potential alternative governments are not seen as competent to run the economy, governments can remain relatively popular, or at least secure re-election, even under adverse economic circumstances (Duch and Stevenson, 2008, p. 12).

Three of these contextual effects, or 'contingency dilemmas', are emphasized in contemporary studies of economic voting, to such an extent that one recent review is titled 'The End of Economic Voting? Contingency Dilemmas and the Limits of Democratic Accountability' (Anderson, 2007). The first contextual effect is the responsibility that political parties in a national government can be made to assume when policies or government actions are specified. In particular, coalition governments, common in the European context and regularly necessitated by proportional representation electoral systems, may disperse power and responsibility for economic policy within any given government. When the economy deteriorates, which party in a coalition is to blame – the one that provides the Prime Minister, the one that provides the Minister of Finance, or some smaller coalition partner that may have influenced the situation? The second important contextual effect has to do with the institutions of a country's government, for example, the number of chambers of a legislature, the importance of committees, and the degree of independence of central banks. All of these institutional structures may affect the chain of responsibility for some economic conditions. Indexes have been developed which take account of the degree of institutional and governmental responsibility in a country combined (Powell and Whitten, 1993) or separately (Hobolt, Tilley and Banducci, 2010).

The third and potentially most important contextual effect is 'globalization'. With the levers of economic policy making increasingly transferred to international bodies like the EU, the G-20, the International Monetary Fund, or international corporations, national governments are becoming increasingly powerless when it comes to exercising control over the direction of their own economies (Hellwig, 2010). Some countries are more globalized than others, and indexes have been developed that measure factors associated with this phenomenon (Dreher, 2006; Vujakovic, 2010); the country ranking or score on a globalization index is increasingly built into comparative studies of economic voting (Hellwig, 2010). Globalization may combine with a lack of institutional or governmental responsibility to make it difficult for the public to hold governments accountable for economic decline.

The economic voting literature, by taking these and other contingency and contextual effects into account, has injected considerable measures of realism and nuance into what was originally seen as a rather mechanical connection between trends of economic indicators of growth, inflation, unemployment, and electoral outcomes. Several of the factors considered in recent studies will be important to look at in our subsequent analysis of the recent elections in Europe. However, one key element of the literature limits its utility in the current instance, because the economic conditions, either positive or negative, which are its components, do not extend to encompass situations of economic crisis. For example, van der Brug, van der Eijk, and Franklin explicitly outline a 'caveat' to their economic voting analysis of 15 countries by saying, 'We do not have a random sample of economic contexts.... Our range of economic conditions does not contain cases of hyperinflation.... We do not analyse circumstances in which economic growth was strongly negative.... Dramatic economic developments... may well lead to effects on party support and election outcomes that are much larger, and conceivably of a different character, than those that we are able to observe...' (2007, pp. 80–1). Likewise, we cannot speculate here on possible future events of an entirely different nature, such as the exit of one or more countries from the Eurozone or the longer-term constraints imposed by the Stability and Growth Pact.

The analyses presented in Tables 4.2 and 4.3 look at the variation in popularity of government parties between the last national election and the 2009 EP election and also, for those EU countries that held national elections between June 2008 and June 2010, the variation in their popularity between that election and the previous national election. We will look first at the zero-order correlations between these electoral outcomes and economic and contingency factors and then at regressions which enable us to weigh their relative importance.

The zero-order correlations shown in Table 4.2 yield some moderately strong relationships between the economy and electoral outcomes, though none reaches statistical significance because of the small number of cases (27 EP elections from 2009, and 14 national elections in EU countries).[2] Of the main economic indicators relevant to the crisis, GDP growth/decline does relate to national government vote loss and the defeat of that government. Similarly, the perception in 2009 that the economy had gotten worse is related to vote loss for the government, particularly in the EP elections of that year. When it comes to those countries holding national elections, however, it is the *perception* that the economy is likely to worsen in the next year that is more important than past evaluations of its condition. Prospective expectations of the state of the economy are indeed predicted by some economic voting literature (Duch and Stevenson, 2008) to condition voting.

The regression analyses summarized in Table 4.3 show that the variables identified from the economic voting literature have some impact on the results in the 2009 EP election and the national elections held in EU countries in the 2008–10 period. In the EP election, negative public attitudes about the seriousness of the past economic situation create a classic punishment situation, quite consistent with previous findings that national governments are vulnerable in EP elections to a variety of negative evaluations of their performance. When it comes to the national elections, however, the key factor is more likely to be prospective than retrospective. Government vote loss is also somewhat less in more globalized countries and is substantially more in countries with high governmental clarity, where responsibility can be more easily pinned on particular politicians and parties.

National and European electoral contexts

If the national elections in this period provided a milieu in which voters might be expected to punish governing parties for poor economic

Table 4.2 Correlations between electoral outcomes and economic conditions

		GDP	UNEM	RETRO	PROS	GLOB	INST	GOV	EPLS	NATLS
Net growth 2009*	[GDP]									
Unemployment 2009	[UNEM]	**–0.56**								
'Much worse' economic conditions – retrospective	[RETRO]	**–0.80**	**0.60**							
'Much worse' economic conditions – prospective	[PROS]	**–0.59**	**0.45**	**0.61**						
Dreher globaization Index	[GLOB]	0.22	–0.19	–0.10	**–0.56**					
Institutional clarity Index	[INST]	–0.32	0.32	0.17	0.23	–0.11				
Government clarity Index	[GOV]	0.19	0.29	0.03	0.04	–0.03	**0.46**			
Net loss for governing party in EP election	[EPLS]	–0.05	0.05	0.36	0.08	0.19	0.26	**0.44**		
Net loss for governing party in national election	[NATLS]	–0.12	0.00	0.31	**0.51**	–0.10	0.09	0.36	**0.59**	
Government defeated	[DFEAT]	–0.35	0.00	0.44	**0.54**	–0.30	0.21	0.26	0.20	**0.57**

Bold sig < 0.050

*Coding is positive in the direction specified for all variables, for example, *higher* growth, *higher* unemployment, *higher* percentage citing much worse economic conditions, *greater* globalization, *greater* clarity, *higher* loss for governing party, and so on. Government defeat is coded 0–1 (1 = defeat).

Table 4.3 OLS regression coefficients – economic conditions and political outcomes in the EU

		Govt defeat	Net loss [NAT]	Net loss [EP]
Net growth 2009*	[GDP]	−0.85	−0.47	0.40
Unemployment 2009	[UNEM]	−0.68	−0.52	−0.40
'Much worse' economic conditions – retrospective	[RETRO]	−0.35	−0.27	0.92
'Much worse' economic conditions – prospective	[PROS]	0.48	0.85	−0.08
Dreher globalization Index	[GLOB]	0.08	0.47	0.10
Institutional clarity Index	[INST]	−0.26	−0.34	0.22
Government clarity Index	[GOV]	0.78	0.75	0.37
N		14	14	25
R^2		0.54	0.60	0.52

Bold sig < 0.05.
*See note in Table 4.2 recoding direction of variables.

performance, the EP elections provide another arena in which negative evaluations of national governments could be expected to appear as 'second order effects' (Reif and Schmitt, 1980; van der Eijk, Franklin and Marsh, 1996; Marsh, 1998; Schmitt, 2004). We know from this literature, as well as from empirical analyses of previous EP elections, that national governing parties generally do poorly in these elections for a number of reasons and that EP elections can often provide fertile electoral ground for smaller parties and/or single issue or protest parties (Curtice, 1989; Irwin, 1995; Marsh, 1998; LeDuc, 2007). We might well expect such effects to be magnified in the 2009 European elections as a result of the adverse economic circumstances.

In 23 of the 27 countries voting in the 2009 EP elections, governing parties[3] performed more poorly than in the preceding national election. The average decline for governing parties from that level was –7.8 per cent (Table 4.1). Among the four exceptions to this pattern is Poland, which was the only country in the EU still displaying positive economic growth in mid-2009. Cyprus, although negative, also had better growth statistics (–1.7 per cent) than the EU average (–4.2 per cent). Both of these countries also had lower levels of unemployment (Cyprus 5.3 per cent; Poland 8.1 per cent) for this period than the EU average (8.9 per cent). Noting the other two exceptions in which governing parties improved their electoral performance even in the face of deteriorating economies (Lithuania and Slovakia), all others (23) follow a pattern that is consistent, both with the typical 'second order' tendencies of EP elections and with the electoral expectations generated by weak economies.

We find a similar pattern in the national elections that took place in the 15 countries that held them during this period (Table 4.1). Among the countries holding national elections between June 2008 and June 2010, governing parties lost support in 12 of them, the average level of decline across all of the cases being –7.9 per cent – about the same level of decline as was found in the EP elections. However, whereas governing parties in four cases improved their standing in the EP elections in spite of poor economic conditions, only in Slovakia, as previously noted, and in Luxembourg, did governing parties succeed in improving their electoral performance in national elections in comparison with that of the previous electoral cycle. In all of the other 12 cases, governing parties lost ground, and in a few of those instances (Bulgaria, Hungary, The Netherlands, Romania), the loss was devastating to the party in power (Table 4.1).

Of course, it is not possible to tell from these statistics alone whether the losses sustained by governing parties in the June 2009 EP elections, or in their own national elections during the period of the economic crisis, can be attributed to the determination of voters to punish governments for poor economic performance. We have already noted that it is 'normal' for governing parties to do poorly in EP elections, and it is not unusual to see an electoral swing in national elections against an incumbent party, even in better economic times. One useful comparison that can be made here is with previous electoral cycles, particularly those taking place under conditions more favourable than those prevailing in 2008–10. A comparison of the EP results with those of the previous (2004) cycle finds that the loss by governing parties in 2009 was actually *less* than that which occurred five years earlier (Figure 4.1). Governing parties lost an average of –9.3 per cent in the 2004 EP elections – substantially more than in 2009. And, economic conditions at the time of the 2004 EP elections were much more favourable, with an average growth rate for EU countries of +2.5 per cent and unemployment at 8.8 per cent.

A slightly different pattern emerges in the comparison of national election results for the 14 countries with those of a previous electoral cycle. In the most recent electoral cycle for these countries, governing parties lost an average of –7.9 per cent of the vote from their performance in the previous national election. This is about two percentage

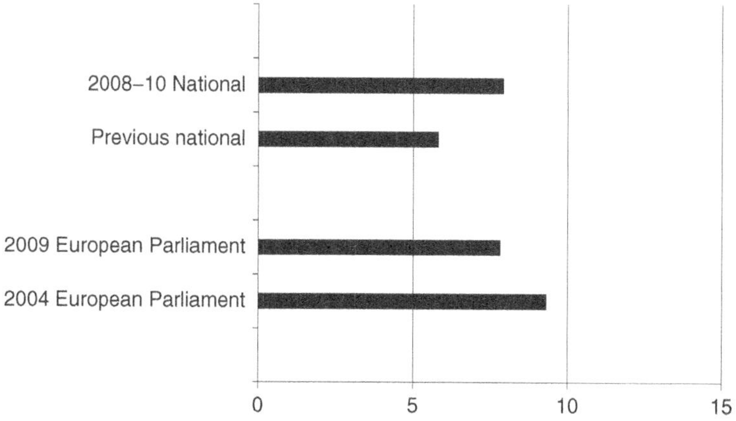

Figure 4.1 Net percentage decline in vote for governing parties in two European Parliament and national election cycles

points *higher* than the loss sustained by governing parties in the previous national electoral cycle for the same countries (–5.8 per cent). Thus, the trend that exists in the national election cycle is somewhat more consistent with an economic voting hypothesis than that of the EP election cycle. Voters *did* punish governments to a greater extent in national elections held after the onset of the economic crisis than they did in the previous national cycle when times were better. However, considering the difference in economic circumstances between the two cycles, the overall effect on electoral outcomes is relatively modest.

Despite the lack of dramatic differences between the two electoral cycles compared in Figure 4.1, 2008–10 was not a benign electoral time for incumbent governments. Among the 15 countries that held national elections during this period, governments were defeated in nine of them. In the Czech Republic, where a caretaker government was in place during the year preceding the May 2010 election, the Civic Democratic Party (ODS), which had won the previous (2006) election and governed until a parliamentary defeat, saw its vote share decline from 35.4 to 20.2 per cent. And even in some instances where a governing party avoided losing office, it suffered substantial losses. The Socialist Party (SPÖ), which had led a grand coalition in Austria, declined –6.1 per cent from the previous election, and the Socialists in Portugal dropped –8.4 per cent. Only in Luxembourg (+1.9 per cent) and in Slovakia (+5.7 per cent) did the governing party improve its vote share. In Slovakia, however, that party (SMER) was dislodged from power despite its success in increasing its vote. In Germany, the Christian Democratic Union/Christian Social Union (CDU/CSU) gained seats, but its share of the vote nevertheless declined by a modest –1.4 per cent.

Other trends are discernible in the outcome of elections during this period. In a number of instances in which a governing party was defeated, a government of the centre-left was replaced by one of the centre-right. In Bulgaria, Hungary, Lithuania, and the United Kingdom, the election was a clear and decisive defeat for Social Democratic governments. In Germany the Social Democratic Party (SPD), which had been in a grand coalition with the CDU/CSU since 2005, registered one of its worst ever electoral performances (–11.2 per cent). The main social democratic party in the Czech Republic (CSSD) likewise saw its vote share drop by more than 10 per cent, in spite of the fact that it had not been part of either the previous governing coalition or the caretaker government leading up to the election. With only a few exceptions, elections held during the period of the economic crisis spelled disaster for parties of the left.

The clear exceptions were Greece and Slovenia, in which governments of the centre-right were defeated by a centre-left party. In Greece, New Democracy, which had governed for two terms, was decisively defeated by the Socialists (PASOK). In Slovenia, a rejuvenated SPD toppled a centre-right coalition, and a new centre-left party (Zares) also made gains. In most other instances, however, parties of the right improved their positions, sometimes at the expense of socialist or social democratic parties and in other cases as part of a swing against a centre-right government. In The Netherlands, for example, the Christian Democrats, which had led coalition governments since 2002, were decisively defeated. However, the principal gains were made not by Labour (PvdA) but by other parties of the right – the Liberals (VVD) +5.8 per cent and Geert Wilders' Party for Freedom (PVV) +9.6 per cent.

There were several other countries where parties on the more extreme right end of the political spectrum also made gains in national elections during the 2008–10 period. In Austria, the Freedom Party, by no means a new party and one which had some previous experience in government, gained 6.5 per cent of the vote over its level in the previous (2006) election to reach a total of 17.5 per cent, a solid third place finish. In addition, the Alliance for the Future of Austria (BZÖ), formed after Jörg Haider broke with the Freedom Party, won 10.7 per cent. Combining the vote for those two parties means that the extreme right in Austria had vote totals similar to those of the traditional establishment parties: the Socialists and the People's Party.

In citing countries where far-right parties made gains, Hungary must also be mentioned. Jobbik, an anti-immigrant and anti-Roma party that was formed to contest the 2006 election, but got few votes, surged in 2010, to a total of 16.7 per cent. The Netherlands is in some ways similar to Hungary. The PVV led by Geert Wilders was established to very modest support in 2006 but finished third in 2010, with 15.5 per cent of the vote. In addition, Bulgaria saw the formation of two new far-right parties, the Blue Coalition (SK) and Order, Law and Justice (RZS), which combined to take over 10 per cent of the vote in the July 2009 election. In Lithuania, the newly founded populist National Resurrection Party won 15 per cent of the vote in the October 2008 election, and the socially conservative Order and Justice Party held steady at over 10 per cent.

In other countries, however, the far-right did not gain, and in some cases lost heavily. In Romania, Greater Romania (PRM) declined to 3 per cent, from 13 per cent in the previous election, and in Slovakia the Slovak National Party saw its vote cut in half. In many other European countries, the far-right vote was either negligible or held steady at a relatively low percentage. So although some European political contexts provided support for the thesis that the far-right would gain during the economic crisis, other cases did not.

Accounts of the election campaigns in the 15 countries holding national elections since September of 2008 generally disclose a pattern of downplaying the impact of the economic crisis on the campaign.[4] In some cases (Austria, Slovenia, Lithuania) the election occurred as the economic crisis was just beginning, making interpretation of its full impact difficult. In other cases, governments seeking re-election were already besieged by problems from other sources, making perceived incompetence in dealing with the crisis 'just one more thing' to persuade people to turn away from them (Hungary, Greece). In the Czech Republic the previous government, having suffered a parliamentary defeat, had been replaced by a non-partisan caretaker regime for over a year prior to the election.

In most 'normal' situations, the state of the economy provides a backdrop to the election campaign, and once the financial crisis hit in the Fall of 2008, the uncertainty about future prospects became the aspect of the economy that dominated discussion. The way the crisis was discussed varied to some extent according to the stage that had been reached. At the very beginning, the potential effect on the national economy of countries outside the United States was unclear. By mid-Fall of 2008, a consensus had developed that help to, or relief of, heavily affected sectors such as banking and manufacturing was necessary. The discussion in countries holding elections in 2009 (Bulgaria, Germany, Greece, Luxembourg, and Portugal) revolved around which party could best administer the stimulus measures, which all agreed by that time were needed. Later, as the policy consensus evolved towards the need for deficit reduction and debt control in the near future, the discourse in election campaigns centred on which party was best positioned to administer a programme of austerity. In countries holding elections in 2010 (Belgium, Czech Republic, Hungary, The Netherlands, Slovakia, and the United Kingdom) such positions of possible retrenchment were framed in terms of economic responsibility. Given the general agreement of major parties on such policy directions, discussion of the ways to address the crisis itself was surprisingly muted.

The economic crisis may also be examined for potential effects on voter turnout. Though turnout has been declining in most countries in the last two decades, the intensity of the economic crisis might have been a stimulus to increased interest in politics and hence to a revival in participation rates. However, the helplessness of national governments in the face of the crisis, together with the degree of consensus between major electoral contenders regarding the proper policy response, would lead to the opposite hypothesis that voting turnout in the 2008–10 period would likely continue its decline, or begin to stabilize. In the event, there was a record low overall turnout in the 2009 EP elections, for reasons that may have had little to do with the crisis, as turnout in EP elections has steadily declined ever since their inception in 1979. In the 15 national contexts considered here, turnout declines are present in almost all of them. Sometimes these were declines in the most recent election (Germany, Greece, Portugal, Romania, The Netherlands), while at other times the turnout decline was in the previous election and the current one was virtually unchanged (Austria, Hungary, Lithuania). In a few cases, the national election in the 2008–10 period saw a small increase in turnout, such as in the United Kingdom (+4 per cent), Slovenia (+2 per cent), Slovakia (+4 per cent), Bulgaria (+3 per cent), but these small increases do not show evidence of reversing the long-term downward trend even in these countries. Thus, the turnout decline, which has been observed over the longer term in many European countries, was not reversed by the onset of the economic crisis, and may have even been exacerbated by it as voters came to realize that a change in government in itself would not provide a solution.

The 2008–2010 crisis in summary

In Table 4.4, we summarize the voting patterns across the 15 countries that held national elections during the period of the economic crisis. The symbol ■ denotes a strong or clearly observable trend in the hypothesized direction, while □ indicates a weaker or more uneven trend. With respect to government defeats, the trend is clear, with such defeats occurring in nine of the cases. And as noted earlier, in most other elections, governing parties lost support even if they avoided outright electoral defeat. Only in Luxembourg did a governing party both improve its vote share and remain in power.

A clear trend in support for parties of the centre-right is observable in 10 of the 15 countries. In most of these, it is quite strong. Exceptions were Greece and Slovenia, where governing centre-right parties were defeated by parties of the centre-left. In most of the others, elections taking place during the period of the economic crisis spelled defeat for socialist or social democratic parties, particularly those that had the misfortune to be in power at the time of the crisis. On the face of it, it is not clear why this should be the case. If it is true that governing parties fare badly in a deteriorating economic environment, this should affect *all* types of parties which have the misfortune to be in government at such a time. The fact that this was not the case leads us to consider some of the reasons why parties of the centre-right weathered the crisis better than their counterparts on the other side of the political spectrum that found themselves in the same position. It may be that the rhetoric of election campaigns that gravitate around economic issues is more suited to parties of the right, which tend to stress increased trade and investment, or necessary austerity, as solutions to a country's economic difficulties. Left parties, by contrast, are more likely to advocate public sector solutions, such as job creation or the protection of workers displaced by the downturn. The data examined here are not sufficient to provide a clear answer to this question, but it is clear that difficult economic times, for the most part, would seem to be even more difficult times for parties of the left.

Smaller parties also appear to have benefited from the political conditions that existed in Europe over the two-year period examined here, and in some cases (Austria, Hungary, The Netherlands), the leaders of this trend were parties of the far-right. But this tendency to support the extreme right was weak or non-existent in many other countries and should not necessarily be attributed to the economic crisis. It may be that the political advantage accruing to smaller parties in general

Table 4.4 Summary of electoral outcome patterns for 15 European countries: June 2008–June 2010

			Gains by				
	Election date	Govt. defeat	Centre-right	Centre-left	Far-right	Small parties	Turnout decline
Austria	28-Sep-08				■	■	■
Belgium	13-Jun-10	■	□	□		■	
Bulgaria	05-Jul-09	■	■		□	□	□
Czech Republic	29-May-10		■			■	□
Germany	27-Sep-09		□			□	■
Greece	04-Oct-09	■		■			■
Hungary	25-Apr-10	■	■		■	□	■
Lithuania	12-Oct-08	■	■		□	□	□
Luxembourg	07-Jun-09		■				
Netherlands	09-Jun-10	■	□	□	■	□	■
Portugal	27-Sep-09			□			□
Romania	30-Nov-08	■					■
Slovakia	12-Jun-10		■	□		■	□
Slovenia	21-Sep-08	■		■			□
UK	06-May-10	■	■			□	

in many countries is simply a function of the swing against the larger mainstream parties.

Finally, we note that the elections held during this period almost all seem to display a lower turnout of voters. In a few instances, this may reflect disillusionment with a governing party's handling of the economy, coupled with a lack of confidence in other parties to do any better. But, the pattern of turnout decline in many countries is part of a longer-term demographic trend, which predates the onset of the economic crisis. At most, the crisis may have exacerbated or moderated a trend that was already well in place. But it is noteworthy that voters were not rushing to the polls in great numbers to defeat incumbent governments. In most cases, it was a smaller percentage of the electorate that participated in bringing about such events.

The second economic crisis and new elections in Europe

This chapter has examined the electoral impact of the economic crisis of 2008–10 on electoral results in Europe. Even though the origins of this crisis were widely perceived to be external to the European countries concerned, the effects were evaluated domestically, as having an impact on banking, manufacturing, employment, and growth of individual countries. The shaky state of key industries in the face of the crisis led to actual or proposed layoffs of workers, as well as declines in the values of shares on stock exchanges. Some faced bankruptcy, leaving governments with stark choices about emergency loans. In their response to this situation, national political parties tended to interpret the crisis as an external shock, not attributable to the country's own weaknesses. The specific nature or direction of economic policy was not therefore often in dispute with other parties. Parties were in general agreement in the initial phase of the crisis that vulnerable components of their own economies needed to be supported; later the general agreement shifted towards the view that the 'stimulus packages' and 'bailout funds' that were established to do this would need to be counterbalanced by an ensuing period of austerity, where cutbacks to support these programmes, and perhaps to governments themselves, would bring the nations' finances back into line, if not into balance. The state of the economy continued to be thought of as a valence issue, where the political battles are not over the specific methods to produce growth, but over who can be trusted to undertake the attempt.

In the European Parliament elections of 2009 and the surrounding national elections examined in this article, the economic crisis provided a background to the campaigns, rather than a central point of policy dispute between the electoral combatants. The internal national focus of concern meant that relations with other countries, especially other countries in Europe, were scarcely mentioned, except to note that other countries were in the same boat. But generally, national political parties, whether fighting the EP elections, or their own national battles, paid little attention to how other countries were faring.

The initial crisis in Europe was transformed after 2009 into one involving deficits, debt, and the currency, while still including concerns about the banking sector. This 'euro crisis' did not necessarily become more widespread, but changed its form, in that the economic and diplomatic relations of European states with one another have become more prominent in its interpretation. This development has also changed the underlying electoral dynamic in ways still to be determined. The state of the national economies in countries like Greece, Italy, and Spain has introduced a dramatic new electoral context there and in other EU Member States. Compared to the 2008–09 period analysed above, international relations between European states now provide a context for the discussion of economic policy in all the countries of the EU, not just those most affected by the economic downturns. Views about the role of the EU and other prominent European countries are more likely to come directly into play.

One could speculate that this change may be felt most clearly in the EP elections of 2014, whether or not solutions to the crisis have been put in place by that time. Heretofore, the primary theme in analysis of voting in EP elections has emphasized the weakness of 'European-ness' in the voting. We have already mentioned the 'second order' characterization of these elections (Reif and Schmitt, 1980), whereby EP elections are typically fought by national parties over national issues and are often substantially affected by the popularity of national governments in their domestic political milieu. EP elections, up to and including that of 2009, did not give much attention either to the activities of European institutions or to the circumstances of other countries conducting parallel campaigns during the same period. The second phase of the European economic crisis, however, is truly EU-wide. It involves not only the state of national economies but also the role played by both EU institutions (such as the European Central Bank) and other prominent governments, particularly that of Germany. European issues, such as the amount and nature of aid to distressed EU members and the amount of austerity they should be forced to undergo, will be forced onto the electoral agenda.

The consequences of these developments, as manifested in the nature of shifting electoral discourse, may make for a 2014 EP campaign that is dramatically different from its predecessors. The possible consequences may be hypothesized to be of three sorts. First, the campaign may gain in salience to the public, perhaps leading to a reversal of the long-term turnout decline. The turnout for the elections to the EP has seen a steady decline from their inception in 1979. In 2009, the lowest EP turnout on record, only 44 per cent of eligible voters decided to cast a ballot. With more attention on the role of the European institutions in creating policies to address the crisis, more prospective voters may take an interest. Second, coincident with a potential influx of new electors, parties will have more of substance to say about the economic policy of the community, and second-order effects deriving from national politics may be more muted. Parties that benefited politically from the first economic crisis may struggle, particularly if they came to power or became part of a governing coalition during the first economic crisis. As subsequent events in Greece have shown, the party (PASOK) that gained the most in 2009 suffered severe losses in the two subsequent elections held in 2012. Such patterns could open the door to greater support for new parties or more extreme parties, either of the left or the right. Third, the public discourse in the European election may be more about Europe as a whole than usual and more about the influence of other countries in the process of policy formation. EU policies to bring the whole community out of the economic crisis will be called for, and consequent subjects such as future enlargement, the single market, Schengen and external relations could well be raised. Those who have hoped for a more 'Europe-focused' EP election process may finally get their wish (Farrell and Scully, 2007).

This changed situation will also affect national elections. An interesting arena to observe the changed electoral context will come in Germany in 2013 when the Bundestag is next chosen. Germany has been in the forefront of community economic policy towards the defaulting Member States, and the demands for austerity have been present both in Germany's own direct relations with states like Greece and in their important influence over the EU policy as a whole. Just as the candidates for the French Presidency differed in their approaches to EU policy in the 2012 election in France – strict austerity from Sarkozy and encouragement of moderate growth from Hollande – so the candidates for Chancellor in Germany in 2013 will be expected to bring such economic policy discussion to the fore. But in the 2013 German election, this will also involve economic relations with other countries, not just the domestic repercussions of particular positions.

Some indication of the economic attitudes which will provide the context for the next campaign in Germany may be found in the recent report by the Pew Research Center's *Global Attitudes Project* (Pew Research Center, 2012). The survey of the German population contained in this report shows that Germans are almost evenly divided and highly polarized on the question of whether the country 'should provide financial assistance to other European Union countries that have major financial problems' (p. 32) – 49 per cent are in favour and 48 per cent opposed, with only 4 per cent having no opinion. Other German attitudes towards Greece are highly negative, with the country being considered 'the least hardworking' in Europe (p. 39). Germans also consider Italy and Spain, other potential candidates for EU financial aid, not to be hardworking, as well as high in corruption (p. 39). The integrity of the Eurozone and the future of European integration, in general, are likely to be lively issues of discussion in the 2013 German Bundestag election.

Conclusion

The successive economic crises that have affected Europe have raised questions, not only about the efficacy of conventional economic models of voting but also about the ability of electoral institutions to effectively mobilize public participation in the face of dire economic circumstances. Economic voting models, as we have shown earlier, are preoccupied with the effects of economic conditions on the support for incumbent governments. But in a perverse twist on the initial logic of the modelling, the more severe the economic circumstances, especially when they can be attributed to an external source, the less the situation allows for its direct attribution to an incumbent, unless other events render that government unpopular to begin with. Thus, governing parties actually did slightly better in the 2009 EP election than they had in the previous election cycle and only slightly worse in the national election cycle, even though they suffered losses. And election campaigns, both at the EP level and at the national level, do not show a particular tendency to dwell on the crisis as an election issue, except in the usual valence terms of which party can best be trusted to deal with the economy.

The ensuing 'Eurocrisis', which began in earnest in 2010 and continues at the time of this publication, has, we have speculated, more likelihood of producing differentiated public policy responses on the part of political parties, and therefore more likelihood of involving the public in deliberation on a variety of specific economic issues. This is because the current economic crisis involves the efficacy of EU institutions, which seek to balance the interests of various Member States of the community. The 'Eurocrisis' also forces individual member states to consider their relations with other EU members and with the Union itself. Given the divisions in public opinion on these questions, as opposed to the generality of supporting economic growth, we may expect more engagement on the part of both the public and the political parties in European countries. Whether this will contribute to, or detract from, the ultimate likelihood of finding a solution is an open question at the moment.

Notes

1. For a review of the earlier literature, see Miller (1989).
2. The Czech Republic is not included in these calculations, since a non-party caretaker government was in office both at the time of the June 2009 EP election and the subsequent (May 2010) national election.
3. We define 'governing party' here, in the case of coalitions, as the largest party or the party leading the coalition.
4. A number of brief accounts of these can be found in the election notes section of *Electoral Studies*. See, for example, Wolfgang C. Müller, 'The Snap Election in Austria, September 2008', *Electoral Studies* 28, 514–17.

Bibliography

Anderson, C.J. (2007) 'The End of Economic Voting? Contingency Dilemmas and the Limits of Democratic Accountability', *Annual Review of Political Science* 10, 271–96.

Brug, W. van der, C. van der Eijk and M. Franklin (2007) *The Economy and the Vote: Economic Conditions and Elections in Fifteen Countries* (Cambridge: Cambridge University Press).

Butler, D. and D. Stokes (1969) *Political Change in Britain* (New York: St. Martin's).

Clarke, H.D., J. Jenson, L. LeDuc and J.H. Pammett (1979) *Political Choice in Canada* (Toronto: McGraw-Hill Ryerson).

Clarke, H.D., D. Sanders, M.C. Stewart and P. Whiteley (2004) *Political Choice in Britain* (Oxford: Oxford University Press).

Curtice, J. (1989) 'The 1989 European Election: Protest or Green Tide?', *Electoral Studies* 8, 217–30.

Dreher, A. (2006) 'Does Globalization Affect Growth? Evidence from a New Index of Globalization', *Applied Economics* 38(10), 1091–110.

Duch, R.M. and R.T. Stevenson (2008) *The Economic Vote: How Political and Economic Institutions Condition Election Results* (Cambridge: Cambridge University Press).

Eijk, C. van der and M. Franklin (1996) *Choosing Europe: The European Electorate and National Politics in the Face of Union* (Ann Arbor: University of Michigan Press).

Eijk, C. van der, M. Franklin and M. Marsh (1996) 'What Voters Teach Us About Europe-Wide Elections: What Europe-Wide Elections Teach Us About Voters', *Electoral Studies* 15, 149–66.

Evans, J.A. (2004) *Voters and Voting: An Introduction* (London: Sage).

Farrell, D. and R. Scully (2007) *Representing Europe's Citizens: Electoral Institutions and the Failure of Parliamentary Representation* (Oxford: Oxford University Press).

Hall, P.A. (1986) *Governing the Economy: The Politics of State Intervention in Britain and France* (Cambridge: Polity Press).

Hellwig, T. (2010) 'Voting and the Economy', in L. LeDuc, R.G. Niemi and P. Norris (eds), *Comparing Democracies 3* (London: Sage), 184–201.

Hix, S. and M. Marsh (2007) 'Punishment or Protest: Understanding European Parliament Elections', *Journal of Politics* 69, 495–510.

Hobolt, S.B., J. Tilley and S.A. Banducci (2010, 13–14 May) 'Electoral Accountability in Context: How Political Institutions Condition Performance Voting'. Paper presented at the 2nd Political Science and Political Economy conference, London School of Economics.

Irwin, G. (1995) 'Second Order or Third Rate?: Issues in the Campaign for the European Parliament – 1994', *Electoral Studies* 14, 183–99.

Katona, G. and B. Strumpell (1978) *A New Economic Era* (New York: Elsevier).

Kramer, G. (1971) 'Short-Term Fluctuations in U.S. Voting Behavior', *American Political Science Review* 65, 131–43.

Krieger, J. (1986) *Reagan, Thatcher and the Politics of Decline* (Oxford: Polity Press).

LeDuc, L. (2007) 'European Elections and Democratic Accountability: The 2004 Elections to the European Parliament', in J. DeBardeleben and A. Hurrelmann (eds), *Democratic Dilemmas of Multilevel Governance* (Basingstoke: Palgrave Macmillan), 139–57.

Lodge, J. (ed.) (2001) *The 1999 Elections to the European Parliament* (London: Pinter).

Marsh, M. (1998) 'Testing the Second Order Election Model After Four European Elections', *British Journal of Political Science* 28, 591–607.

Miller, W.L. (1989) 'Studying How the Economy Affects Public Attitudes and Behavior: Problems and Prospects', in H.D. Clarke, M.C. Stewart and G. Zuk (eds), *Economic Decline and Political Change: Canada, Great Britain, the United States* (Pittsburgh: University of Pittsburgh Press), 143–72.

Perrineau, P., G. Grünberg and C. Ysmal (eds) (2002) *Europe at the Polls: The European Elections of 1999* (Basingstoke: Palgrave Macmillan).

Pew Research Center (2012) *European Unity on the Rocks: Greeks and Germans at Polar Opposites*, http://www.pewglobal.org/2012/05/29/european-unity-on-the-rocks/http://pewglobal.org, 29 May (accessed on 10 July 2012).

Powell, G.B. and G.D. Whitten (1993) 'A Cross-National Analysis of Economic Voting: Taking Account of the Political Context', *American Journal of Political Science* 37, 391–414.

Reif, K. (1984) 'National Electoral Cycles and European Elections', *Electoral Studies* 3, 244–55.

Reif, K. and H. Schmitt (1980) 'Nine Second-Order Elections: A Conceptual Framework for the Analysis of European Election Results', *European Journal of Political Research* 8, 3–44.

Schmitt, H. (2004) 'The European Parliament Elections of June 2004: Still Second Order?' *West European Politics* 28, 650–79.

Solomon, R. (1999) *The Transformation of the World Economy*, 2nd ed., (Basingstoke: Palgrave Macmillan).

Thomas, N.C. (1989) 'Adapting Policy-Making Machinery to Fiscal Stress', in H.D. Clarke, M.C. Stewart and G. Zuk (eds), *Economic Decline and Political Change: Canada, Great Britain, the United States* (Pittsburgh: University of Pittsburgh Press), 27–52.

Vujakovic, P. (2010) 'How to Measure Globalization? A New Globalization Index (NGI)', *Atlantic Economic Journal* 38(2), 237.

Part II

The EU's Global Role and International Institutions

5
Do the Rules of International Trade Constrain Protection? Global Recession and EU Trade Policy

Crina Viju and William A. Kerr

Introduction

Many feared that governments around the world would resort to protectionism in the wake of the global financial meltdown and economic recession that commenced in 2008. Protectionism tends to be pervasive during economic downturns and the Great Depression experience proved that beggar-thy-neighbour trade wars have disastrous effects. However, governments have a predilection for imposing trade restrictions in times of economic hardship to shelter domestic industries from foreign competition and to save jobs. During the Summit on Financial Markets and World Economy of 15 November 2008, the leaders of the Group of Twenty (G20) declared that they understand the devastating effects of trade protectionism and that they would refrain from imposing new barriers to trade and investment (G20, 2008). Based on the Great Depression experience, however, not many believed those promises.

In 2009, Pascal Lamy, the Director General of the World Trade Organization (WTO), reported that trade was as open at the time as it was before the crisis and asked the WTO members who imposed any additional trade restrictions to start removing them once their economies start to recover (WTO, 2009).

According to various WTO assessments, the new protectionist measures affected a maximum of 1 per cent of world trade in 2009, only 0.4 per cent between November 2009 and May 2010, followed by an increase to 0.8 per cent of trade during the period June 2010 to October 2010 and, finally, decreasing again to 0.53 per cent of trade between mid-October 2010 and April 2011 (WTO, 2011). The new measures were primarily border and export restrictions on sensitive sectors such as textiles, clothing, steel, iron, footwear, electronics, and agriculture.

Thus, the fear that governments would resort to protectionism proved to be unfounded. A question still remains: why such a muted trade policy was not expected, given that most economists have shown that trade liberalization is welfare enhancing? (Perdikis and Kerr, 1998). There is even a general acceptance by policy makers that trade wars have destructive effects and trade agreements promote cooperation. However, the idea that exports are good and imports bad still remains pervasive and deeply rooted (Gaisford and Hester, 2007). Exports are good as they add jobs, while imports just give away the jobs to foreigners. This idea gains more prominence when the economy passes through a recessionary period and when politicians are under heavy pressure to do something that would lessen the unemployment. Imposing trade restrictions is tempting for policy makers as it seems to be the easiest way to satisfy the vocal vested interests. There is, however, always the risk that the trading partners would react in the same way and a beggar-thy-neighbour trade war will be precipitated. Unfortunately, this is what happened during the Great Depression.

Except for the 'quick fix' effect that trade restrictions have, politicians find protectionism attractive for other reasons as well. For example, by restricting imports all the costs are transferred to foreigners, who are not able to vote. One alternative to trade restrictions is fiscal stimulus measures, which in short run can be funded by government borrowing, but in long run may eventually result in increased taxes, thus affecting those that vote. Hence, it is not a politically attractive solution. Further, raising taxes prior to economic recovery can result in additional economic hardship through reduced consumption and investment. The other way of financing fiscal stimulus, large government borrowing, increases the risk associated with government bonds. This is exactly the situation that Greece was forced to deal with starting in 2010. As the government was heavily indebted prior to the crisis, during the economic downturn lenders lost faith in the government and increased the cost of new borrowing. This imposes a large cost on the voters. By examining the implications of some of the alternatives to trade policy, it is not hard to understand why trade restrictions that impose the costs on foreigners[1] are very appealing to politicians.

While politicians may wish to raise trade barriers during a recession, they are constrained by both domestic institutional arrangements that require political capital to be expended and by the international commitments made in trade agreements (Perdikis and Kerr, 1998). It is important to understand the nature of both of these constraints to fully understand the absence of the expected trade policy response to the economic downturn precipitated by the financial crisis of 2008.

This chapter begins by outlining the economic and trade implications of the global economic crisis of 2008–11. A discussion of the development of constraints on protectionist initiatives that are embedded in European Union (EU) institutions follows. The main reasons for the absence of global protectionism observed in the wake of the latest financial crisis are analysed in Section 3. The chapter ends with a summary and conclusions.

Trade effects of the global financial and economic crisis that commenced in 2008

During the global financial and economic crisis that commenced in 2008, international trade suffered the most important decline since the most Great Depression. In the past 50 years, global trade suffered steep declines during three worldwide recessions; in the 1970s by 11 per cent and in both 1982 and 2001 by 5 per cent. However, between the third-quarter of 2008 and the second-quarter of 2009, global trade dropped by 15 per cent, registering a total reduction of 12.2 per cent in 2009 (Baldwin, 2009). In 2010, global trade in goods rose by 14.5 per cent (WTO, 2011).

The major trading regions suffered sharp declines in trade with exports dropping by 14.8 per cent in the EU-27, 14.4 per cent in North America, and 11.1 per cent in Asia and imports decreasing by 14.5 per cent in the EU-27, 16.3 per cent in North America, and 7.9 per cent in Asia (WTO, 2010). While gross domestic product (GDP) declined by 3–4 per cent in 2009 in the two of the largest markets, the United States and the EU, international trade dropped almost five times more compared to the GDP reduction (Baldwin, 2009). Surprisingly, the major explanations for the large trade decline are not protectionist measures, but demand shocks manifested through commodity prices and consumption delays (Baldwin, 2009), global supply chain rigidities, and lack of financing (Kee, Neagu and Nicita, 2010). Exchange rate fluctuations have also impacted global trade with the US dollar appreciating against other currencies in September of 2008, but depreciating between March and October of 2009 by 12 per cent against a basket of currencies and by 15 per cent against the euro. As a result, commodity prices rose, with the price of oil increasing from US$40/barrel to US$80/barrel in 2009 (WTO, 2009).

The effects of the crisis on foreign direct investment (FDI) started to be felt only in the second half of 2008, with an estimated decline in global FDI inflows of about 15 per cent in 2008. A large drop of 25 per cent in FDI was registered in developed countries (Filipov and Kalotay, 2009).

Despite the fact that FDI flows to G20 countries registered an increase of 3 per cent in 2010 compared to 2009, global FDI inflows remained 25 per cent below the pre-crisis average of 2005–07 (OECD and UNCTAD, 2011). The main causes of the decline in FDI relate to tighter credit, lower profits, and decreased business confidence.

A number of macroeconomic measures were implemented by governments in an effort to boost economic activity and to recover from the deep economic downturn. Not many of those measures were, however, trade restrictive. A maximum of 1 per cent of global trade was affected by new trade measures implemented during the period from October 2008 to October 2009 and only 0.53 per cent of trade between October 2010 and April 2011 (WTO, 2011). Most of the trade restrictions implemented are explained by spikes in tariffs, new non-tariff barriers (NTBs), stricter application of Sanitary and Phytosanitary (SPS) and Technical Barriers to Trade (TBT) regulations, additional export measures, and custom procedures (WTO, 2011). As suggested above, those new measures were mostly implemented in sectors that have been traditionally protected, known as the sensitive sectors. It also should be mentioned that different economies have introduced trade opening measures such as lower tariffs, removal of some NTBs, and elimination of various restrictions on trade in services (WTO, 2009). As an example, Canada decided to remove custom duties on more than 1500 items starting in March of 2010 (WTO, 2010). Except for the trade restrictions, other macroeconomic measures have impacted trade, such as fiscal stimulus, bailout packages, and, more importantly, local buy/hire requirements.

Some WTO members did raise their applied tariffs; this was, however, on a very limited scale, with the largest markets, the United States and the EU, continuing to reduce their applied tariffs during the crisis. However, an increase could be observed in NTBs, especially in the number of anti-dumping (AD) investigations. Between July 2008 and June 2009, the number of AD cases increased by 15 per cent, only to be followed by a reduction of 10 per cent during the period of October 2010 to April 2011 compared to the period from October 2009 to April 2010 (WTO, 2011). An interesting aspect worth mentioning is that most of the AD investigations were initiated by developing countries against developing countries (mostly China) and in the sectors with the most AD cases having been opened over the years, such as chemicals, plastics, and metals (WTO, 2010). On the other hand, the number of countervailing duty (CVD) investigations increased from October 2008 to October 2009. As was the case for AD, the increase in CVD cases was followed by a sharp decline of 36 per cent from October 2010 to April 2011 compared to October 2009–April 2010 (WTO, 2011). In terms of safeguard initiations, the number increased from 11 in 2008 to 26 in 2009. The increase was slowed in 2009, being followed by a decline of 46 per cent in October 2010–April 2011 compared to October 2009–April 2010 (WTO, 2011).

For SPS notifications, the number increased. A total of 633 regular SPS notifications and 95 emergency SPS notifications were submitted by WTO members during the period between October 2008 and October 2009 as compared to 782 notifications and 107 emergency notifications during the same period of time in 2007–08 (WTO, 2009). From November 2009 to May 2010, 635 regular notifications and 50 emergency notifications were submitted (WTO, 2010), meaning that the number of regular notifications recorded during 2009–10 significantly increased, with developing countries being the main users. Despite that, during 2010–11 the number of notifications from developing countries has returned to the previous level. However, a threefold increase in the number of regular notifications from the United States was recorded (WTO, 2011). One problem is that WTO members do not take into account internationally developed standards, especially in regard to certain animal diseases (bovine spongiform encephalopathy, avian influenza, and foot-and-mouth disease) when they impose different import restrictions (Kerr, 2009). As a consequence, the SPS committee of the WTO has decided to include a new transparency rule starting in December 2008 to encourage all WTO member countries to follow the international standards when providing notifications. In the case of TBT, an increase in the number of notifications and trade concerns can be observed during October 2008–October 2009 with 1450 notifications and 127 specific trade concerns compared to 1274 notifications and 90 trade concerns during the same time in the previous period. However, in 2010, the number of notifications dropped by 5 per cent, this signalling increased regulatory activity or better implementation of the TBT agreement (WTO, 2010).

Moving on to trade in services, the crisis did not trigger significant new market access barriers. However, a concern relates to the protection of local labour markets through increases in barriers to international migration. For example, due to high levels of unemployment, a number of EU Member State governments have introduced measures to protect labour markets. As Sward (2009) describes, in 2008 the level of immigration from Poland to the United Kingdom was at its lowest since 2004. In addition, the immigration rules for non-EU skilled migrants were tightened by requiring visas for doctors, nurses, and secondary-school teachers. In Spain, the large increase in the unemployment rate to 17 per cent by the middle of 2009 and to 28 per cent among foreign workers, resulted in the decision by the government to offer bonuses to non-EU workers if they agreed to return to their home countries for at least three years (Martin, 2009). However, the bonuses did not have a large uptake by immigrants as they preferred to remain in Spain. Martin (2009) also points out that there were four sectors most affected by job losses: construction, financial services, manufacturing, and travel-related services. However, countries have refrained from imposing major barriers to immigration.

Trade restrictions, however, represent just a small per cent of measures implemented by governments during the latest global crisis. The bulk of measures are represented by fiscal stimulus and bailout packages.

In the United States, the support programmes were approximately US$12 trillion and in the EU around US$8 trillion for 2009. Within the EU, the fiscal rescue packages represented 28 per cent of GDP in the United Kingdom and 19 per cent of GDP in Germany and France. Those rescue packages were much larger than the ones originally announced in 2009; for example, 1–1.5 per cent of GDP in the United Kingdom and France and 2.8 per cent of GDP in Germany (WTO, 2009). However, according to the WTO (2011), from October 2010 to April 2011 only a few additional government stimulus measures were implemented and these were mainly extensions of existing programmes. Some government support measures were phased out. For instance, the EU announced in December 2010 the gradual phasing out of the economic stimulus measures that it had taken to combat the global financial and economic crisis. The question that is raised is whether fiscal stimulus can have any trade effects. The direct answer would be it depends on the type of the fiscal measure. Tax cuts, for example, can have trade effects, while 'buy local' requirements for government procurement can raise at least three important trade concerns. First, foreign suppliers are excluded; second, the costs to domestic producers in countries implementing such regulations can be increased; and, third, which is probably the most important from a trade perspective, they can lead to retaliation. For example, during the latest economic crisis, the 'buy American' requirement of the US stimulus legislation was followed by 'buy Chinese' regulations.[2] Bailouts and scrapping schemes have benefited mostly the banking and automobile sectors. Even the fiscal stimulus and bailout packages have allowed governments to be more involved in industries affected by crisis, their involvement has started to follow a decreasing trend.

The development of European Union trade policy institutions

An assessment of EU trade policy institutions is important for understanding the weakness of protectionist measures in the recession that started in 2008. Individual European countries were very active in the trade war of the 1930s. Some EU Member States are still known for being in favour of protectionism. Looking back at the 1930s, most economists agree that the protectionism that originated from the United States worsened the depression by setting off a non-cooperative beggar-thy-neighbour trade war. The US Smoot–Hawley Tariff imposed on 17 June 1930 was the beginning of the global trade war. The US action was followed by the United Kingdom, which through the Abnormal Importations Act (AIA), passed on 19 November 1931, permitted the imposition of tariffs up to 100 per cent. The British Board of Trade immediately raised tariffs to 50 per cent on 23 classes of, primarily, European goods. The result was that the imports of the specific products effectively ceased. A 10 per cent general tariff increase followed, but not for countries that belonged to the British Empire. Additionally, the British imposed restrictive quotas on Japanese textiles and those of other countries dependent on access to the British market.

Germany reacted next by imposing strict import licensing and by turning to bilateral trading arrangements, followed by France which imposed a 15 per cent *ad valorem* exchange surtax on British goods, while 65 per cent of imports were restricted through an import quota system (Saint-Etienne, 1984). Bilateral or regional agreements were increasingly relied upon and, by the mid-1930s, much of world trade had been reduced to barter arrangements.

After the Second World War, most of these Depression era trade restrictions remained in place. While European countries engaged in the General Agreement on Tariffs and Trade (GATT) negotiations, progress on trade liberalization was slow and the European market remained economically fragmented. European economies remained weak. Once the European Economic Community (EEC) was formed in 1957, under the Treaty of Rome, the EEC's internal trade policy was concentrated mostly on removing cross-border tariffs, while in the 1980s, after the completion of the single market, national level NTBs were eliminated, resulting in all trade policy being decided at the EU level. In effect, this meant that if Member States wished to have imports restricted, they had to make their case at the European Commission (EC), and any trade barriers imposed would affect all Member States. Currently, the EU Common Commercial Policy covers the main measures affecting trade in goods and services and other trade-related issues such as standards and technical regulations, intellectual property rights (IPRs), and so on. Delegating trade policy authority to the EU level acted to insulate trade policy makers from protectionist pressures to a considerable degree (Dür, 2008). Further, policy makers within Member States no longer had the unilateral ability to impose formal trade barriers, such as tariffs and import quotas, thus making them less useful to those seeking protection (Gaisford, Kerr and Perdikis, 2003).

The common commercial policy is based on uniform principles in regards to tariff changes, conclusion of trade agreements, commercial aspects of intellectual property, FDI, and export policy. After the Treaty of Rome, despite a commitment to a unified commercial policy, in practice, the EU Member States still had a large degree of autonomy regarding external policy. Even after 1968, when the EU adopted a single set of external tariffs, the Member States still retained the control over the application of NTBs, such as health, safety, and technical standards and border controls, which can explain the protectionism during subsequent economic downturns (Hine, 1985).

While stripped of their powers to impose tariffs and other direct barriers to trade, individual governments have continued to intervene through new regulations in labour and capital markets and by offering subsidies to different vulnerable sectors, through fiscal stimulus packages and price and wage controls. Some Member State governments have blamed persistent unemployment on growing imports, particularly from Japan. Different types of NTBs such as Voluntary Export Restraints (VERs) and Orderly Market Arrangements (OMAs) have been negotiated with foreign governments to restrict imports.[3] In the EU, the number of VERs increased five times from the 1970s to the 1980s, mostly in sensitive sectors such as electronics, automobiles, steel, and agriculture, where competition from outside the EU was particularly intense. The number of AD measures increased from 5 in 1973 to 187 in 1984. Quotas for textiles and apparel were tightened under the Multi-Fiber Arrangements (MFA) of 1973, and were reduced under the MFA renewals of 1978 and 1982 (Hanson, 1998). In the automobile sector, imports of Japanese cars were restricted by VERs. Various European governments imposed 'local-content requirements' on Nissan and Toyota cars produced in Europe. The steel industry benefited from large subsidies in the EU (especially in the United Kingdom) (Erixon, 2009). In effect, since the 1970s these non-tariff regulatory barriers have represented the most important trade barriers to non-EU products.

The completion of the single market brought a change in the institutional context in which external policy is made and, thus, has reduced the opportunity for Member States to use national policy tools to protect sensitive sectors. The single market resulted in the elimination of NTBs between the EU Member States and the launching of a programme that would allow the harmonization or mutual recognition of product standards (Hanson, 1998). Thus, even if Member State governments wish to put in place national trade restrictions, these would impede indirect imports (transhipment of non-EU goods through other EU Member States) from other Member States in violation of Treaty commitments. The result is that the institutional setup under which EU trade policy is made impedes the ability of Member States to put barriers to trade in place.

Before the Lisbon Treaty was ratified in 2009, trade policy at the EU level was determined by the community process, meaning that the EC would propose and the Council would adopt the negotiating mandates. Once the limits of what could be negotiated were agreed at the political level, the EC, in consultation with the Article 133 Committee, would negotiate the agreements, with the Council subsequently approving, or not, what had been negotiated by majority voting. The Article 133 Committee is composed of trade officials from each Member State, who are appointed by the Council. Thus, if any Member State wished to have a trade barrier imposed, it would have to convince both the EC and the other members of the Article 133 Committee. The reality was even more complicated because EU level trade policy was usually decided by consensus, due to the mix of agreements covering issues exclusive to EU competencies (such as tariffs) and issues under joint EU and Member State competencies, such as investment or IPRs. A proposal from the EC to increase EU competencies was resisted by the Member States in a number of intergovernmental conferences (IGC). For topics that were not under the EU competence, unanimity was, in general, required. However, a single Member State, even a large one, could not block the adoption of an already negotiated trade agreement as the Council tried to work towards an agreement that could be accepted by all Member States. Processes for changing trade policy were equally complex. The institutional structure of trade policy making was also time consuming, meaning that a quick response to requests for protection could not be expected. In reality, there were more tensions in reaching agreements on topics under EU competence, such as agriculture, than on topics under mixed competencies such as services or IPRs (Woolcock, 2010). Prior to the Lisbon Treaty, the European Parliament (EP) had limited trade policy powers. The EP could ratify a trade agreement only when it had budgetary or institutional implications, and when the trade agreement would result in the modification of certain EU legislation adopted by co-decision of the EP and the Council or in case of an association agreement.

The Lisbon Treaty brought important changes to the trade policy process. First, according to Article 207 (1) of the Lisbon Treaty, all aspects of external trade, including services, IPRs and FDI are under exclusive EU competence. As a result of some Member State and non-governmental actors' pressure, special provisions were implemented regarding audiovisual, health, educational, and social services specified in Article 207 (4). Thus, unanimity in EU decision-making is required when negotiations are performed in the specified fields, when the agreements 'risk prejudicing the Union's linguistic and cultural diversity' and 'risk seriously disturbing the national organization of such services and prejudicing the responsibility of Member States to deliver them'. Decisions on other topics are based on qualified majority voting. Second, the Lisbon Treaty enhances the role of the EP in external policy. The EP now shares responsibility with the Council for developing the regulations for the implementation of the common external policy. The EP also has the ability to influence the EC during trade agreement negotiations, and the EP has the power to ratify or not (Woolcock, 2010). The Lisbon Treaty, however, does not significantly change the institutional arrangement within the EU regarding trade policy processes. The extension of EU areas of exclusive competence means a reduction in the possibility for Member States to block policy by withholding unanimity. Thus, as the changes in the institutional setup within the EU since the Treaty of Rome have as main goals an enhanced integration of the EU economies and a unique voice on the global market, Member States' capabilities and roles in imposing and deciding on the EU common external policy have been gradually reduced. There are still sensitive sectors where Member States have the right to veto, and, thus, can still influence the outcome of trade policy, but starting in December 2009, when the Lisbon Treaty was ratified, the options have been reduced to a minimum. Further, initiating an increase in trade barriers through EU-wide measures is an extremely complex and time-consuming process and, hence, not a viable option for a government wishing to quickly respond to an economic downturn. In the 1930s, European countries faced no such constraints.

Have the lessons of the 1930s affected the link between recession and trade barriers?

The last international economic downturn of a somewhat similar magnitude to that which began in 2008 was the Great Depression of the 1930s, so it is probably natural to look to it for insights as to what to expect as events unfold in the post-2008 period. The experience of the 1930s suggests three major lessons: (1) protectionist pressure will be intense as economies face widespread business losses and there are widespread job losses – pressured politicians will find difficult to resist; (2) the trade barriers put in place will both deepen and, in particular, lengthen the economic downturn; and (3) once in place, the trade barriers will be difficult to remove. Many of the trade barriers in existence today originated in the 1930s.

As during the Great Depression, protectionist voices have been shrill as economies spiralled into decline in the wake of the 2008 financial crisis. Increased protection, however, has not been forthcoming to any measurable degree. The question is why? There are two answers. First, policy makers did learn from the experience of the Great Depression. Second, the economic environment has changed in significant ways since the 1930s. As a result, it may be that there is not much which will be useful that can be gleaned from examining the Great Depression. There is one constant, however, that protectionists are resilient, able, and expert of tapping public sympathy. They never 'go away'. Prior to the 1930s, there were virtually no international coordinating institutions in existence. Thus, the Great Depression was dealt with by individual countries acting alone. There was no cooperation and there were no rules. This lesson was not lost by policy makers at the end of the Second World War. In fact they saw it as the major reason the depression of the 1930s became 'Great' and many believed the lack of institutions to deal with international tensions was a major contributor to the second major war in a generation. Based on these conclusions, the war's winners, largely the United States and the United Kingdom, decided to create a 'New World Order' based on strong international institutions. They perceived four major sources of international conflict and attempted to put in place an institution to deal with each of them. The four sources of conflict were as follows: (1) political disagreements;

(2) international differences in standards of living – the term development had not yet gained common currency; (3) strategic devaluations; and (4) beggar-thy-neighbour trade wars.

The ill-fated and relatively toothless League of Nations that had been established at the end of the First World War to deal with political conflict was judged as a failed institution, and a new United Nations (UN) with more powers and institutional resilience was put in place. The World Bank was created to deal with different levels of economic well-being – first in Europe where economies had been destroyed in the war and later in what became known as 'underdeveloped countries'. The International Monetary Fund (IMF) was to deal with strategic devaluations – at the time fixed exchange rates were the norm.

Finally, to deal with trade barrier retaliations, a new International Trade Organization (ITO) was negotiated. It was, however, the only one of the four institutions of the New World Order that was never put in place. While the US Administrative arm had agreed to the ITO in the negotiations, in the US system the Congress would have had to approve it. Protectionists were sufficiently influential in Congress that it became clear that it could not be ratified and the ITO was never presented to the legislators (Kerr, 2010). Hence, the ITO was stillborn. All was not lost; however, one of the ITO's sub-agreements, the GATT, became the *de facto* multinational trade institution, but was never on the same level as the UN, the World Bank, and the IMF. Only in 1995, with the advent of the WTO, an equal institution to deal with international trade conflicts came into being.

A set of obligations was made the central element of the GATT: (1) bound tariffs; (2) non-discrimination; (3) transparency; and (4) accepted retaliation (Kerr, 2000). Since 1947 when the GATT came into being, these obligations have not changed, but have been added to and made stronger. As a result, members of the WTO (which is based on the original GATT) are constrained in how they can respond to the pleadings of protectionists. As shown by the discussion of the EU above, outlets for protectionism do remain (anti-dumping, unfair subsidies, and safeguard actions), but each of these has tight institutional procedures that prevent their use as a means to raise the level of protection on a broad basis.

The international trade institutions appear to have worked as intended in response to protectionist pressure in the post-2008 era. Unlike the 1930s, there has been no beggar-thy-neighbour trade war. Of course, in the 1930s there were no venues such as the Group of Eight (G8) or G20 where world leaders meet face to face – the transport technology simply did not allow it. In the post-2008 recession, political leaders meeting in such forums have consistently pledged to eschew raising trade barriers.

Prior to the 1930s, governments did not intervene to any great degree in the economy. The macroeconomic orthodoxy of the time required balanced budgets. As tax receipts fell rapidly during the economic decline, to balance budgets, expenditures were cut. This 'austerity' further reduced demand and contributed to the downward economic spiral. There was no thought of government being responsible for job-creation and welfare payments were, at best, considered a necessary evil to prevent social unrest. It was the era of small government. Trade policy was one of the few mechanisms by which governments could legitimately intervene in the economy. Given the desperation of the times, they were not shy to use it. Of course, it proved to be very counterproductive. The inability of governments to deal effectively with the Great Depression led to a revolution in economic thinking – based on the (at the time radical) economic thinking of the British economist J.M. Keynes. His theory was set out in *The General Theory of Employment, Interest and Money*, published in 1936. The book, and the Keynesian economists that followed, were instrumental in changing what was considered the appropriate roles for government to play in the economy – big and interventionist were the bywords. In particular, when faced with a recession and falling demand, governments should offset the deficiency in demand through deficit spending. After all, consumers worried about their livelihoods and firms facing falling markets cannot rationally be expected to increase their expenditures.

This change in thinking opened the door to widespread intervention in the economy. It became accepted that governments should engage in industrial policy, subsidizing industries they wished to promote. From there it is an easy leap to subsidizing industries considered worth saving – such as automobiles – in an economic downturn. Of course, subsidies alter the competitive economic landscape, just like border measures (e.g., tariffs), but the GATT disciplines are much weaker than those for direct trade barriers. Hence, Member State governments in the EU did not have to resort to seeking trade barriers through the EU to extend aid to struggling sectors. If the subsidies do not turn out to be temporary then one might expect more widespread initiation of unfair subsidy actions.

Many of the subsidies initiated by countries to stimulate their flagging economies are targeted – from transport infrastructure to water treatment plants to football stadiums. These tend to be non-tradable goods and, hence, minimally trade distorting. As governments activities now account for 40–50-plus per cent of GDP, their procurement expenditures are much more important than in the 1930s. Governments can reserve their procurement for domestic suppliers. Again, WTO disciplines on procurement are much weaker than those that constrain the use of tariffs. In the pre-Keynesian era of small government, procurement was too small to be much used in supporting local firms.

The calls for government assistance are just as strong as in the Great Recession, but governments now have a much wider range of economic leavers that they can pull. Many, if not most, of these economic leavers are much less encumbered by international constraints than trade policy. It seems clear that governments now both understand that the use of trade barriers is counterproductive in a recession and that they cannot be used without voiding international obligations. There are simply easier ways to satisfy requests for support.

Conclusion

As the global financial and economic crisis that began in 2008 has become the biggest global crisis since the Great Depression, many have attempted to draw parallels between the two events. One of the effects of the Great Depression was increased protectionism resulting in a beggar-thy-neighbour trade war, considered to be one of the triggers of the Second World War. Thus, it is not surprising that increased protectionism was forecast by some as the global economy was hit by the latest economic downturn, especially when global trade suffered a sharp decline of 12.2 per cent in 2009. However, up to the time of this writing, January 2012, no major trade protectionist measures have been implemented in the world's major trading nations. Thus, this chapter looks at the major institutional and policy changes that have taken place at the global level since the Great Depression, and within the EU in particular.

At the global level, two major changes have taken place since the 1930s. Firstly, four important international institutions have been created with the main goal of mitigating state-to-state conflicts: the UN, the IMF, the World Bank, and, lastly, the GATT/WTO. One of the major roles of GATT/WTO is to prevent increased protectionism and beggar-thy-neighbour trade wars and the recession of 2008 can be considered a first real test for this institution. Generally, governments have respected their GATT/WTO obligations. Secondly, the role of the government in the economy has expanded greatly since the Great Depression. If in the

1930s trade policy was the only instrument that governments could use to assist firms, during the latest crisis governments have additional policy options, such as subsidies and government procurement, which are much less constrained by international institutions than trade policy.

It is still too early to state that the international trading system has escaped unharmed as the global economic crisis that started in 2008 is not over. The Keynesian fiscal policy prescription followed during the latest recession has resulted in large public deficits and debt levels, especially for the EU countries. Thus, the debate on how governments will deal with budgetary imbalances when economic recovery is not guaranteed still continues. Will countries, especially the smaller ones, resort to trade protectionism if the recession continues? For the troubled EU countries such as Greece, Spain, Italy, and Portugal, the adoption of euro has further complicated domestic policy making. If a country like Greece would still have its national currency, in a recessionary period the government could use a currency devaluation policy at least temporarily. For a short period of time, exports could be stimulated, imports restricted, and government revenues increased. Thus, the latest economic crisis has exposed some problems with the monetary union and has raised questions regarding whether some countries should be part of this European project.

Similar to devaluation, the use of trade policy is no longer a viable option for individual Member States of the EU. The EC's Directorate General for Trade, which is responsible for the EU's external trade policy, is charged with ensuring that international trade commitments are lived up to. It is unlikely to propose trade barriers that would breach provisions of international trade agreements. Given that, institutionally, the EC must bring forward suggestions for changes to trade policy, Member States do not have an easy avenue to promote trade restricting policies. Getting agreement among the 27 members of the Article 133 Committee is also difficult and time consuming. In the 2008 recession it appears that Member States have realized that seeking new trade measures is too slow and costly to be pursued through EU institutions. Subsidies and other policies are not so constrained.

The interaction of the constraints imposed by international commitments and the trade policy-making processes in the EU provides an excellent case study into how the world has changed since the 1930s. Given how cumbersome increasing protection can be, protectionists and governments chose to concentrate on policy alternatives such as subsidies and restrictions on government procurement to obtain/provide economic relief. One lasting legacy that should arise from the absence of trade policy measures in the wake of the current recession is that there will not be trade barriers to remove when the global economy begins to recover. It has taken more than 60 years to remove the trade barriers put in place during the Great Depression. As a result, the economic recovery from the current recession should be much swifter than it was in the 1930s.

Notes

1. Of course, tariffs and other border restrictions increase costs for domestic consumers, but the transmission of these costs between border measures and the prices of goods is seldom transparent for consumers.
2. An important development took place at the beginning of 2010 regarding government procurement; the Canada–US bilateral agreement on government procurement addresses the trade frictions resulting from the 'buy American' requirements included in the American Recovery and Reinvestment Act of 2009. The main two elements of the agreement are, first, the permanent and reciprocal commitment under the WTO Government Procurement Agreement (GPA) regarding procurement at all levels of government and, second, provision of additional and reciprocal guarantees of access on a temporary basis (WTO, 2010).
3. VERs are negotiated with foreign governments that 'voluntarily' agree to restrict their exports, the economic effect of which is similar to an importing country imposing barriers on imports. OMAs are also negotiated with foreign governments and normally specify complicated triggering arrangements whereby export flows are restricted. Of course, to obtain agreement from foreign governments either concessions in other areas must be offered or a credible threat must be made (Gordon, Hannesson and Kerr, 2001).

Bibliography

Baldwin, R. (2009) 'The Great Trade Collapse: What Caused It and What Does It Mean?', in R. Baldwin (ed.), *The Great Trade Collapse: Causes, Consequences and Prospects* (Brussels: Centre for Economic Policy Research and VoxEU.org).

Dür, A. (2008) 'Bringing Economic Interests Back into the Study of EU Trade Policy Policy-Making', *British Journal of Politics and International Relations* 10(1), 27–45.

Erixon, F. (2009) 'Containing Creeping Protectionism: A Realist Agenda for the G20', *Policy Brief*, European Centre for International Political Economy (ECIPE), http://www.ecipe.org/publications/ecipe-policy-briefs/containing-creeping-protectionism-a-realist-agenda-for-the-g20/PDF, accessed on 10 August 2011.

Filipov, S. and K. Kalotay (2009) 'Foreign Direct Investment in Times of Global Economic Crises: Spotlight on New Europe', *United Nations University Working Paper Series*, http://ideas.repec.org/p/dgr/unumer/2009021.html, accessed on 10 August 2011.

Gaisford, J.D. and A. Hester (2007) 'Why Are There Trade Agreements?', in W.A. Kerr and J.D. Gaisford (eds), *Handbook on International Trade Policy* (Cheltenham: Edward Elgar), 57–70.

Gaisford, J.D., W.A. Kerr and N. Perdikis (2003) *Economic Analysis for EU Accession Negotiations* (Cheltenham: Edward Elgar Press).

Gordon, D.V., R. Hannesson and W.A. Kerr (2001) 'Of Fish and Whales: The Credibility of Threats in International Trade Disputes', *Journal of Policy Modeling* 23(1), 83–98.

Group of Twenty (G20) (2008) 'Declaration Summit on Financial Markets and the World Economy', http://g20mexico.org/images/stories/canalfinan/docs/brazil/01summitdec.pdf, accessed on 1 March 2012.

Hanson, B. T. (1998) 'What Happened to Fortress Europe? External Trade Policy Liberalization in the European Union', *International Organization* 52(1), 55–85.

Hine, R.C. (1985) *The Political Economy of European Trade: An Introduction to the Trade Policies of the EC* (New York: St. Martin's Press).

Kee, H.L., C. Neagu and A. Nicita (2010) *Is Protectionism on the Rise? Assessing National Trade Policies during the Crisis of 2008* (World Bank Policy Research Working Paper 5274), http://econ.worldbank.org/external/default/main?pagePK=64165259&piPK=64165421&theSitePK=469372&menuPK=64166093&entityID=000158349_20100419121819, accessed on 20 August 2011.

Kerr, W.A. (2000) 'A New World Chaos? – International Institutions in the Information Age', *Journal of International Law and Trade Policy* 1(1), 1–10.

Kerr, W.A. (2009) 'Political Precaution, Pandemics and Protectionism', *Journal of International Law and Trade Policy* 10(2), 1–14.

Kerr, W.A. (2010) 'GATT-1947: A Living Legacy Fostering the Liberalization of International Trade', *Journal of International Law and Trade Policy* 11(1), 1–11.

Keynes, J.M. (1936) *The General Theory of Employment, Interest and Money* (London: Macmillan).

Loppacher, L.J. and W.A. Kerr (2006) 'The GATS Impact on Private Investors: Is It "Much Ado About Nothing?"', *Investment Management and Financial Innovations* 3(4), 79–88.

Martin, P. (2009) *The Recession and Migration: Alternative Scenarios*, Working Papers 13 (Oxford: International Migration Institute), http://www.imi.ox.ac.uk/pdfs/wp13-martin, accessed on 20 August 2011.

Organisation for Economic Co-operation and Development (OECD) and United Nations Conference on Trade and Development (UNCTAD) (2011) *Fifth Report on G20 Investment Measures*, http://www.unctad.org/en/docs/unctad_oecd2011d5_en.pdf, accessed on 10 August 2011.

Perdikis, N. and W.A. Kerr (1998) *Trade Theories and Empirical Evidence* (Manchester: Manchester University Press).

Saint-Etienne, C. (1984) *The Great Depression, 1929–1938: Lessons for the 1980* (Stanford: Hoover Institution Press).

Sward, J. (2009) 'Migration and the Financial Crisis: How Will the Economic Downturn Affect Migrants?' *Briefing*, 17 (Development Research Centre on Migration, Globalisation & Poverty, Sussex Centre for Migration Research), http://www.research4development.info/PDF/Outputs/MigrationGlobPov/BP17.pdf, accessed on 20 August 2011.

Woolcock, S. (2010) *The Treaty of Lisbon and the European Union as an Actor in International Trade* (ECIPE Working Paper 1), http://www.ecipe.org/publications/ecipe-working-papers/the-treaty-of-lisbon-and-the-european-union-as-an-actor-in-international-trade, accessed on 20 August 2011.

World Trade Organization (WTO) (2009) 'Overview of Developments in the International Trading Environment. Part A: Trade and Trade-Related Developments in 2009', *Annual Report by the Director-General*, http://www.wto.org/english/news_e/news09_e/lamy_20nov09_e.htm, accessed on 1 March 2012.

World Trade Organization (WTO) (2010) 'World Trade 2009, Prospects for 2010', *Press Release*, http://www.wto.org/english/news_e/pres10_e/pr598_e.pdf, accessed on 15 May 2011.

World Trade Organization (WTO) (2011) *Report to the TPRB from the Director-General on Trade-Related Developments*, WT/TPR/OV/W/5, http://wto.org/english/news_e/sppl_e/sppl196_e.htm, accessed on 15 July 2011.

6

A Climate of Crisis: The Impacts of the Economic Crisis on EU Climate Change Policy

Matthew Paterson

Introduction

The European Union (EU) has long claimed a leadership role in the global response to climate change. At least since the withdrawal of the United States from the Kyoto Protocol in March 2001, the EU had expressly arrogated to itself such a leadership role in international climate negotiations (Christiansen and Wettestad, 2003; Hovi, Skodvin and Andresen, 2003; Schreurs and Tiberghien, 2007). This has been important both to international climate change policy, keeping up momentum in the face of the challenge of US non-participation, and in relation to the EU's external identity – its construction of an identity around leadership in a range of non-military, but important diplomatic issues, along the lines of what Ian Manners (2002) calls 'normative power Europe'.

The EU has also backed up these claims to leadership with targets and policies to limit its greenhouse gas (GHG) emissions that were more ambitious than anywhere else in the world. In the period leading up to the end of the Kyoto Protocol's first commitment period (2008–12), the EU has succeeded in achieving deeper cuts in emissions than other industrialized countries and, in particular, in integrating climate change policy measures relatively deeply into its economic strategy. The central plank of EU climate policy has been its Emissions Trading Scheme (EU ETS), which effectively creates a novel financial market around the trading in permits to emit carbon dioxide, the principal GHG.

It is a commonplace assertion in environmental policy debates that economic policy and environmental policy are often in tension with each other and that in times of economic crisis the pursuit of economic growth takes precedence over dealing effectively with environmental challenges. This assumed tension can be seen on both sides of the environmental debate. On the one hand, the 'limits to growth' arguments are central to many environmental discourses (Meadows et al., 1972; Dryzek, 1997), while on the other hand many economists, business actors, and political elites resist the idea of limiting growth in order to pursue environmental policy (Beckerman, 1974; Lomborg, 2001). Both arguments accept the premise that there is a basic tension between the two goals.

Since the late 1980s, it has become more prevalent to question this presumed opposition between growth and the environment. First under the rubric of sustainable development (WCED, 1987), and more recently under the banner of 'ecological modernization' (Mol, 2001), a range of analysts and policy makers increasingly argue that there is no necessary tension. Even relatively conventional economists argue that the pursuit of environmental goals can stimulate technological innovation and increase economic efficiencies (Porter and van der Linde, 1995; von Weizsäcker, Lovins and Lovins, 1998). Policy makers have increasingly internalized this sort of a 'win-win' discourse. But even with this general shift in political discourse, in the context of economic crises, such as the one that started in 2008, many expected environmental policy to take a back seat in response to the crisis.

In some countries, notably Canada (perhaps paradoxically since the Canadian economy was far less affected by the crisis than many other countries), governments have adopted a discourse emphasizing the conflict between economy and environment (e.g., Scoffield, 2010).[1] But in many other contexts, the expectation that the crisis would have a negative impact on environmental policy, particularly climate change policy, appeared not to play out. In particular, many countries adopted significant 'green' economic stimulus packages, notably in terms of increased investment in public transport (Bernard et al., 2009; Goldenberg, 2009; Robins, 2010). Overall, there was a wide variation in the green component in the stimulus packages, from 9 per cent of the total stimulus spending in Canada to 79 per cent in South Korea. The EU's green component was amongst the highest, at 64 per cent (Robins, 2010, p. 7). Moreover, some political leaders also used the crisis as leverage to engineer changes in corporate environmental performance. President Obama, for example, used the situation to impose a 30 per cent improvement in the Corporate Average Fuel Economy (CAFE) standards, while many elements in the stimulus package entailed switches in investment and subsidies both towards non-petroleum-based technologies for cars and from the car sector to alternative transport modes.

In this context, this chapter explores the impact of the economic crisis on EU climate change policy. It suggests that as in the above illustrative examples, the impact of the crisis has been far more complex than simply producing a retrenchment of the ambitions of the EU's climate policy. The chapter proceeds by first exploring the impacts of the crisis on the EU ETS, suggesting that these have been twofold: a collapse in emissions and thus in permit prices, and a series of scandals that critical movements have used to undermine the legitimacy of the EU ETS. Second, the chapter examines the impact of the crisis on European climate policy more generally, concluding with a discussion of how this has affected European leadership in international climate politics.

The crisis and the EU Emissions Trading Scheme (EU ETS)

The EU ETS is the principal element in the EU's response to climate change. It is a 'cap and trade' regulatory system where emitters are required to hold a number of allowances (known as European Union Allowances, or EUAs) equivalent to their emissions. These allowances are, however, tradable, and any actor can engage in trading these allowances. In the EU, the scheme is imposed on the large emitters of carbon dioxide, the principal GHG; around 11,000 installations are included, covering around 45 per cent of the EU's total emissions.[2]

The standard logic behind such a system is that since the marginal costs of reducing emissions vary considerably amongst emitters, the introduction of trading possibilities greatly reduces the overall cost of meeting specific emissions targets and enhances the fairness of the system by imposing in effect the same costs on all actors. Each actor is faced with the option of reducing its emissions to the specified target, not reducing its emissions and purchasing extra allowances to cover those emissions or exceeding the target in order to have allowances to sell. The price of allowances in the market that emerges will reflect the balance of supply and demand expressed in these choices and will thus create an incentive to the actors to shift their strategy accordingly – the higher the price, the greater the incentive the actors have to reduce their emissions rather than seek to purchase allowances.

This market logic became increasingly dominant in international discussions of climate change during the second half of the 1990s. At first, it was pushed heavily by the United States in the negotiations that led to the Kyoto Protocol in 1997, where the United States made acceptance of the three market mechanisms – emissions trading, the Clean Development Mechanism (CDM), and Joint Implementation – a condition for it signing the Protocol. The EU was initially sceptical of such market mechanisms, only accepting them late in the Kyoto negotiations, but shifted position rapidly after Kyoto was agreed. The EU started work in 1998 to develop its own ETS as a means of implementing its Kyoto target (van Asselt, 2010) and introducing the ETS Directive in 2003 for a system that started its first phase of implementation in 2005.

The EU also integrated its ETS into the mechanisms created by the Kyoto Protocol directly. In the 2004 Linking Directive, the EU allowed companies regulated under the EU ETS to purchase credits generated by the two Kyoto mechanisms, the CDM and Joint Implementation, and to use those credits against their obligations under the EU ETS. The success of the CDM in particular is largely due to this directive, which has created enormous demand for projects in developing countries under that mechanism, far exceeding the expectations of the CDM's designers. The EU's role in underpinning demand in the CDM has also been important in sustaining its overall leadership in international climate politics. The EU ETS and the CDM are now comfortably the two largest carbon markets in the world, accounting for around 85 per cent of trades in these markets in 2009 (Kossoy and Ambrosi, 2010, p. 1).

The collapse in European Union Allowance (EUA) demand

The economic crisis has had two principal impacts on the EU ETS. The first and the most immediate has been on emissions themselves and thus, because of the structure of EU ETS, also on EUA prices.

The EU had been able to produce a modest (but greater than other countries) decline in emissions in line with its Kyoto Protocol commitments. Between 2008 and 2009 overall EU emissions declined by 6.9 per cent, while emissions in the sectors covered by the EU ETS declined by 11.2 per cent. This decline was particularly evident in energy-intensive sectors such as iron and steel, chemical, and cement, which are especially responsive to an economic downturn (European Environment Agency, 2010).

The EU ETS, along with policies to promote renewable energy and energy efficiency, played a role in producing this decline. But, the recession produced a significant decline in emissions. As a consequence, EUA prices declined dramatically during the recession. EUA prices declined from a peak of €31 in July 2008 to a trough of €9 in February 2009. This decline also drove down prices in the CDM market, from €25 at the peak to €7 at the trough (Kossoy and Ambrosi, 2010, p. 5). The explanation here is fairly straightforward. The recession entailed reductions in productive capacity and triggered cuts in expenditures, which in turn involved contractions in energy use and thus declines in electricity and fossil fuel commodity prices. Regulated companies therefore needed to hold fewer EUAs, primarily because their emissions were declining as a direct result of the recession. More companies went into a position of surplus in their EUA holdings and thus tried to offload them, triggering a reduction in prices.[3]

On the one hand, this decline in emissions and EUA prices meant that it would now become much cheaper to meet existing EU emission targets. According to Egenhofer et al. (2011), while the Commission had assumed that meeting the 2020 target (a 20 per cent GHG reduction) would involve a carbon price of around €32 per tonne for the period 2013–20, after the recession, this cost was estimated downwards to €16. On the other hand, it meant that the *de facto* incentive to invest in further low-carbon development was significantly reduced, since companies could expect to need to hold fewer EUAs over the medium term. The objective of the EU ETS to stimulate such low-carbon development, therefore, was significantly compromised by the recession, even while it produced a short-term decline in emissions.

Legitimacy crises in the EU ETS: 'subprime carbon'

The second impact of the financial crisis and recession on the EU ETS was more indirect. Critical social movements opposed to the use of market mechanisms to deal with climate change were given an opportunity in the financial crisis to reframe the EU ETS as a problem of 'subprime carbon' (Chan, 2009). Groups like Carbon Trade Watch and Friends of the Earth attempted to delegitimize the EU ETS by associating the various financial practices involved with those that generated the financial crisis. They were helped by a number of scandals in the EU ETS that broke during 2009. I focus here on just three such scandals, although a large number can be identified.

The Value Added Tax (VAT) fraud scam

The essence of VAT fraud is that, given that VAT rates vary across the EU and the items on which VAT is applied also vary, traders can buy EUAs in a jurisdiction where VAT is not applied, sell them on in one where it is, pocket the VAT, and shut the company down, taking the VAT with them. It is referred to as 'carousel tax fraud', in response to the fact that this sort of trading can be repeated continuously. In a report issued on 1 December 2009 by Europol, which started investigating this in June

2009, tax authorities in the EU may have lost up to €5 billion in tax revenues due to this scam. As much as 13 per cent of all EUA trades, and up to 90 per cent in some countries, were associated with this tax fraud scam, according to Bloomberg New Energy Finance, a news and research organization on carbon markets (Point Carbon, 2010a).

Throughout the second half of 2009, traders moved from one country to another taking advantage of these VAT differences. The scandal was first identified in France, where a spike in trade volumes on Bluenext (the French exchange platform) was noticed on 2 June. During June, the French government acted to make EUAs free from VAT by reclassifying them as financial products, not as goods (Gourlay, 2009). The United Kingdom (UK) government acted similarly in July (Kanter, 2009). On 15 July, the Dutch government noticed a 49 per cent increase in EUA trade volumes in June on the Climex exchange that operates in Amsterdam, despite an overall drop in EUA trades that month. It did not directly find evidence of VAT fraud but did see 'clear indications' of such fraud and changed the rules to make buyers and not sellers responsible for paying the VAT (*Reuters*, 2009). On 19 August, seven traders were arrested in the UK, suspected of £38m of fraud (Kanter, 2009).

In December, just on the eve of the 15th Conference of the Parties to the UN Framework Convention on Climate Change in Copenhagen, Europol, which had been investigating this fraud since June, reported that in some countries up to 90 per cent of trades were associated with tax fraud and that up to €5 billion in tax revenue had been lost (Phillips, 2009; Mason, 2009; ENDS Report, 2009). At the same time, four individuals were arrested in Belgium for a scam. Three UK nationals and a Dutch national 'bought CO_2 credits in Britain and sold them to Belgian banks, taking home the 21 per cent sales tax charged in the country' (Inman, 2010). At the end of April 2010, there were swoops both in Germany and in the UK. In Germany, the offices of several companies including Deutsche Bank (one of the main banks involved in EUA trading) and RWE (a major German electricity generator) were raided, and in the UK, 22 were arrested on suspicion of involvement (Twidale, 2010).

The Certified Emissions Reduction (CER) recycling scam

This was a crisis that erupted in March 2010. On 9 March, the Hungarian government sold 1.743 million CERs (the CDM credit unit) to Hungarian Energy Power; these CERs had earlier been surrendered by Hungarian companies to meet their obligations under the EU ETS (Point Carbon, 2010b). These CERs had been 'surrendered' (by the companies to the government) but not 'retired' (sent on to the Kyoto Protocol system as part of Hungary's obligations there). Hungary sold them on to the power company with a rider that they could not be sold back into the EU ETS system – if the company sold them, it had to be outside the EU. The logic here was that if the CERs were bought by another country, this sale would then be 'backed' by Hungary's Assigned Amounts Units (AAUs, the basic Kyoto unit), and since Hungary had a surplus of AAUs compared to its needs, due to the economic collapse from 1990 onwards, there would be no fraud in the Kyoto system (they could sell on AAUs directly, but these sold at a lower market price than CERs). The most likely end point outside the EU for the credits would be Japan, and there was some evidence that that was where Hungarian Energy Power was trying to sell them, via traders based in London (Point Carbon, 2010e).

However, in part because of the complexity of the EU ETS and the difficulties in surveillance, the recycled CERs found their way back into the system within a week, through the French-based exchange Bluenext. On 16 March, Bluenext told the Hungarian government it had found 7000 of the recycled CERs in its account (Point Carbon, 2010f). How they had gotten there remains a mystery, but the consequence is that these credits could in principle be used twice by different firms for compliance purposes within Europe. The announcement thus caused an immediate crisis in CER trading in Europe, with CER prices tumbling from around €11.50 to €1.50; Bluenext and NordPool (based in Oslo) suspended CER trading immediately (Point Carbon, 2010g). After some speculation that other governments, especially in Eastern Europe (many of whom had AAU surpluses), might do the same (Point Carbon, 2010c), EU governments quickly agreed not to sell on surrendered CERs even if they had an AAU surplus. The International Emissions Trading Association, the main lobby group for carbon market actors, weighed in asking the European Commission to act quickly to shore up any reputational crisis for the ETS (IETA, 2010). The EU Commission also announced, on 18 March, a temporary ban on surrendering CERs for EUAs within the system (Point Carbon, 2010d).

Windfall profits

There had long been criticism of windfall profits for certain companies regulated under the EU ETS. This was principally because companies that could pass all the costs of the carbon price onto consumers were getting a free allocation of allowances. Electricity generators in particular gained substantial windfalls especially in Phase I of the EU ETS (2005–7). But, in the context of the recession, this became exacerbated by the rapid decline in industrial production during 2009. For sectors whose production reacts very quickly to economic downturns, like steel or cement, companies found themselves holding more EUAs than they would need to comply with their EU ETS obligations. Even with the declines in EUA prices mentioned above, many companies were then able to use EUA sales to stabilize their financial position.

The research-oriented non-governmental organization Sandbag produced a report in February 2010 detailing the principal beneficiaries and losers from this process. They showed that it was principally steel and cement companies, such as Arcelor Mittal, Lafarge, Corus, and SSAB-Svenske Stal, that benefited from surplus allocations. The principal losers in this process were electricity generators, especially the large German-based firms with Europe-wide operations, RWE and E.On, who remained 'short' in their EUA allocations and invested disproportionately in emission reductions compared to others. Sandbag labelled the big winners the 'Carbon Fat Cats' (Sandbag, 2010). Collectively, the surplus permits these companies held in 2008 were worth around €500 million at current EUA prices.

Connecting the EU ETS to the financial crisis

There has been a considerable amount of anti-carbon market activism since the inception of such markets. They have been variously criticized as a distraction from the real task of reducing GHG emissions, as engendering new sorts of colonialism or as simply being unethical in the way they commodify the atmosphere (see variously: Bachram, 2004; Lohmann, 2006; Smith, 2007; Böhm and Dabhi, 2009; Gilbertson and Reyes, 2009). In the context of the financial crisis, these critiques were updated and reframed through the phrase 'subprime carbon' (see, especially, Chan, 2009). The main intent of this reframing is to delegitimize carbon markets, in this context the EU ETS, by presenting such markets as prone to similar sorts of overly complex financialized trading that can be easily gamed for profits, and thus likely to experience bubbles and collapses, in the same way as the subprime mortgage phenomenon in the United States, and especially the complexity of products like Collateralized Debt Obligations, triggered the financial crisis in 2008.

At times, a simple populist argument is used – to suggest that the link lies in the fact that the same players are present in both carbon trading and the financial sector. In Annie Leonard's popular online polemic 'The Story of Cap & Trade', which has received considerable exposure, one of the main themes is that the carbon trading 'solution' to climate change was brought to us by the same actors that brought us increasingly complex derivative financial instruments. A common figure to appear in this narrative is Richard Sandor; he was not only key to the futures markets innovations in the 1970s on the Chicago Board of Trade, but also a pusher for emission markets for acid rain in the late 1980s and climate change throughout the 1990s, as well as founder of the Chicago Climate Exchange in 2001 (Lohmann, 2009, p. 26). Also playing a frequent role is Enron, whose John Palmisano was an important promoter of emissions trading in the United States in the 1990s. The main trading houses – Goldman Sachs, Merrill Lynch, and so on – also come in for a good deal of criticism.

But, the more common argument is in fact subtler than the populist rant against the big financial wheeler-dealers. This critique is more focused on the borrowing of a range of financial practices into environmental policy. The EU ETS, and by extension carbon markets more generally, are crisis prone because they involve directly analogous practices to those that produced the financial crisis. The two fullest expressions of this critique are in the US Friends Of the Earth report 'Subprime carbon' and in the Cornerhouse briefing by Larry Lohmann 'When Markets are Poison: learning about climate policy from the financial crisis' (Chan, 2009; Lohmann, 2009).

A number of arguments are made here. First, these critics argue that carbon markets are derivative markets. This is largely because they are primarily sold as forward or future contracts (Chan, 2009, p. 2). Second, they argue that the potential for 'subprime' carbon is considerable, principally because of the trading of forward contracts in CERs from projects that have not yet got CDM approval. This means that there is a risk of non-performing carbon contracts, especially as the offset markets expand rapidly as and when a US cap-and-trade system with offset allowances emerges (Chan, 2009, p. 3). Third, they suggest that there is a danger of a bubble economy in carbon markets because of the role of speculators who have an interest in arbitrage and thus price volatility (Chan, 2009, p. 4; Lohmann, 2009, pp. 27–8). Fourth, they claim that there is a trend towards more complex securitized deals in carbon markets akin to mortgage backed securities, picking up, in particular, on a deal by Credit Suisse in 2008 that 'bundled together carbon credits from 25 offset projects *at various stages of UN approval*, sourced from three countries, and five project developers' (Chan, 2009, p. 6, emphasis in the original). Fifth, they argue that the underlying value of assets in such markets is particularly difficult to assess, especially once carbon commodities are bundled in the same way as the Credit

Suisse deal was (Chan, 2009, p. 6). Sixth, they suggest that because many companies are in conflict of interest, acting as both investors in offset projects and speculators in the derivative markets, this can lead to excessive risk taking (Chan, 2009, p. 6; Lohmann, 2009, pp. 52–5). Finally, and perhaps most fundamentally, Lohmann (2009) argues that carbon markets share the construction of an abstract commodity. Namely, because carbon markets are so fundamentally abstracted from the social context (the classic commodity fetishism, in fact) and because they are dependent on extraordinarily complicated calculative techniques in their production (especially in the offset markets) and permit the elaboration of complex financial strategies, carbon markets share many of the features that generated the financial crisis. Specifically, they permit the generation of strategies that appear to spread risk, but in practice transform individualized risk management into systemic risk production.

These arguments were developed in particular by the US Friends of the Earth, and activists around Carbon Trade Watch circulated through the mainstream media during 2009 and 2010, serving to keep up the pressure on the legitimacy of the EU ETS. The allegations called into question the environmental effectiveness of the market – whether it could actually play a role in reducing emissions or was just a new avenue for financial speculation. This discursive framing provides a context within which one can understand the development of EU climate policy in the aftermath of the crisis.

The impact of the crisis on EU climate policy

What impact did these two developments – the collapse in emissions and in EUA prices and the delegitimization of carbon markets by critical social movements – have on EU climate change policy? There are two principal effects. First, perhaps paradoxically, they generated a process by which the EU made its climate change policy more ambitious; and second, it created considerable pressure to start to regulate the EU ETS market as a financial market.

Upping the ante on GHG targets

While it is commonplace to assume that in a recession, environmental policy is put on hold until the economy recovers (see above), this did not take place in relation to EU climate policy. In fact there has been considerable pressure to make EU climate change policy more, not less, ambitious, in the context of the economic crisis.

Early on in the crisis, there was pressure from some quarters in the EU to relax EU climate policy because of the recession. As Bowen and Stern suggest:

> Before the European Union summit in October 2008, eight EU members suggested that carbon-dioxide emissions targets ought to be revised in the light of current 'serious economic and financial uncertainties'. And the Prime Minister of Italy told a press conference, 'our businesses are in absolutely no position at the moment to absorb the costs of the regulations that have been proposed'.
>
> (Bowen and Stern 2010, p. 139, citing a BBC news report, 15 October 2008)

But this pressure was resisted by other EU actors, who then went on the offensive to suggest the opposite should be the case. The Environment Directorate in the Commission first suggested revisiting the target to reduce EU GHG emissions by 20 per cent by 2020, and then more specifically, in May 2010, floated the idea that the EU move to a unilateral 30 per cent reduction target for 2020. The economic crisis was the clear context for suggesting such a move (European Commission, 2010, pp. 3–4). According to the Commission, this meant that the costs of meeting the 20 per cent reduction by 2020 were reduced from €70 to €48 billion (European Commission, 2010, p. 3). Shifting the target to 30 per cent would entail overall costs of €81 billion, much cheaper than would have been the case without the recession, and only €11 billion more than the previously estimated cost of meeting the 20 per cent target (European Commission, 2010, p. 8). There was some to and fro within EU institutions over the next few months, but in March 2011, the Commission formally proposed to shift the EU target from 20 to 25 per cent, despite intense lobbying by energy intensive industries (Harvey, 2011; European Commission, 2011).

Why did the EU engage in this counter-intuitive policy shift in the midst of a recession? First, during the course of the recession, a number of analyses were carried out that showed that GHG emissions in 2020 (the most commonly suggested target date for 'post-Kyoto' negotiations) would be considerably lower than previously thought. For example, the International Energy Agency's Energy Outlook (WEO) report of 2008 (essentially pre-recession) projected that GHG emissions for Annex I countries (i.e., industrialized countries) would be 2 per cent above 1990 levels, while in the WEO 2009 report this projection was changed to a 6 per cent reduction in emissions because of the impact of the economic crisis (Amann et al., 2009). This was assuming no more action to limit emissions other than that which countries had committed to under the Kyoto Protocol. In the EU specifically, this changed from a projected 5 per cent cut to a projected 16 per cent cut over 1990 levels (Amann et al., 2009, p. 13). In effect, while the EU was projected to meet its Kyoto commitment in any case, the recession made doubly sure and meant that Annex I countries collectively would be comfortably able to do so. It also meant that the EU was already close to meeting projected commitments for 2020 (the EU at that point had a commitment to reduce emissions by 20 per cent by 2020 over 1990 levels).

As a consequence, the projected gross domestic product (GDP) impacts of emission reductions were also lowered considerably. For an impact of 0.1 per cent of 2020 GDP, Annex I countries (aggregated) could achieve 27 per cent reductions in GHG emissions, whereas in the WEO 2008, such an economic impact would have only achieved 17 per cent emission cuts (Amann et al., 2009, p. 15, Figure 3.2).

Second, a range of actors were able to mobilize rapidly around the idea that tackling the financial crisis, the recession, and climate change could be done simultaneously. At the broad institutional level, Ban Ki-moon was instrumental, making a number of interventions along these lines (e.g., Ki-moon and Gore, 2009). In the European context, the Centre for European Policy Studies produced a series of early reports arguing that the recession offered an opportunity to make European climate policy more, not less, ambitious and that stimulus investment could be directed towards a low-carbon economy (e.g., Behrens, 2008). In particular, the argument was made that in a recession, a good deal of industrial capacity is lost; as the economy recovers, this entails significant investment in new plant, and the objective should be to make sure that these investments should be simultaneously directed towards decarbonization (e.g., Bowen and Stern, 2010). These arguments were helped by arguments like those of Sandbag, that the recession had in effect eliminated the incentive effect of the EU ETS, because the carbon price had collapsed.

Perhaps the most comprehensive form of this mobilization was the coalition of actors coalescing around the idea of a 'green new deal' (Green New Deal Group, 2008). The 'green new deal' discourse referred to a 'triple crunch', articulating the financial crisis with climate change and the coming energy 'crunch', and suggested that a large-scale package of re-regulation and economic reform, on the scale similar to the reforms of the 1930s and 1940s, was necessary (Green New Deal

Group, 2008). The package was taken up, in particular, by United Nations Environment Programme (e.g., UNEP, 2009).[4] The mobilization by these actors was important in shaping the discursive environment within which European politicians worked, making it possible to imagine investment in climate change as the appropriate response to the economic crisis.

A third reason, although the evidence for this is perhaps less solid, has to do with the design of the EU ETS. Because EU bureaucrats, national policy makers, and corporate leaders all had come to recognize that the EU ETS contains significant ability to cushion companies from the financial risks associated with decarbonization (by creating financial assets, e.g., in the EUAs), policy makers were able to detach the overall impacts of the recession from the specific impacts of environmental regulation on companies. In other words, in many other contexts, when an economy is in recession, regulators try to avoid putting additional regulatory pressure on companies. But with the EU ETS, this additional regulation was simultaneously creating financial assets for companies (at least to the extent that they gained windfall profits, as they had done up to that point for the most part), which offset the regulatory cost and made it possible for policy makers to frame the recession as an opportunity to make climate policy more ambitious. In addition, since policy makers had, with the ETS, developed a system that depended on sending a reasonably reliable price signal to market actors, in order to function properly the only serious way to deal with the effects of the recession was to move to more ambitious targets, in order to restore carbon prices to those that might make the system function as a form of environmental regulation.

Regulating carbon markets

The second impact was that pressure emerged to regulate carbon markets as financial markets. The designers of the EU ETS, as with other environmental markets, tended to see them not as financial markets, but as simple markets in property rights. As such, the regulation is focused on establishing the initial property right (the allowance, in a cap and trade market like the EU ETS, or the credit, in an offset market like the CDM), and on tracking allowances or credits, in order to avoid double counting or fraud. Each allowance thus has its own unique identifier number and can be tracked as it is traded between companies. Each company has to keep its account with a national regulator, and a transaction log exists through which every trade has to be recorded.

But this governance arrangement (while itself fragile in places, as a number of the scandals discussed above illustrate) does not cover trading as a financial transaction at all. It deals only with what is usually referred to as the 'environmental integrity' of the system – that each allowance, or credit, relates to one tonne of carbon dioxide equivalent and that the system cannot be gamed so that companies could double count. But, while still modest in comparison with other financial markets, a range of derivative products quickly emerged – mostly futures, options, and swaps – as well as a range of products available to companies to manage risk related to their obligations under the EU ETS. These are completely unregulated as financial products. There are other ways in which these markets are not governed in financial terms, notably the absence of any internationally agreed accounting standard by which carbon should be treated in company accounting (Thistlethwaite, 2011; Lovell and MacKenzie, 2011). At present, companies can more or less decide for themselves how to treat an EUA in company accounts – whether as asset or liability (it has aspects of both), whether as financial service or commodity (similarly, there are elements of both), and so on. The scandals and the mobilization around them by movement activists have, however, fed pressure to treat the EU ETS and other carbon markets as financial markets. This has perhaps also been fed by a broader shift towards re-regulation of financial markets in the aftermath of the financial crisis, in this context best represented by the 'green new deal' discourse.

The fullest expression of this reaction by political elites is in the Prada Commission report, commissioned by the French government (Prada, Barbéris and Tignol, 2010a, 2010b). The Prada report opens with an acknowledgement that the series of scandals discussed above raise general questions as to the legitimacy of the EU ETS market and more specific questions about the regulation of the carbon market as a financial market (Prada, Barbéris and Tignol, 2010a, p. 12). The Prada report insists that, in general, the ETS market works well in terms of its goals, but that there remain a number of specific risks exposed by the scandals of 2009 and 2010 that need to be addressed through improved regulatory frameworks.

The report details the various existing regulatory frameworks for carbon markets and shows that, in practice, there is minimal oversight of the market (see, generally, Prada, Barbéris and Tignol, 2010a, 2010b, for what follows). There is some regulation of those involved in derivatives trading under the Market in Financial Instruments Directive and the Market Abuse Directive (Prada, Barbéris and Tignol, 2010b, p. 2), but no regulation concerning the over-the-counter market. As a consequence, there is little transparency concerning the transactions in the ETS market. There is virtually no oversight over who can trade in the EUAs. The original design deliberately created an open access framework for involvement in the market. As a result, the possibility of involvement by organized crime is eased. The legal definition of an EUA is left to the Member States, and is thus highly variable, leaving it open for companies (both trading companies and those holding allowances for regulatory purposes) to define an EUA in their accounting according to their own interests.

The report then goes on to identify a number of regulatory changes that should be adopted to ensure the smooth functioning of the carbon market and to minimize the chances of market manipulation. These should be done at the European level in order to minimize the possibility of regulatory arbitrage. Regulations should include: a common legal definition of an EUA; market oversight of all transactions, whether going through exchanges or in the OTC market; tighter verification rules about emission levels, to minimize information asymmetry between regulators and firms, and thus the possibility of insider trading; enhanced oversight over those operating in the market; and use of the European Securities Market Authority as the site of this regulation (albeit recognizing the 'hybrid' character of the carbon market, as both a trading system and a regulatory instrument) (Prada, Barbéris and Tignol, 2010b, pp. 5–7).

Other actors also made arguments for enhanced regulation of the EU carbon market. The UK government elected in May 2011, for example, argued for the creation of price floors in the EU ETS market, because the decline of prices in the wake of the recession reduced the incentive to invest in low-carbon development (e.g., Sandbag, 2009, p. 13). In addition, the problems of the EU market had spin-off effects in the United States. One of the significant changes in legislative proposals in the US Congress for the creation of a carbon dioxide emissions trading system during this period was the introduction of restrictions on access to the market – only those regulated under the cap and trade system would be allowed to participate in the market.

Conclusion

Did the crisis and its impacts on the EU ETS have an effect on the EU's leadership in international climate politics? It is absolutely clear that the EU's leadership in international climate negotiations waned during this period. But, the effect of the economic crisis on this is probably relatively small. As shown in the rest of this chapter, the economic crisis had little overall effect on the EU's climate change policy, and if anything, it generated processes that led to enhanced ambition on the part of the EU in terms of its GHG emission targets. The EU's climate leadership had been based in part on its successful claims to be acting more aggressively than other industrialized countries to limit its emissions. Little has changed in this regard.

The waning of EU leadership thus has more to do with the revival of participation in the climate change negotiations by the United States after the election of Barack Obama, combined with the timing of negotiations to produce a successor to the Kyoto Protocol. The EU had not had diplomatic challengers for leadership since the withdrawal of the United States from active negotiation in March 2001; Obama's election changed this dynamic significantly (see, in particular, Paterson, 2009). The United States could not claim to match the EU in terms of ambition on emission reductions. However, its renewed participation and, in particular, the strategic necessity for US negotiators to prioritize negotiations with large developing countries (especially China) in order to make Senate ratification possible, meant that the EU was no longer in centre stage. This situation opened the door for more aggressive negotiations by China, leading in large part to the collapse of talks in Copenhagen in December 2009.

The timing here was also crucial; Kyoto's first commitment period concludes at the end of 2012, so to have a chance of having a replacement treaty (or an extension of Kyoto) in force by January 2013, it would have to be negotiated by December 2009. In addition, since European leadership had in part been sustained by the way the EU ETS created demand for CDM projects, the uncertainty about the future of the CDM (as an institution that depends on the Kyoto architecture for its existence) drove down demand for new CDM projects. While the recession played a role in the decline of EU ETS prices, uncertainty about the negotiations were more important. Without this timing constraint, the negotiating tactics of Obama might have been different, affecting the EU's leadership potential in the negotiations. But, in any case, the economic crisis and its effects on the EU's climate policy played at best a minor role in this process.

Although the crisis may have had little effect on the EU's international leadership in this area, it did have a number of effects on the EU's international climate change policy. First, it had the paradoxical effect of creating pressures to make EU climate policy more ambitious, since it was easy to show that the costs of meeting more ambitious targets would now be much lower, and since the legitimacy of the ETS had been called into question by the recession and consequent price collapse. Second, social movement actors effectively linked a series of scandals within the ETS during 2009 and 2010 to the problems that produced the financial crisis from 2007 onwards, thus creating pressures to regulate the EU ETS as a financial market. While the outcome of this process is not clear at the time of writing (early 2012), it remains likely that enhanced financial regulation of carbon markets will be effected as a result.

Acknowledgements

I am grateful to Philippe Descheneau for research assistance in the preparation of this chapter.

Notes

1. This is in part an ideological construct in Canada that precedes the crisis. Prime Minister Harper had long operated with such a discourse, describing Kyoto, for example, as 'the job-killing, economy-destroying Kyoto Accord' (Paehlke, 2008, p. 87). More generally, see Juillet and Paterson (2009).
2. For general accounts of the EU ETS, see Skjærseth and Wettestad (2008) or Ellerman, Convery and de Perthuis (2010).
3. There is a more complicated process whereby EUA prices track electricity prices, and those are, later on, affected fundamentally by natural gas prices (natural gas being the swing producer that makes up short-term changes in electricity demand) and thus oil prices, since gas is often co-produced with oil (e.g. Convery and Redmond, 2007 for a general analysis of the determinants of prices in the EU ETS).
4. For an environmentalist critique of this sort of 'Green new deal' logic, see in particular Lohmann (2009).

Bibliography

Amann, M., J. Cofala, P. Rafaj and F. Wagner (2009) *The Impact of the Economic Crisis on GHG Mitigation Potentials and Costs in Annex I Countries* (Laxenburg: International Institute for Applied Systems Analysis, November).van Asselt, H. (2010) 'Emissions Trading: The Enthusiastic Adoption of an Alien Instrument', in A. Jordan, D. Huitema, H. van Asselt, T. Rayner, and F. Berkhout (eds) *Climate Change Policy in the European Union: Confronting the Dilemmas of Mitigation and Adaptation* (Cambridge: Cambridge University Press), 125–44.

Bachram, H. (2004) 'Climate Fraud and Carbon Colonialism: The New Trade in Greenhouse Gases', *Capitalism, Nature, Socialism* 14(4), 5–20.

Beckerman, W. (1974) *In Defence of Economic Growth* (London: Jonathan Cape).

Behrens, A. (2008) *Financing Climate Change Bailing out the Environment in the Long-Term May Be Just As Important As Bailing Out Financial Markets Now* (CEPS Commentary, 7 October) (Brussels: Centre for European Policy Studies).

Bernard, S., S. Asokan, H. Warrell and J. Lemer (2009, 2 March) 'Which Country Has the Greenest Bail-Out?', *Financial Times*, http://www.ft.com/cms/s/0/cc207678-0738-11de-9294-000077b07658.html#axzz1M576mQ63, accessed on 12 May 2011.

Böhm, S. and S. Dabhi (eds) (2009) *Upsetting the Offset: The Political Economy of Carbon Markets* (London: Mayfly Books).

Bowen, A. and N. Stern (2010) 'Environmental Policy and the Economic Downturn', *Oxford Review of Economic Policy* 26(2), 137–63.

Chan, M. (2009) *Subprime Carbon? Re-Thinking the World's Largest New Derivatives Market* (Washington: Friends of the Earth US).

Christiansen, A. and J. Wettestad (2003) 'The EU as a Frontrunner on Greenhouse Gas Emissions Trading: How Did it Happen and Will the EU Succeed?' *Climate Policy* 3(1), 3–18.

Convery, F. and L. Redmond (2007) 'Market and Price Developments in the European Union Emissions Trading Scheme', *Review of Environmental Economic Policy* 1(1), 88–111.

Dryzek, J. (1997) *The Politics of the Earth: Environmental Discourses* (Oxford: Oxford University Press).

Egenhofer, C., M. Alessi, A. Georgiev and N. Fujiwara (2011) *The EU Emissions Trading System and Climate Policy towards 2050: Real Incentives to Reduce Emissions and Drive Innovation?* (CEPS Special Report) (Brussels: Centre for European Policy Studies).

Ellerman, D., F. Convery, and C. de Perthuis (2010) *Pricing Carbon: The European Emissions Trading Scheme* (Cambridge: Cambridge University Press).

ENDS Report (2009) 'Carbon Trading Scam Reaches Epidemic Levels', *ENDS Report* 419 (December), 8.

European Commission (2010) 'Analysis of Options to Move Beyond 20% Greenhouse Gas Emission Reductions and Assessing the Risk of Carbon Leakage', COM (2010) 265 final, Brussels, 26 May (Brussels: European Commission).

European Commission (2011) 'A Roadmap for Moving to a Competitive Low Carbon Economy in 2050', COM (2011) 112 final, Brussels, 8 March (Brussels: European Commission).

European Environment Agency (2010) 'Recession Accelerates the Decline in EU Greenhouse Gas Emissions', http://www.eea.europa.eu/highlights/recession-accelerates-the-decline-in, accessed on 9 June 2011.

Gilbertson, T. and O. Reyes (2009) 'Carbon Trading: How It Works and Why It Fails', *Critical Currents* 7 (November) (Uppsala: Dar Hammarskjöld Foundation).

Goldenberg, S. (2009, 24 February) 'Great Clean-Up – Can Economic Rescue Plans Also Save Planet?' *The Guardian*, http://www.guardian.co.uk/environment/2009/feb/24/obama-environment-economic-rescue, accessed on 1 June 2011.

Gourlay, P. (2009) 'Innocent Companies Face VAT Fraud Bill: KPMG', *Point Carbon*, 14 July.

Green New Deal Group (2008) *A Green New Deal: Joined-up Policies to Solve the Triple Crunch of the Credit Crisis, Climate Change and High Oil Prices* (London: New Economics Foundation).

Harvey, F. (2011, 8 March) 'Connie Hedegaard Wins Battle For 25% Carbon Emissions Cut', *The Guardian*, http://www.guardian.co.uk/environment/2011/mar/08/connie-hedegaard-25-per-cent-carbon-emissions, accessed on 9 June 2011.

Hovi, J., T. Skodvin, and S. Andresen (2003) 'The Persistence of the Kyoto Protocol: Why Other Annex I Countries Move on Without the United States', *Global Environmental Politics* 3(4), 1–23.

Inman, P. (2010, 11 January) 'Three Britons Charged Over €3m Carbon-Trading "Carousel Fraud" ', *The Guardian*, http://www.guardian.co.uk/business/2010/jan/11/eu-carbon-trading-carousel-fraud, accessed on 7 June 2011.

International Emissions Trading Association (IETA) (2010), *IETA's Concerns over Recycled CERs*, Press Release, Geneva, 15 March.

Juillet, L. and M. Paterson (2009) 'Une difficile modernisation écologique: l'evolution de la politique canadienne sur les changements climatiques', in L. Cardinal and D. Karmis (eds) *Les politiques publiques au Canada: Pouvoir, conflits et idéologie* (Québec: Presses de l'Université de Laval), 251–80.

Kanter, J. (2009, 20 August) 'Carbon Traders Arrested for Tax Fraud', *New York Times*, http://green.blogs.nytimes.com/2009/08/20/carbon-traders-arrested-for-tax-fraud/, accessed on 1 June 2011.

Ki-Moon, B. and A. Gore (2009, 17 February) 'Green Growth is Essential to Any Stimulus', *Financial Times*.

Kossoy, A. and P. Ambrosi (2010) *State and Trends of the Carbon Market 2010* (Washington: The World Bank).

Lomborg, B. (2001) *The Skeptical Environmentalist: Measuring the Real State of the World* (London: Cambridge University Press).

Lohmann, L. (2006) 'Carbon Trading: A Critical Conversation on Climate Change, Privatization and Power', *Development Dialogue* 47, 1–356.

Lohmann, L. (2009) 'Climate as Investment', *Development and Change* 40(6), 1063–83.

Lovell, H. and D. MacKenzie (2011) 'Accounting for Carbon: The Role of Accounting Professional Organisations in Governing Climate Change', *Antipode* 43(3), 704–30.

Manners, I. (2002) 'Normative Power Europe: A Contradiction in Terms?', *Journal of Common Market Studies* 40(2), 235–58.

Mason, R. (2009, 10 December) 'Copenhagen Climate Summit: Carbon Trading Fraudsters in Europe Pocket €5bn', *The Daily Telegraph*, http://www.telegraph.co.uk/earth/copenhagen-climate-change-confe/6778003/Copenhagen-climate-summit-Carbon-trading-fraudsters-in-Europe-pocket-5bn.html, accessed on 7 June 2011.

Meadows, D., D. Meadows, J. Randers and W. Behrens (1972) *The Limits To Growth* (London: Pan).

Mol, A. (2001) *Globalization and Environmental Reform: The Ecological Modernization of the Global Economy* (London: MIT Press).

Paehlke, R. (2008) *Some Like It Cold: The Politics of Climate Change in Canada* (Toronto: Between the Lines).

Paterson, M. (2009) 'Post-Hegemonic Climate Politics?', *British Journal of Politics and International Relations* 11(1), 140–58.

Phillips, L. (2009, 10 December) 'EU Emissions Trading An "Open Door" For Crime, Europol Says', *EU Observer*, http://euobserver.com/885/29132, accessed on 7 June 2011.

Point Carbon (2010a) 'Carbon Market Growth to Stall in 2010: Report', *Point Carbon*, 18 January.

Point Carbon (2010b) 'Hungary Sells "Recycled" CERs', *Point Carbon*, 11 March.

Point Carbon (2010c) 'Market Braces For More "Recycled" CER Sales', *Point Carbon*, 12 March.

Point Carbon (2010d) 'Hungary Lifts Lid On Controversial CER Deal', *Point Carbon*, 14 May.

Point Carbon (2010e) 'Japan Will Not Ban Use of Recycled CERs', *Point Carbon*, 18 March.

Point Carbon (2010f) 'Bluenext Confirms Sales of Used CERs', *Point Carbon*, 16 March.

Point Carbon (2010g) 'Bluenext, Nord Pool Suspend Spot CER Trading', *Point Carbon*, 17 March.

Porter, M. and C. van der Linde (1995) 'Toward a New Conception of the Environment-Competitiveness Relationship', *Journal of Economic Perspectives* 9(4), 97–118.

Prada, M., J. Barbéris and A. Tignol (2010a) *The Regulation of CO_2 Markets*, Report Commissioned by the French Ministry of Finance, Paris.

Prada, M., J. Barbéris and A. Tignol (2010b) *The Regulation of CO_2 Markets*, Executive Summary of Report Commissioned by the French Ministry of Finance. Paris.

Reuters (2009, 15 July) 'Dutch Ministry Acts On VAT Fraud In CO_2 Market'.

Robins, N. (2010) *Overview of Global Green Stimulus Spending* (London: HSBC Global Research, February 17), http://csis.org/files/attachments/100217_NRobins.pdf, accessed on 1 June 2011.

Sandbag (2009) *ETS S.O.S: Why the Flagship 'EU Emissions Trading Policy' Needs Rescuing* (London: Sandbag).

Sandbag (2010) *The Carbon Rich List: The Companies Profiting from the EU Emissions Trading Scheme* (London: Sandbag).

Schreurs, M. and Y. Tiberghien (2007) 'Multi-Level Reinforcement: Explaining European Union Leadership in Climate Change Mitigation', *Global Environmental Politics* 7(4), 19–46.

Scoffield, H. (2010, 29 January) 'Harper Urges "Enlightened" Foreign Policy, But Faces Criticism On Climate', *The Canadian Press*, http://www.citytv.com/toronto/citynews/news/national/article/69016–harper-urges-enlightened-foreign-policy-but-faces-criticism-on-climate, accessed on 10 June 2011.

Skjærseth, J.B., and J. Wettestad (2008) *EU Emissions Trading: Initiation, Decision-Making and Implementation* (Aldershot, England: Ashgate).

Smith, K. (2007) *The Carbon Neutral Myth: Offset Indulgences For Your Climate Sins* (Amsterdam: Carbon Trade Watch).

Thistlethwaite, J. (2011) 'Counting the Environment: The Environmental Implications of International Accounting Standards', *Global Environmental Politics* 11(2), 75–97.

Twidale, S. (2010) 'UK Arrests 22 As CO_2 Tax Probe Widens', *Point Carbon*, 30 April.

United Nations Environment Programme (UNEP) (2009) *Global Green New Deal: An Update for the G20 Pittsburgh Summit* (Nairobi: United Nations Environment Programme).

van Asselt, H. (2010) 'Emissions Trading: The Enthusiastic Adoption of an Alien Instrument', in A. Jordan, D. Huitema, H. van Asselt, T. Rayner, and F. Berkhout (eds) *Climate Change Policy in the European Union: Confronting the Dilemmas of Mitigation and Adaptation* (Cambridge: Cambridge University Press), 125–44.
von Weizsäcker, E., A. Lovins and H. Lovins (1998) *FactorFour: Doubling Wealth – Halving Resource Use: The New Report to the Club of Rome* (London: Earthscan).
World Commission on Environment and Development (WCED) (1987) *Our Common Future* (Oxford: Oxford University Press).

7

The Role of the IMF in the International Financial and Eurozone Crises

Patrick Conway

On 23 September 2007, Dominique Strauss-Kahn was named the Managing Director of the International Monetary Fund (IMF). In his speech on that day (as reported in Weisman, 2007), he summarized the challenges facing the IMF as 'relevance and legitimacy'. Eighteen months later, the final communiqué of the Group of Twenty (G20) meeting of April 2009 (G20, 2009) voted to triple IMF lending capacity and authorized a substantial expansion in the stock of special drawing rights in circulation. By the end of 2010, the IMF had partnered with the European Union (EU) to design and administer financial relief packages for Greece and Ireland (IMF, 2011). The IMF went in short order from a supernumerary role to a central place on the world stage. What brought about this shift?

The first section of this chapter describes the causes and effects of the international financial crisis, with special attention to the impact in Europe and to IMF forecasts. The second and third sections address the role that the IMF played as a global financial actor, and how it unfolded in the context of the 2008–09 crisis and in the subsequent Eurozone crisis. Underlying this analysis is the question of why the IMF moved to centre stage. Was it due to its ability to anticipate the crisis and its effects, to its facility in lending-cum-conditionality or simply as a manifestation of a 'lender of last resort' function, when other financial intermediaries were reluctant to lend? The argument made here, based on the evidence from the crises, is that the IMF's central role in the crises stems from (a) a global desire to re-establish a lender of last resort for the crisis and (b) a perceived need on the part of creditors for the IMF's traditional lending-cum-conditionality product.

The emergence of the international financial crisis and the IMF

In this chapter, the term 'international financial crisis' refers to the economic crisis that affected advanced economies, first and foremost beginning in 2008 and then spread to emerging and developing economies through both trade and financial channels. Output growth in the advanced economies began its collapse earlier and became more recessionary than in most emerging and developing economies. Among the emerging and developing economies, those countries with closest economic links to Europe and the United States were on average more strongly affected, including the post-communist states of Eastern Europe. In 2010, the *World Economic Outlook* (IMF, 2010, p. 6) predicted a 'multi-speed' recovery over the next few years – IMF shorthand for rapid growth among emerging and developing markets coupled with an anaemic recovery in the advanced economies.

There is widespread agreement that the trigger for the crisis was the downturn in housing values in US real estate markets in the mid- to late-2000s. The controversy begins with the possible explanations for why such a relatively minor event should trigger a global recession. The suspected causes have been summarized elsewhere (e.g., Conway, 2010). At its base, this international financial crisis is similar to those that came before and is rooted in a speculative bubble. Kindleberger (2000) was an early expositor of this behaviour, and documented that speculation will lead to a rapid run up in price followed by a crash. In the current instance, the bubble was found in the US real estate market. While the speculators believed that their purchase of credit default swaps had hedged their risks, the failure of American International Group (AIG), the major issuer of these swaps, appeared to return the risk to the speculators.

There was no direct connection between the IMF and the collapse of the sub-prime housing market in the United States. While the IMF has been accused in the past of creating an environment in which international lending to developing countries is excessive and in which developing country governments take insufficient steps to address systemic economic problems (two aspects of moral hazard, see Conway, 2006), this crisis erupted in parts of the international economy in which an IMF 'guarantee' carried no weight. Bernanke (2005) put forward the hypothesis that the global imbalance of the 2000s was due to a 'savings glut': too many countries wishing to save too much, leading to low interest rates and greater induced borrowing. If this explanation is accepted

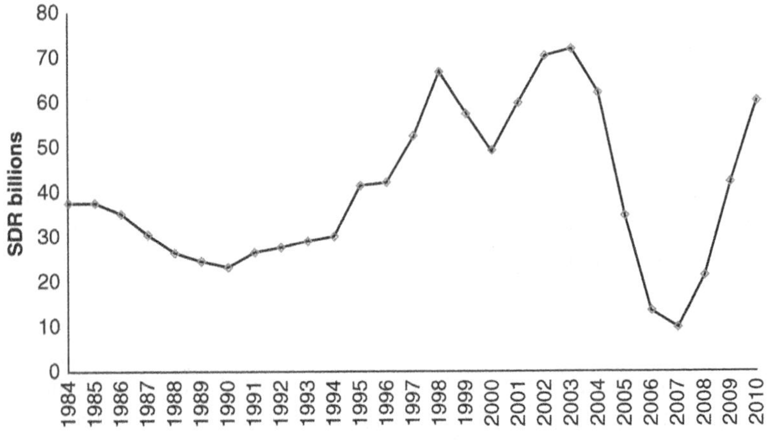

Figure 7.1 IMF credit outstanding (as of 31 December of year listed)
Source: IMF (2011). Includes both GRA and PRGT purchases.

as a cause of the financial crisis, it is inappropriate to treat the IMF as an intermediary for that saving. As is evident from Figure 7.1 (plotted by the author from data available in IMF, *Annual Reports*, 1984 through 2010), the IMF's role in international lending was declining during the period that Bernanke identifies with the 'savings glut'.

IMF failure to anticipate the crisis

The IMF saw a US-driven crisis during this period as a possibility, but was focused on a different potential crisis, one based in global saving imbalances. The IMF has annual Article IV consultations with the US government about international financial issues, just as it does with all its members.[1] In 2005, for example (IMF, 2005), the key advice from the IMF concerned global imbalances, and specifically means to raise US saving and reduce the US current account deficit. The IMF found itself in broad agreement with the US monetary policy of the time. By 2008, as Faruqee (2008) reports, the IMF recognized that the financial crisis would cause economic slowdowns in the United States and Europe – and saw that as good news, in part because it reduced global imbalances. Blanchard (2008), currently chief economist of the IMF, had a similar focus on the threat of global imbalances. The IMF's projections of the impact of the crisis in the United States and Europe are in retrospect very similar to those of government agencies. When the consensus forecasts of real economic growth in the United States by the IMF and the Federal Reserve's Federal Open Market Committee (FOMC) are compared, the IMF projections appear to match actual outcomes more closely for 2008 and 2009.[2] Neither agency anticipated the magnitude of the drop in 2009 growth, prior to 2009.

An examination of the Latvian case illustrates the failure of the IMF to anticipate the crisis. Latvia experienced a number of years of rapid economic growth during the mid-2000s. This growth was in large part financed through a credit boom. The Latvian financial sector, dominated by local subsidiaries of Scandinavian banks, intermediated the credit through its own borrowing from European commercial banks. Latvia participated in IMF-supported programmes beginning in 1992, but by 2004 had no outstanding loans from the IMF.[3] The Latvian government, just like other member governments, conducted annual Article IV consultations with the IMF about macroeconomic performance. A review of published IMF documents prepared subsequent to IMF-Latvia consultations between 2004 and 2008 (e.g., IMF, 2005) indicates growing concern by IMF staff about Latvia's credit boom, excessive growth, and financial-sector vulnerability. By April 2007, the mission counselled an urgent and immediate contractionary demand-management policy. In December 2008, the IMF and the Republic of Latvia announced a Stand-by Arrangement (SBA). The advice given by the IMF did anticipate a crisis but not necessarily due to the world financial crisis; it seemed to be more a prediction of the adverse consequence of a Latvian speculative bubble than of the transmission of the shock from the international crisis.

This conclusion is reinforced by the examination of biannual IMF forecasts. Every six months, IMF staff prepared a forecast for Latvia's real economic growth, and it is reasonable to believe that concerns about transmission of the international financial crisis would be reflected in these forecasts. Figure 7.2 summarizes the forecasts provided in each successive edition of the publication between April 2007 and April 2010.[4] As is evident, the forecasts in April 2007 and October 2007 predicted only a small downturn in economic growth in 2008. In April 2008, the forecast was for lower, but still positive growth in 2009–11, while in October 2008 the forecast was for small reductions in real gross domestic product (GDP) during 2008 and 2009. It is only in April 2009 that the large negative growth rate, similar to what was actually observed, was predicted for 2009. A similar and slowly evolving realization of the possibility of crisis is evident in *World Economic Outlook* forecasts for the current account of Latvia from the same source.

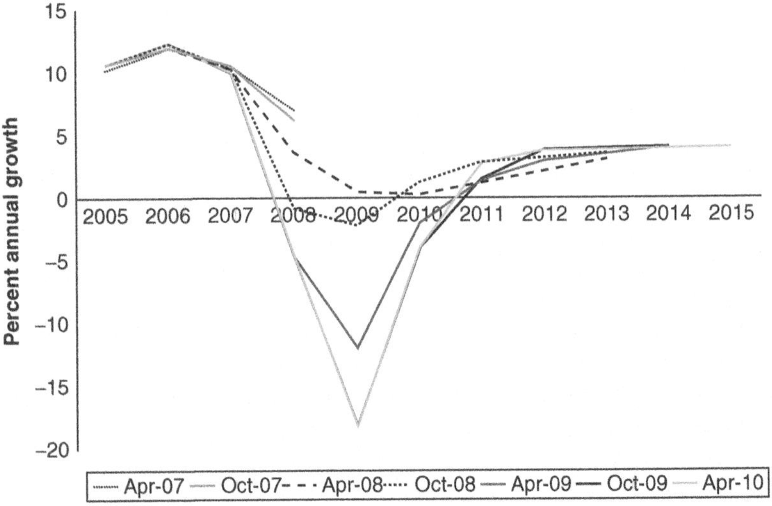

Figure 7.2 IMF forecasts of Latvia's real economic growth
Source: IMF (2007 through 2010).

While the IMF did not anticipate the scope of the crisis in Latvia, the private sector, apparently, also did no better. When ratings by Standard and Poor's and Moody's for medium-term foreign currency denominated bonds issued by the government of Latvia are considered, we observe two risk adjustments.[5] The Standard and Poor's rating was reduced in two steps in the first quarter of 2007 from A- (stable) to BBB+ (negative). Moody's rating remained higher (at an equivalent of an A), but was reduced from positive to stable outlook in September 2007. Both ratings remained above the investment grade cut-off during this period. The large downgrading of Latvian sovereign debt began in August 2008, subsequent to a run on Parex Bank, Latvia's second-largest (and largest domestic owned) bank, and bottomed out in the last quarter of 2009. The rating agencies thus showed a modest increase in their assessment of risk in early 2007, but the largest downgrades only occurred after the run on Parex Bank – when everyone recognized that a crisis was in full swing. The IMF, therefore, did no worse and no better than these private agencies in predicting the crisis in Latvia.

Propagation of the financial crisis and differential impacts

The rapid propagation from the United States to other economies can be attributed to three features of the behaviour of financial institutions in advanced economies. First, collateralized debt obligations provided an opportunity for speculators throughout the world to participate in the bubble. These assets lost value as the US crisis intensified, causing commercial banks in advanced countries to reduce their liabilities in synchronized fashion. Second, the expansion of bank balance sheets throughout the world was disproportionately financed through issuance of US dollar denominated short-term liabilities. When the crisis began, all commercial banks had difficulty in 'rolling over' these liabilities. Third, Kamin and De Marco (2010) attribute the majority of the propagation effect across borders to what they call 'indirect contagion'. In their view, financial actors throughout the advanced economies observed the US experience. They also observed that banks in other countries had adopted a similar, highly leveraged, business model. This observation triggered a synchronized run on banks in advanced economies.

As a result of these propagation channels, the financial crisis in each country took a similar form. A subset of financial institutions became insolvent due to their bets on these collateralized debt obligations; a large percentage of financial institutions faced a shortage of liquidity (short-term borrowing) in the aftermath of the crisis, and a majority of commercial borrowers in the advanced economies found that short-term borrowing was either very costly or impossible. Countries with strict banking supervision, whether advanced (Canada) or emerging (China), escaped the worst of the financial shock. This supervision discouraged not only the speculation in collateralized debt obligations but also the overleveraging that amplified the crisis in other countries. Åslund (2009) and Berkmen et al. (2009) also identified the exchange-rate regime as a critical factor. Countries with inflation-targeting monetary policies performed significantly better in response to the financial shock than those with 'exchange-rate targeting' policies: 'inflation targeting' requires a flexible exchange rate.

The impact of the crisis on the emerging economies varied substantially across regions. This was due to the dual channels for transmission to these countries. While it was not common for emerging-economy financial institutions to hold the speculative collateralized debt obligations, some emerging economies faced substantial financial shocks due to the crisis. In addition, the reduction of growth in the United States, Japan, and Western Europe led to a reduction in demand for emerging-economy exports. Those emerging economies that were most affected by the financial crisis were those in which multinational banks had become dominant and less regulated. Dooley (2010) remarks that the

Asian countries were largely spared by the financial shock as they continued the close supervision of their home financial sectors that began in the aftermath of the Asian crisis. The Asian financial institutions were not allowed to become overleveraged or to follow the 'risky business' model of the advanced-economy financial institutions and so were largely insulated from the financial shock. Eastern European countries, by contrast, had banking systems dominated by foreign-owned banks.

Emerging economies that dodged the financial shock, however, did not escape unscathed from the crisis. The study by te Velde et al. (2010) reported a number of negative effects of the crisis on emerging economies through changing developed-economy behaviour, including reduction in portfolio investment flows (due to the flight to safe havens), reduction in direct foreign investment in emerging and developing economies (due to the economic downturn), reduction in remittances (due to the economic downturn), and reduction in exports of tradable goods and services to the advanced economies.

The crisis has had quite a differentiated impact in the various countries of Eastern Europe. When the real annual growth rate by country (as reported by the IMF, *World Economic Outlook*, 2010) is considered for the year 2009, over 2008, there is great variation in country experience. The Eurozone at –4.1 per cent was a poor outcome, but Latvia, Ukraine, and Lithuania had negative growth rates of over 15 per cent. Poland joined Azerbaijan, Kosovo, Albania, and (barely) Belarus with positive growth rates. If these countries were all tightly linked to the EU-15, we would not expect such differences – and such magnification of the negative impact of the crisis. Figure 7.3 illustrates the time path of the crisis for the Eurozone and selected Eastern European countries using economic growth statistics reported by the IMF (*World Economic Outlook*, 2007 through 2010). The Eurozone growth path indicates the 'sine wave' path from 2004 to the present: rising and then declining growth through 2009, with a slight upturn thereafter. Iceland's economy, provided as another comparison, illustrates the magnification effect, due to what is in 'old Europe' an egregious case of overleveraging. The magnification observed in Latvia and Ukraine is much greater, with higher growth in 2006 and 2007 followed by much larger contraction in 2009 and 2010. Trade linkages are unlikely to provide such magnification; the most likely outcome with trade linkages will be for the countries to follow the same growth 'sine wave' as the Eurozone but with only limited dispersion around that path. The large differentiation of country experience in Figure 7.3 points to a financial-market cause.

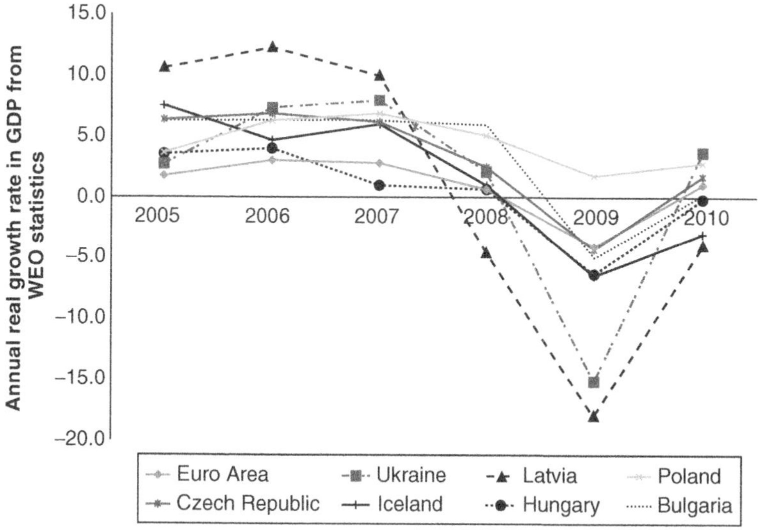

Figure 7.3 Economic growth in selected East European countries
Source: IMF (2007 through 2010).

The share of foreign ownership in the banking sector was one of the major differences between Eastern Europe and the rest of the world during this crisis period. While foreign participation was less than 50 per cent in Latin America and less than 20 per cent in emerging Asia through the 2000s, it was 70 per cent and was rising in emerging Europe. By the time the crisis hit, nearly 90 per cent of the financial-sector assets in emerging Europe were foreign owned. This had led to substantial on-lending by the subsidiaries in Eastern Europe. The growth of cross-border credits as reported by the Bank of International Settlements reflects this on-lending (e.g., Hermann and Mihaljek, 2010). From 2001, credits into the Eurozone followed a 'boomerang' pattern: the value of credits increased 200 per cent by June 2008. From that time on, the value of credits into the Eurozone did not grow further, but rather declined slightly. Iceland experienced a classic financial bubble; when compared to 2001 values, growth of credits into Iceland were roughly 13 times higher by June 2008, falling to four times higher by March 2010. The Icelandic bubble pales, however, when compared to the experience of Ukraine and Latvia; once again compared to 2001, there was growth at the height of the bubble of 39 and 26 times, respectively, with a large portion of that given back in the aftermath. Poland, by contrast, observed only a slight financial bubble in cross-border lending. Rapid growth leads to an imbalance of cross-border assets and liabilities. When European financial institutions faced the financial crisis, they reduced these cross-border flows and caused 'sudden stops' in the Eastern European countries.

The IMF response to the 2008–09 crisis

The important role that the IMF took on in relation to the 2008–09 crisis requires some explanation, as prior to that it appeared that its role as an important global lender was on the decline. As noted above, the IMF was not particularly foresighted in anticipating the crisis and its effects, so other explanations for its increased role need to be explored. To do this, it is important to place the IMF's role in the 2008–09 crisis in historical context.

The Articles of Agreement of the IMF (as reported by Boughton, 2006, p. 19) define two responsibilities for the organization. First, the IMF extends short-term credit to countries with balance-of-payment deficits, 'conditional on the country's commitment to implement economic policies that will restore equilibrium'. Second, the IMF conducts periodic consultations with member governments about their exchange-rate arrangement and external balance and provides advice as appropriate on macroeconomic and exchange-rate policy reforms.

As Kenen (1986) notes, the IMF was first envisioned as a type of international credit union. Countries subject to adverse external shocks would approach it for credit; there would be no distinction between creditor and borrower country, since each member would be both at different times. Over time this has, of course, evolved into a different type of group activity. Conway (2007) describes the current situation: a large number of recidivist borrowers and a smaller number of advanced economies that rarely or never (until the recent euro crisis) use the credit facility. Kenen (1986) concludes that by 1986 the IMF was operating more like a bank than a credit union, intermediating funds from creditor members to borrower members.

Tirole (2002) advanced a more complex view of the IMF's role. While its form may be similar to a stand-alone bank, its unique contribution to the international financial market stems from its ability to complete an incomplete contract between private lenders and borrowers. Tirole characterizes the contract between the private lender (e.g., Deutsche Bank) and the private borrower (e.g., Latvia's electricity corporation) as subject to dual agency.[6] The private lender enters a contract with the private borrower but recognizes that the ability of the borrower to repay will depend critically upon the actions of the sovereign government (e.g., the government of Latvia). IMF programmes with the sovereign government 'complete' the contract and encourage private lending.[7] As Jeanne, Ostry, and Zettelmeyer (2008) put it, the IMF is more effective than uncoordinated private investors in eliciting policy adjustments from crisis countries. The IMF has its own technology associated with lending that creates a commitment device for government adjustment. This conditionality is welfare improving in the absence of moral hazard. Moral hazard (less than optimal government adjustment *ex ante* because of the understanding that the IMF will be there to assist during crises) can lead to welfare reduction.[8] This highlights the importance of *ex ante* conditionality.

As a bank, the IMF has had a decided disadvantage until very recently in attracting customers. The IMF practice of attaching conditionality to its credit, while enshrined in the Articles of Agreement, has traditionally been a very unpopular feature of its lending.[9] There have been periods in which IMF lending was in heavy demand, including the period after the dissolution of the Soviet Union and the period subsequent to the Asian financial crisis. However, as Figure 7.1 indicates, by mid-2007 the use of its credit was at a recent low.

In the aftermath of the Asian crisis of 1997 and the Russian crisis of 1998, there was a loud and concerted objection to the IMF's implementation of its crisis lending programme. Many informed observers (e.g., Sachs, 1997; Feldstein, 1998; IFIAC, 2000; Stiglitz, 2002) attributed the slow recovery from the crisis to the IMF's behaviour. The critique was targeted at both tactical and strategic choices of the IMF. On the tactical front, Sachs, Feldstein, and Stiglitz criticized the conditionality that the IMF attached to its lending to crisis countries in Asia. While they differed in particulars, they agreed that the IMF's insistence on widespread financial-sector reform as a condition for lending was inappropriate. Sachs (1997) viewed the crisis as analogous to a 'run on the bank'. The IMF's insistence on market-reform conditions in this context just deepens the loss of confidence that caused the 'bank run' while causing the affected country to undertake unnecessary and costly policy changes. Feldstein (1998) argued that the IMF recommended austerity measures inconsistent with the Asian countries' economic needs just because that is the customary policy reform. Stiglitz (2002) echoed these criticisms, adding that the IMF's insistence on contractionary monetary policy during the crisis was counterproductive. On the strategic front, Feldstein (1998) and the International Financial Institutions

Advisory Commission Report (IFIAC, 2000) argued that IMF-supported programmes, by their nature, bail out unwise private lenders and create moral hazard in international lending. The International Financial Institutions Advisory Commission, also known as the Meltzer Commission, called for the IMF to cease lending except to emerging economies having met specific economic and financial pre-conditions.

These criticisms led to substantive reforms at the IMF in lending and in surveillance. In the early 2000s, the IMF came up with new guidelines for programme (now known as *ex post*) conditionality. One of the hallmarks of the new approach was to be 'country ownership' of the programme, as outlined in IMF (2001) and Boughton (2006). Another was to have greater flexibility, with less stress on meeting quarterly targets before tranche disbursements can occur (IMF, 2002). The IMF also introduced the Contingent Credit Line (CCL) in 1999: a precautionary line of defence for members with sound policies but vulnerable to contagion effects from capital account crises in other countries (IMF, 2004). Under the facility, an IMF member that met the eligibility criteria (now known as *ex ante* conditionality) could draw on a large pre-specified amount of resources if hit by a financial crisis due to factors outside of the member's control. This was a direct response to the IFIAC recommendation, but in its five year existence no country chose to complete the necessary pre-certification.

From the beginning of the 2008–09 financial crisis, the IMF moved swiftly to expand its lending. The IMF created a successor to the CCL. The Flexible Credit Line (FCL) was established in March 2009, requiring *ex ante* conditionality and providing unrestricted access to large amounts of credit (up to ten times quota in some cases). Mexico, Poland, and Colombia have already been approved for these lines of credit, with unrestricted access to US$82 billion in total. The G20 meeting of 2 April 2009 voted to triple the IMF lending capacity in the current crisis, from roughly US$250 to US$750 billion, through an expansion of the IMF's existing Arrangements to Borrow.[10] The G20 also supported the issuance of a new allocation of special drawing rights valued at US$250 billion to increase liquidity in the world economy.

As Figure 7.1 illustrates, the IMF's lending activity has expanded substantially from its low at the beginning of 2008. Table 7.1 lists the total value of lending programmes in place as of 31 December 2010. Note that the programmes in the left-hand column (Stand-by, Extended, and FCL facilities) were all arranged after the beginning of the financial crisis. The programmes in the right-hand column are for the most part lending to least developed countries through the Poverty

Table 7.1 IMF lending arrangements (in thousands of SDRS, on 31 December 2010)

Stand-By and Extended Arrangements (SBA, EFF)				**Poverty Reduction and Growth Trust Extended Credit Facility (ECF) 1/**			
Member	**Date of arrangement**	**Expiration**	**Total amount agreed**	**Member**	**Date of arrangement**	**Expiration**	**Total amount agreed**
Angola	23-Nov-09	22-Feb-12	858,900	Afghanistan, Islamic Republic of	26-Jun-06	25-Jun-10	81,000
Armenia, Republic of	06-Mar-09	05-Jul-11	533,600	Burundi	07-Jul-08	06-Jul-11	46,200
Bosnia and Herzegovina	08-Jul-09	30-Jun-12	1,014,600	Central African Republic	22-Dec-06	30-Jun-10	69,620
Costa Rica	11-Apr-09	10-Jul-10	492,300	Comoros	21-Sep-09	20-Sep-12	13,573
Dominican Republic	09-Nov-09	08-Mar-12	1,094,500	Congo, Democratic Republic of	11-Dec-09	10-Dec-12	346,450
El Salvador	17-Mar-10	16-Mar-13	513,900	Congo, Republic of	08-Dec-08	07-Dec-11	8,460
Gabon	07-May-07	06-May-10	77,150	Cote d'Ivoire	27-Mar-09	26-Mar-12	373,980
Georgia	15-Sep-08	14-Jun-11	747,100	Djibouti	17-Sep-08	16-Sep-11	12,720
Guatemala	22-Apr-09	21-Oct-10	630,600	Gambia, The	21-Feb-07	20-Feb-11	24,880
Hungary	06-Nov-08	05-Oct-10	10,537,500	Ghana	15-Jul-09	14-Jul-12	387,450
Iceland	19-Nov-08	31-Aug-11	1,400,000	Grenada	18-Apr-10	17-Apr-13	8,775
Iraq	24-Feb-10	23-Feb-12	2,376,800	Guinea	21-Dec-07	20-Dec-10	69,615
Jamaica	04-Feb-10	03-May-12	820,500	Liberia	14-Mar-08	13-Mar-11	239,020
Latvia, Republic of	23-Dec-08	22-Dec-11	1,521,626	Malawi	19-Feb-10	18-Feb-13	52,050
Maldives	04-Dec-09	03-Dec-12	49,200	Mali	28-May-08	27-May-11	27,990
Moldova, Republic of	29-Jan-10	28-Jan-13	184,800	Mauritania	15-Mar-10	14-Mar-13	77,280
Mongolia	01-Apr-09	01-Oct-10	153,300	Moldova, Republic of	29-Jan-10	28-Jan-13	184,800
Pakistan	24-Nov-08	30-Dec-10	7,235,900	Nicaragua	05-Oct-07	04-Oct-10	78,000
Romania	04-May-09	03-May-11	11,443,000	Niger	02-Jun-08	01-Jun-11	23,030

Table 7.1 (Continued)

Stand-By and Extended Arrangements (SBA, EFF)				Poverty Reduction and Growth Trust Extended Credit Facility (ECF) 1/			
Member	**Date of arrangement**	**Expiration**	**Total amount agreed**	**Member**	**Date of arrangement**	**Expiration**	**Total amount agreed**
Serbia, Republic of	16-Jan-09	15-Apr-11	2,619,120	Sao Tome & Principe	02-Mar-09	01-Mar-12	2,590
Seychelles	23-Dec-09	22-Dec-12	19,800	Sierra Leone	10-May-06	09-May-10	51,880
Sri Lanka	24-Jul-09	23-Mar-11	1,653,600	Tajikistan, Republic of	21-Apr-09	20-Apr-12	78,300
Ukraine	05-Nov-08	04-Nov-10	11,000,000	Togo	21-Apr-08	20-Apr-11	84,410
				Zambia	04-Jun-08	03-Jun-11	220,095
Total			**56,773,196**	**Total**			**2,562,168**

Flexible Credit Line (FCL)				Exogenous Shock Facility (ESF)			
Member	**Date of arrangement**	**Expiration**	**Total amount agreed**	**Member**	**Date of arrangement**	**Expiration**	**Total amount agreed**
Colombia	11-May-09	10-May-10	6,966,000	Ethiopia	26-Aug-09	25-Oct-10	153,755
Mexico	25-Mar-10	24-Mar-11	31,528,000	Kyrgyz Republic	10-Dec-08	09-Jun-10	66,600
Poland, Republic of	06-May-09	05-May-10	13,690,000	Maldives	04-Dec-09	03-Dec-11	8,200
				Mozambique	30-Jun-09	29-Jun-10	113,600
Total			**52,184,000**	Senegal	19-Dec-08	18-Jun-10	121,350
				Tanzania	29-May-09	28-May-10	218,790
USD $1 = 0.684 SDRs 1 SDR = USD $1.462				**Total**			**682,295**

Source: IMF (2008 through 2010).

Reduction and Growth Facility (PRGF) and represent only about 3 per cent of total IMF commitments at this time.[11] Presbitero and Zazzaro (2010) document this underservice of least developed countries; they also conclude that the IMF lending during this crisis has been skewed towards countries that share political positions with the largest funders of the IMF. IMF-supported programmes were predominantly of two types prior to the crisis: PRGF lending and 'precautionary' programmes, that is, those agreed upon with the express desire not to draw them down unless circumstances for the borrower deteriorated sufficiently to require it. Among the programmes approved in 2008–10, these two types of lendings continue, but are joined by lending to countries – often European countries – in financial crisis. As is evident in the amounts approved, the lending to crisis countries is many orders of magnitude larger than the PRGF and precautionary lending to Central American countries.

The question arises as to whether the IMF acted as a lender of last resort in this crisis. Bagehot (1873) provides the definition of 'lender of last resort': one with responsibility for accommodating demands for high-powered money in times of crisis at penalty interest rates to 'solvent but illiquid' banks. In the international context, Tirole (2002) describes it as an institution that provides short-term liquidity to a country when commercial lenders no longer want to supply funds. Tirole (2002, p. 111) doesn't see the need for the IMF to play this role; as he says:

> the case for a LOLR [lender of last resort] is weaker than in the case of domestic liquidity because there is plenty of international liquidity to go around.... The limit is not [its] overall availability, but [its] availability to a country with limited international collateral.

While Tirole is likely correct, he did not anticipate the speed with which the definition of international collateral could change with the financial crisis. The crisis centred in the financial sector forced financial intermediaries to retrench and to restrict their lending. This has triggered 'sudden stops' (as described by Calvo, 1998) for many emerging economies – countries with sufficient international collateral to borrow pre-crisis found themselves with no takers when they attempted to float new obligations to roll over their earlier debts. Figure 7.4 illustrates this pattern for Eastern European countries using Bank of International Settlements data on cross-border capital flows, beginning in the second quarter of 2008. For these countries, the IMF credit is, then, lending

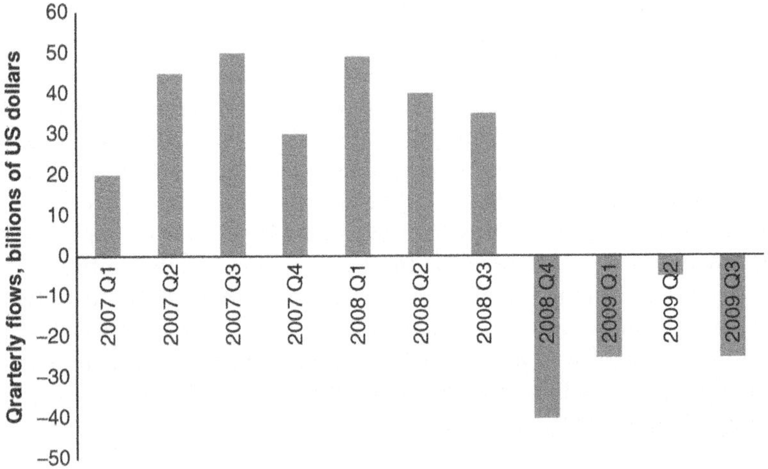

Figure 7.4 Sudden stop in emerging Europe
Source: Bank of International Settlements (various years) *Locational Banking Statistics*, http://www.bis.org/statistics/bankstats.htm, accessed on 2 January 2012.

of last resort designed to lessen the impact of the sudden stop on the emerging economy.

IMF participation in the EU financial stability plan in response to the Eurozone crisis of 2010–11

In this section, we turn to a different, and yet related, crisis: the excessive sovereign debt burden of Greece, Ireland, Portugal, and other members of the EU. This has led not only to financial instability in these countries but also to an ongoing debate over the sustainability of the Euro as the common currency. The recent experience of Greece, Spain, Portugal, Italy, and Ireland in the international bond markets has led to a number of initiatives to support these countries, the euro, and financial stability. In May 2010, Greece reached agreement with the IMF, the European Commission, and the European Central Bank (ECB) on a focused programme to stabilize its economy, to become more competitive, and to restore market confidence with the support of a €110 billion (about US$145 billion) financing package.[12] Simultaneously, the Council of the European Union created the European Stabilization Mechanism 'to present financial stability in Europe' by providing guarantees of up to €500 billion (about US$660 billion) sovereign borrowing from international capital markets (Europa, 2010). The ECB for its part amended its operating procedures to allow purchases of public and private debt obligations from member countries. As Blackstone (2010) reports, the ECB quickly put the plan into action by buying government bonds of Greece, Ireland, Portugal, Spain, and Italy.

This episode has many fascinating strands. There is a 'run on the bank' feature, with the ECB playing the role of lender of last resort to Eurozone commercial banks. There are heavily indebted sovereign governments paying destabilizingly high interest rates to roll over their debts, with the EU willing to provide guarantees to bring those interest rates down to manageable levels. And there is the IMF's participation. But why is this? It would seem that the EU and ECB institutions span the set of mechanisms necessary to deal with this crisis.

IMF participation in the Eurozone rescue has three potential rationales. First, it is a source of bridge financing. EU action through the European Stabilization Mechanism will ultimately be substantial, but disbursements cannot occur immediately. The IMF can provide short-term debt finance until that mechanism is operational. Second, there is agreement within the EU that reforms will be necessary in the debtor countries. EU governments do not want to be seen dictating policy to fellow members, and there may in fact be no consensus among members for the specific conditions to be placed. The EU thus delegates its condition design and monitoring role to the IMF. This is a specific example of the view of Tirole (2002) and Jeanne, Ostry and Zettelmeyer (2008) regarding IMF comparative advantage. In this case, the IMF can also serve to defuse common-agency problems when existing EU members favour different macroeconomic reforms for the destabilized countries. Third, including IMF financing in this programme will lessen the exposure of European countries to the rescue efforts. The increased resources of the IMF have come from many countries, only a few of which are within the EU. By including the IMF in the European initiative, the United States, Japan, China, and other IMF member countries will provide part of the financing necessary.

Eastern Europeans will see both positive and negative aspects of IMF involvement in the Eurozone rescue. The positive will come if IMF participation facilitates a solution to the EU/euro uncertainty. The crisis is centred in the financial systems of the Eurozone, and, as noted above, any disturbance in the European financial system can have magnified effects in Eastern Europe. Further, a healthy 'old Europe' is a large market for the goods and services exports of Eastern Europe. The negative comes from the drain on IMF resources necessary to provide assistance to the Eurozone countries. The financing packages designed by the IMF for Greece, Ireland, and Portugal in 2011 are very large and divert funds that could be provided to reforming countries in Eastern Europe. The Eastern European countries also contribute to the fund through their subscriptions. All members are being called upon to increase their subscription to the IMF, and those are funds that the countries would certainly like to have back.

Conclusion

In the beginning, the IMF was invented to sustain a fixed exchange-rate regime. Its activities were designed in essence to keep small crises from becoming big ones, to keep local imbalances from becoming global crises. Times have changed, and the IMF is now best known as a crisis manager, with a mandate to keep big crises from getting bigger.

Eastern Europe has suffered relatively more when compared to other emerging economies, due to the international financial and Eurozone crises. While propinquity to 'old Europe' and loss of export market due to its current recession is one reason, the size and differentiation in output reduction across these countries indicate that financial-sector causes also play a role. The degree of cross-border financial flows pre-crisis and the predominantly foreign-owned nature of Eastern European banks exacerbated the effects of the crisis, causing 'sudden stops' proportional to the reversal of cross-border flows.

The IMF has gone from an afterthought to a central player in world financial markets, thanks to the financial crisis. It performed as a lender of last resort during the initial days of the 'sudden stop' for those countries that were most severely affected by financial-flow reversal, and its expertise in designing adjustment programmes has been called into action throughout Europe. Its 'relevance and legitimacy' are no longer in question. Private-lender concerns with dual agency had nearly disappeared in the years leading up to the crisis, leaving the IMF's contribution as superfluous. The financial crisis and the Eurocrisis that has grown from it have renewed demand for the IMF's product, both as lender of last resort and as designer of appropriate conditionality. As long as private lenders remain cautious due to the risk that sovereign-government policy will interfere with repayment, the IMF will have a role to play in Europe.

This role is obviously important to Western Europe, but it is important to Eastern Europe as well. Western Europe's recovery is important to resume (or in some cases, continue) economic growth in Eastern Europe. At the same time, Eastern European countries find IMF's attention to the Eurozone costly (in terms of contributed resources). It also distracts the IMF from attention to their own needs.

Notes

1. This refers to Article IV of the IMF's Articles of Agreement signed in 1944. Article IV is entitled 'Obligations Regarding Exchange Arrangements', and commits each signatory to periodic meetings with IMF staff to discuss the country's exchange-rate regime and external balance.
2. This conclusion is based upon comparison of IMF and FOMC forecasts of US economic growth. The IMF projection is as reported in the IMF, *World Economic Outlook* (various years). The FOMC forecast is created by taking the midpoint of the reported 'Central Tendencies' range of forecasts by Federal Reserve presidents and board members in Federal Reserve System (various years). Federal Reserve forecast growth rates are fourth quarter over fourth quarter, while IMF are year-over-year.
3. Latvia first entered a one-year SBA with the IMF in 1992 and negotiated a second SBA, this time for 18 months, in 1993. It drew down a total of 110 million Special Drawing Rights (SDRs) from those two arrangements. Latvia also negotiated 'precautionary' SBAs in 1995, 1996, 1997, 1999, and 2001 but did not make any drawings from these. Latvia made its final repayment on the 1992/1993 SBAs in 2004.
4. This figure is created by the author from real economic growth data reported in the IMF, *World Economic Outlook* (2007 through 2010). For the more recent forecasts, historical data are inserted for earlier years. For example, the April 2010 forecast has historical values for 2005 through 2009.
5. Standard and Poor's (2011) and Moody's (2011).
6. Tirole (2002) also discusses the importance of common agency in international financial contracts, but this is less important in the context of IMF activity.
7. The extensive empirical literature on the catalytic effect of IMF lending (for a recent example, see Bird and Rowlands, 2008) represents a test of this view.
8. Vaubel (1983) presents a strong statement of the negative consequences of moral hazard and continues the logic to argue that the IMF should not lend under any circumstance. There have been numerous empirical tests of moral hazard created by IMF activity; Conway (2006) provides a survey of the literature that includes Dreher (2004) and Dreher and Vaubel (2004).
9. Williamson (1983) provides an early summary of the critique of IMF conditionality. Jeanne, Ostry, and Zettelmeyer (2008) is an excellent recent summary of the evolution of IMF conditionality.
10. The information in this paragraph not otherwise given citation is drawn from Moghadam (2009) and http://www.imf.org/external/np/exr/faq/sdrfaqs.htm.
11. There is a difference between the total 'credit outstanding' in Figure 7.1 and the total value of IMF lending programmes reported in Table 7.1. The table reports the initial contractual value of the loan or credit line, while the figure

reports the amount of the loan or credit line outstanding. Some loans are partially repaid; other loans or credit lines are not yet disbursed.

12. Ireland entered a similar arrangement with the IMF and the other actors in December 2010.

Bibliography

Åslund, A. (2009) *The East European Financial Crisis* (CASE Network Studies and Analyses, Study 395) (Warsaw: CASE Center for Social and Economic Research).

Bagehot, W. (1873) *Lombard Street: A Description of the Money Market* (London: H.S. King).

Berkmen, P., G. Gelos, R. Rennhack, and J. Walsh (2009) *The Global Financial Crisis: Explaining Cross-Country Differences in the Output Impact* (IMF Working Paper 09/280) (Washington: International Monetary Fund).

Bernanke, B. (2005, April) *The Global Savings Glut and the US Current Account Deficit.* Remarks given at the Homer Jones Lecture, St. Louis, Missouri.

Bird, G. and D. Rowlands (2008) 'Catalyzing Private Capital Flows and IMF Programs: Some Remaining Questions', *Journal of Economic Policy Reform* 11(1), 37–43.

Blackstone, B. (2010, 11 May) 'Amid the Storm, Questions about Bank's Role', Markets section, *Wall Street Journal*, vol. 109

Blanchard, O. (2008) *The Crisis: Basic Mechanisms and Appropriate Policies* (MIT Working Paper 09-01) (Cambridge: Ifo Institute for Economic Research).

Boughton, J. (2006) 'Who's in Charge? Ownership and Conditionality in IMF-Supported Programs', in G. Ranis, J. Vreeland and S. Kosack (eds) *Globalization and the Nation State* (New York: Routledge), 19–35.

Calvo, G. (1998) 'Capital Flows and Capital-Market Crises: The Simple Economics of Sudden Stops', *Journal of Applied Economics* 1, 35–54.

Conway, P. (1994) 'IMF Lending Programs: Participation and Impact', *Journal of Development Economics* 45, 365–391.

Conway, P. (2006) 'IMF Essays from a Time of Crisis', *Journal of Economic Literature* 40(1), 114–141.

Conway, P. (2007) 'The Revolving Door: Duration and Recidivism in IMF Programs', *Review of Economics and Statistics* 89(2), 205–220.

Conway, P. (2010, 10 June) *The IMF and the International Financial Crisis.* Paper presented at Egon Sohmen Memorial Conference, University of Tubingen.

Dooley, M. (2010) *Central Bank Responses during Financial Crises* (BIS Papers 51) (Basel: Bank for International Settlements).

Dreher, A. (2004) 'Does the IMF Cause Moral Hazard? A Critical Review of the Evidence', *Social Sciences Research Network*, http://ssrn.com/abstract= 505782, accessed on 26 January 2012.

Dreher, A. and Vaubel, R. (2004) 'Do IMF and IBRD Cause Moral Hazard and Political Business Cycles? Evidence from Panel Data', *Open Economies Review* 15, 5–22.

Europa (2010) *The European Stabilization Mechanism*, press release RAPID, Brussels, 10 May, http://europa.eu/rapid/press-release_MEMO-10-173_en.htm, accessed on 30 November 2012.

Faruqee, H. (2008) 'IMF Sees Global Imbalances Narrowing, But More to Be Done', *IMF Survey Magazine* 30(3), 1.

Federal Reserve System (2011) *Minutes of the Federal Reserve Open Market Committee*, http://www.federalreserve.gov/monetarypolicy/fomccalendars.htm, accessed on 26 January 2012.

Feldstein, M. (1998) 'Refocusing the IMF', *Foreign Affairs* 77(2), March/April.

Group of 20 (G20) (2009) *Final Communique*, 2 April 2009, http://www.g20.org/Documents/final-communique.pdf, accessed on 8 November 2011.

Hermann, S. and D. Mihaljek (2010) *The Determinants of Cross-Border Bank Flows to Emerging Markets: New Empirical Evidence on the Spread of Financial Crises* (BIS Working Paper 315, July) (Basel: Bank for International Settlements).

International Financial Institution Advisory Commission (IFIAC) (2000) *Report* (Washington: Government Printing Office).

International Monetary Fund (IMF) (2001) *IMF Reviews Strengthening Country Ownership of Fund-Supported Programs* (IMF Public Information Notice 1/125) (Washington: International Monetary Fund).

International Monetary Fund (IMF) (2002) *Guidelines on Conditionality*, 25 September 2002, http://www.imf.org/external/np/pdr/cond/2002/eng/guid/092302.htm, accessed on 26 January 2012.

International Monetary Fund (IMF) (2004) *The IMF's Contingent Credit Lines* (IMF Factsheet, March) (Washington: International Monetary Fund).

International Monetary Fund (IMF) (2005) *Staff Report for the 2005 Article IV Consultation for Latvia*, 14 July, http://www.imf.org/external/pubs/ft/scr/2005/cr05282.pdf, accessed on 26 January 2012.

International Monetary Fund (IMF) (2011) *Regional Economic Outlook – Europe* (Washington: International Monetary Fund).

International Monetary Fund (IMF) (2012) *IMF Resources and the G20 Summit*, http://www.imf.org/external/np/exr/faq/sdrfaqs.htm.

International Monetary Fund (IMF) (2003 through 2010) *World Economic Outlook* (Washington: International Monetary Fund).

International Monetary Fund (IMF) (1984 through 2010) *Annual Report* (Washington: International Monetary Fund).

Jeanne, O., J. Ostry, and J. Zettelmeyer (2008) *A Theory of International Crisis Lending and IMF Conditionality* (IMF Working Paper 08/236) (Washington: International Monetary Fund).

Kamin, S. and L. DeMarco (2010), *How did a Domestic Housing Slump Turn into a Global Financial Crisis?* (IFD Discussion Paper 994) (Washington: Board of Governors of the Federal Reserve System).

Kenen, P. (1986) *Financing, Adjustment and the International Monetary Fund* (Washington: Brookings Institution).

Kindleberger, C. (2000) *Manias, Panics and Crashes*, 4th ed. (New York: John Wiley & Sons).

Moghadam, R. (2009) *Review of Recent Crisis Programs*, http://www.imf.org/external/np/pp/eng/2009/091409.pdf, accessed on 26 January 2012.

Moody's (2011) http://www.moodys.com/researchandratings/market-segment/sovereign-supranational/, accessed on 14 November 2011.

Presbitero, A. and A. Zazzaro (2010) *The Global Crisis in Low- and Middle-Income Countries: How the IMF Responded* (MOFIR Working Paper 35) (Ancona: Money and Finance Research Group).

Sachs, J. (1997, 3 November) 'The Wrong Medicine for Asia', *New York Times*.
Standard and Poor's (2011) *Sovereigns Rating List*, http://www.standardandpoors.com/ratings/sovereigns/ratings-list/en/us/, accessed on 14 November 2011.
Stiglitz, J. (2002) *Globalization and Its Discontents* (New York: W.W. Norton).
te Velde, W. et al. (2010) *The Global Financial Crisis and Developing Countries: Phase 2 Synthesis* (Overseas Development Institute Working Paper 316) (London: Overseas Development Institute).
Tirole, J. (2002) *Financial Crises, Liquidity and the International Monetary System* (Princeton: Princeton University Press).
Vaubel, R. (1983) 'The Moral Hazard of IMF Lending', *The World Economy* 6(3), 291–304.
Weisman, S. (2007, 28 September) 'IMF Faces a Question of Identity', *New York Times*, http://www.nytimes.com/2007/09/28/business/worldbusiness/28imf.html, accessed on 26 January 2012.
Williamson, J. (ed.) (1983) *IMF Conditionality* (Washington: Institute for International Economics).

Part III

The Crisis in Central and Eastern Europe

8

Economic Crisis, the Power Vertical, and Prospects for Liberalization in Russia

Joan DeBardeleben and Mikhail Zherebtsov

Economic and financial crises can spur major political change as well as policy adjustments. Those with an exogenous source, such as the 2008–09 crisis, can be unanticipated and introduce into the existing domestic context an external 'surprise' that the system has few resources to cope with. This chapter explores potential effects of the 2008–09 crisis on political relations in Russia, with the goal of assessing whether it produced an impetus for liberalizing reform.

The context of this study is a broader consideration of the prospects for reversing Russia's authoritarian backslide. What could be the impetus for such a correction? One possibility would be the introduction of a reform agenda from within the elite, possibly as a spin-off effect of poor policy decisions. Policy conflict might generate an elite split, triggering political competition. This type of dynamic underlay the liberalizing reforms of the late 1980s under Mikhail Gorbachev. A second impetus could be popular pressure, either electorally or through street protests, strikes, or other extra-systemic actions. A third trigger for liberalization could be external factors, such as contacts between opinion leaders or experts, challenges in the geopolitical environment, an externally generated crisis, or the imposition of new stresses from an external source. This type of explanation is also sometimes offered for the liberalizing Gorbachev reforms.

The dynamics that determine the impact of global economic crises on political relations in authoritarian systems may not be that transparent. However, such systems are not immune to change. The interests of various elite groups may be differentially affected by crisis. While in competitive democratic systems such differential effects may spur regional and political party leaders to try to mobilize public sentiments, in authoritarian systems the public's role may be limited to sporadic protests, and the crisis could nourish elite conflict that is not so visible to the outsider. As Haggard and Kaufman (1997, pp. 266–7) note, economic crises can 'undermine "authoritarian bargains" forged between ruler and key sociopolitical constituents and expose rulers to defection from within the business sector and protest "from below" '. In authoritarian systems, popular protests may be one of the few vehicles available to the public to vent frustrations, so these situations pose a particular risk for the leadership. For example, in the communist period, the Solidarity movement developed in part as a response to Poland's economic decline, which was linked to the tightening of credit in the 1970s. In extreme cases, economic crisis could trigger a level of upheaval adequate to challenge the foundations of the political regime, making authoritarian leaders nervous and provoking measures to exert further control. In mixed systems, where contested elections and a partially free media exist alongside authoritarian tendencies, as in contemporary Russia, the range of vehicles for change expands to include electoral effects and subsequent popular mobilization in response to perceived breaches of electoral fairness.

Prior to 2008, in the short period since the collapse of the communist system, Russia had already faced one acute financial crisis that was linked to a larger global downturn in 1998. Luong and Weinthal (2004) argue that the 1998 crisis spurred an increased appetite for cooperation between Russian oil companies and the government, by revealing their common vulnerability, resulting in an agreement to undertake a successful reform of the tax system. In terms of federal relations, Liasko (1999) argues that the 1998 crisis increased the dependence of regions on the centre, while Petrov and Shklyar (1999, p. 546) conclude that 'the financial crisis and resulting governing paralysis in the center presented regional leaders with vast opportunities to strengthen their power'. These opportunities spurred the governors' ambitions, encouraging them to take matters into their own hands, including measures such as price controls and restrictions. The 1998 crisis took place in a completely different political context from the one that followed in 2008–09, as it preceded Vladimir Putin's efforts to reassert central control over recalcitrant and self-assertive regions. One might speculate that the trends identified by Petrov and Shklyar (1999) reinforced Putin's decision to undertake the recentralizing initiative.

Two features of the Russian political system warrant particular attention when considering the possible impacts of economic crisis. First is Russia's status as a resource-exporting country. Export and specifically resource-exporting economies, such as Russia's (Hanson, 2007), were particularly hard hit by the 2008–09 financial/economic crisis, both due to declining oil and gas prices and because of the drying up of international credit and reduced demand for exports in other countries hit by the crisis. Deryugin (2009) argues that in Russia the crisis most strongly affected the wealthiest highly export-dependent regions of the country. However, due to the relatively rapid recovery of energy prices in 2010, the importance of this structural feature of the Russian economy should not be overestimated. Whether a more sustained depression of energy fuel prices would have produced a stronger incentive for political change cannot be tested with this case.

A second important feature of the Russian political system is the nature of federal–regional relations. Here the broader literature on how economic crisis affects federal systems can be instructive, as Russia remains, in a legal sense, a federal system, despite centralizing measures undertaken in the previous ten years. Comparative analysis suggests that in federal systems the impact of global economic crises may affect a longer-term shift in the balance of power between federal and regional governments or may contribute to slippage or shifts in the definitions of policy jurisdictions. Examples from democratic polities might include the experience of Canada in the Great Depression; facing bankruptcy, some Canadian provinces increasingly needed to turn to the federal government for help, allowing it to develop new capacities to influence provincial politics, including creation of the Bank of Canada, the Canadian Wheat Board, and a national unemployment scheme. A survey of 'federations and the economic crisis' of 2008–09 led George Anderson (2009, p. 37) to conclude that the nature and scope of that particular crisis has 'shifted the weight of decision-making to federal capitals', with variation in terms of the degree to which constituent regions took on responsibility for carrying out federally funded measures or, in some cases, for supplementing them. Differential impacts of economic stress on particular regions within a federation can contribute to a readjustment of fiscal federal relations or can serve to shift patterns of inequality between regions in such a way as to trigger new demands, both from regional leaders and from the public at large.

Conceptual framework and methodology

The hypothesis tested here is that the type of crisis that unfolded in 2008 fuelled political change via a number of mechanisms: at the central level through elite-initiated reforms or the emergence of more effective in-system political opposition; at the civil society level by forcing government responsiveness to public demands or affecting election outcomes; and in the sphere of centre-regional relations by challenging the vertical structure of executive power as regions articulate new demands. If the hypothesis is rejected, then this might be an indicator that power relations are less fragile than some analysts expect. The time framework for testing the hypothesis may be too short to offer definitive conclusions, and the apparent receding of economic crisis conditions earlier than expected may also make change less likely. However, in this chapter we look at indicators that might suggest a link between economic crisis and system reform or change.

At the central level, these indicators could include modernization measures announced by the federal government or changes in relations within the political elite. In terms of civil society, both electoral outcomes and the nature of public protests associated with the economic crisis are important. For centre–regional relations, indicators for change would include overt challenges to the vertical structure of executive power, established by Vladimir Putin since the year 2000, or shifts in the existing federal–regional balance of power. The realm of centre–regional relations is particularly important because creation of the 'power vertical' was of cardinal significance for Putin's centralizing reforms that set in place a quasi-authoritarian trajectory, the redline indicator being the elimination of gubernatorial elections in 2004. The effort to establish a 'unified system of executive power' involves a circular flow of power, in which governors depend on the Kremlin's favour for political survival; they in turn reinforce the Kremlin's power through their acquiescence in supporting the dominance of the establishment party, United Russia, and in ensuring its electoral success as well as by promoting within their regions an analogous pattern of political dependence. This symbiotic, but asymmetrical, power relationship has in part depended on the ability of the federal government to provide benefits to compliant regions and regional leaders. With decreasing flows of resource revenues to feed regional budgets and public consumption and with a slowdown in economic growth, maintaining benefit flows becomes more difficult. Here, the economic crisis could pose challenges to the power vertical by encouraging increasingly autonomous action by regional elites, due to: (a) reduced rewards (and thus reduced incentives) for adherence to federal directives and (b) an increased necessity to respond to local challenges as they arise, if federal help is not available. Working against this dynamic might be other factors (that could contradict our hypothesis): economic crisis could reinforce the power vertical because the federal centre would have increased incentives to maintain control in the face of potential social unrest or regional self-assertion, and governors, dependent on the centre, would have minimal resources to pursue an independent policy.

This chapter is primarily concerned with political liberalization, which refers to the expansion of real opportunities for the exercise of effective political opposition through a competitive electoral system (thus by extension including more traditional definitions of civil liberties, such as freedom of speech, press, and association). By contrast, economic liberalization involves support for a competitive market system, with a reduction in overt government intrusion into market relations. Whether economic liberalization alone encourages longer-term political liberalization is beyond the scope of this chapter.

Assessing whether economic crisis may engender systemic change requires a definition of factors that might trigger such change. While economic stress is highly likely to engender conflict and tensions, such conflict does not necessary facilitate political liberalization. Table 8.1 provides a scheme for evaluating effects of the crisis that might have the potential to feed deeper political liberalization. The left-hand column specifies the three mechanisms identified above – changes at the central level, in civil society activism, and in centre–regional relations. The second and third columns indicate some of the forms that these types of conflict may take, distinguishing between those that have a greater or lesser liberalizing potential. The right-hand column draws out potential systemic implications of each factor, including feedback effects on other political relations.

At the national elite level, interests of particular groups may be threatened by fallout from the crisis, and conflicts may emerge over the distribution of scarcer resources and about policy choices. If these types of conflict take on a public character, with differing forces or leaders associated with distinct policy options, then such conflict can have a liberalizing impact by producing an increasingly pluralist political landscape. Within authoritarian systems that still allow some form of electoral competition, this renewed type of elite conflict could translate into a more competitive electoral environment, even if only between 'loyal' parties, opening the way for the mobilization of the public in support of one force or the other. The Orange Revolution in Ukraine provides a case in point, even if the context for those events was not an economic crisis but rather a falsified electoral outcome.

In terms of civil society, economic crisis can engender popular protests, which, in authoritarian systems, can take the form of demonstrations, strikes, or other public manifestations of discontent. We posit

Table 8.1 Indicators of liberalizing dynamics in economic crisis conditions

Type of indicator	Evidence of liberalizing potential of the indicator	Evidence of minimal liberalizing potential of the indicator	Implications for other dynamics
Elite conflict at the federal level	• If evidenced in enhanced party competition or electoral gains for the opposition • If elite split becomes public • If conflict is perceived as reflecting diverse issue positions	• If limited to conflicts over distribution of resources • If depicted as conflict over personal power	• Providing opening for mobilization of other interests by various elite groups • Uncertainly provides opening for self-assertion by regional elites
Civil society activism – public protests or actions	• If connected to broader critique of power relations • If the protests gain wide media coverage or lead to a broad social coalition • If actions cause significant economic disruption	• If focused on specific local economic issues • If placated by local concessions	• Destabilizing potential that could nurture regional self-assertion • Opening for mobilization by regional elites • Spurring repressive measures by central or regional authorities • Stimulating sense of shared interested among regional and central elites
Conflict with or self-assertion by regional elites	• If accompanied by *de facto* assertion of autonomous authority • If accompanied by challenges to central authority • If public or other interests are mobilized in support.	• If mainly verbal, as way of gaining additional resources or concessions from the centre • If centre is able to deflate demands	• Nurturing elite split at the central level • *De facto* undermining of central authority • Spurring repressive measures by central

that these are less likely to have a liberalizing impact if they are localized geographically and are focused on particular economic issues such as wage arrears, layoffs, or cutbacks in benefits. When such economic demands become widespread enough to engender a broader movement, they take on a greater liberalizing potential because they are more likely to be politicized, harder to accommodate without more significant concessions, and in themselves reflect an expression of collective power that seeks to hold the political authorities accountable. The same is true if these actions have significant economic repercussions and if they receive extensive national media coverage. The destabilizing potential of popular protest can give regional leaders leverage with the centre and provide them with a bargaining tool to gain concessions, even substantial ones, from the central authorities. On the other hand, public activism can spur more repressive actions, on the part of either regional or federal authorities, and may lead officials at both levels to join forces to resist popular pressures.

Finally, in terms of regional elites, conflict and new demands may arise if the centre is not effectively responding to the crisis, making regional leaders less able to deal with popular discontent; this could trigger self-assertion by regional leaders, as happened to some extent in Russia in the context of the 1998 crisis, as well more generally during the economic downturn of the 1990s. To the extent demands are distributional (thus subject to accommodation through limited concessions by the centre), rather than political, jurisdictional, or bolstered by overt public support, they are less likely to challenge the power vertical and be liberalizing.

Sources for this study are primarily media reports and some (scarce) secondary literature and experts' appraisals to assess trends in federal–regional relations under the influence of the economic crisis. Material was drawn from the interviews with experts, searches of databases of major political newspapers and magazines, such as *Ekspert, Kommersant-Vlast', Kommersant-Dengi, Kommersant-Daily, Nezavisimaia gazeta, Izvestiia, Rossiiskaia gazeta,* and several regional media sources. The methodology included utilization of publishers' own search engines and the Yandex search engine.

Federal government reactions to the crisis

Immediate economic impacts of the crisis in Russia included devaluation of the rouble, a decline in the inflow of money from abroad, a plummeting stock market, reduced state revenues, higher unemployment, reduced work hours, and wage arrears (Aleksashenko, 2009; Osborn and Cullison, 2008). As indicated in Table 8.1, the peak effect occurred in late 2008 and early 2009. From positive growth rates in the previous ten years, Russia moved to a dramatic fall by the first quarter of 2009 (Figures 8.1 and 8.2).

Unemployment rates reached levels not seen since the beginning of Putin's first presidential term. While the crisis did not push Russia back to the disastrous economic situation of the 1990s, the dramatic shift in economic performance may have reminded Russians of the potential

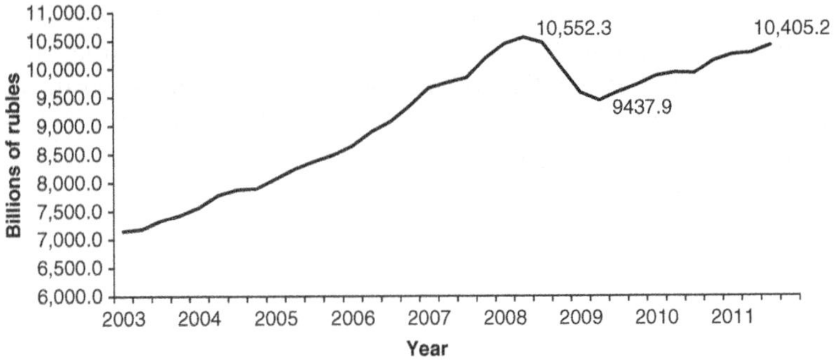

Figure 8.1 Dynamics of GDP growth in Russia quarterly: 2003–11 (in 2008 prices)
Source: Rosstat DataBase, accessed in March, 2012.

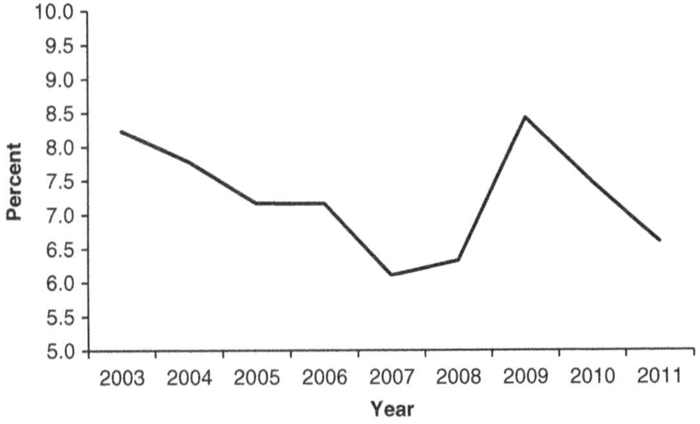

Figure 8.2 Unemployment rate: 2003–11 (in %)
Source: Rosstat DataBase, accessed in 2011.

fragility of the economic recovery that Russia had experienced over the previous ten years.[1] Both small and large businesses sought government support, in the form of bailouts, access to credit, or subsidies.

In reviewing Russian federal responses to the crisis, Deryugin (2009) notes that efforts to maintain social welfare systems through provision of special grants to the regions, support for companies of strategic importance, and tax reductions (which also impacted negatively on regional budgets) lessened some of the impacts. Given the strong public reaction to efforts to 'monetarize' social benefits in 2004–05, the federal government avoided cutbacks in social welfare measures, since such actions could be particularly provocative, as happened in Barnaul when pensioners launched protests over cuts to public transit subsidies (Osborn and Cullison, 2008). The existence of the Reserve Fund and Prosperity Fund (generated in the previous period from high oil and gas revenues) provided a buffer against the worst effects. In particular, the reserve funds were used to cover current budgetary expenses and reinforcement of the banking sector (Konishcheva, 2008; *Lenta.ru*, 2009). Government responses were directed at averting bankruptcies of large financial institutions and increasing cash flow into the banking sector. Particular banks were targeted to receive help, including giants such as Sberbank, Gazprombank, and Vneshtorgbank, along with the provision of credit to other financial institutions to prevent cash flow shortages (Dement'eva and Chaikina, 2008). In particular, the government adopted the Federal Anticrisis Program for 2009 (Russian Federation, 2009).

Economic crisis, elite conflict, and the modernization agenda

The Russian government's federal anti-crisis programme (Russian Federation, 2009) contained not only remedial but also modernizing measures. On 10 September 2009, in a much discussed essay entitled 'Go Russia' President Dmitry Medvedev (2009) laid out a modernization plan for Russia,[2] acknowledging that 'the world crisis has shown that our current state of affairs leaves much to be desired'. Medvedev pointed to Russia's continuing dependence on resource exports, a faltering infrastructure, lack of technological innovation, low economic efficiency, corruption, and a weak civil society. In concrete terms, he proposed what might seem rather modest measures to address these deficiencies, including development of five strategic vectors: 'efficiency of production, transportation, and energy use'; 'nuclear technologies';

modernized 'information technologies'; ground and space 'transmission of... information'; and advanced medical equipment. Medvedev acknowledged that there must be important political corollaries of technological advancement: 'technological progress is inseparable from progress of political systems'. He also suggested that the innovation strategy he outlined would create 'unprecedented opportunities for realizing such fundamental political values as freedom of speech and assembly', as well as providing the potential for controlling corruption. Associated trends would be alteration in power of parliamentary parties, 'civilized political competition', and a culture of compromise and consensus, along with respect for rule of law and continuing reform of the judicial system.

Medvedev's 'Go Russia' essay elicited widespread public debate both inside and outside of Russia. Critics, such as respected Russian economist Vladislav Inozemtsev, considered the generation of 'made in Russia' technological innovations that would be competitively viable as unrealistic; rather, there should be a focus on 'importing technologies, attracting investments, providing a basis for opening foreign manufactures' (Inozemtsev, 2010). Medvedev may have heard the message; in 2010 he reached out to foreign partners (including the European Union and Germany) to push forward the modernization effort, including continued rhetorical support for Russia's World Trade Organization (WTO) accession and limits on protectionist measures (Europa, 2010). Other commentators pointed to limited action to realize Medvedev's modernization plan after its announcement.

The closely intertwined interests of oligarchic business elites with the Moscow political leadership removed a potential impetus for systemic change. It appears that the government resisted the introduction of significant institutional reform in the business sphere. Owners of large corporations, financial and industrial groups are deeply intertwined with political decision makers involving reciprocal, but mainly informal and non-institutionalized, relations. The close links between oligarchic capital and the government reduced the likelihood of effective political pressure for systematic change from these quarters. However, despite conclusion of a 'friendly alliance' with the dominant political party (United Russia) in August 2007 (Rodin, 2007), in October 2008 the Russian Union of Industrialists and Entrepreneurs itself issued criticisms of the federal anti-crisis programme for the lack of transparency in the distribution of federal support and for engaging in dialogue with only a small group of companies (Sergeev, 2008). Measuring the evidence of reform impetus at the central level against the indicators in

Table 8.1, neither policy reform nor elite conflict at the central level took on a momentum adequate to fuel liberalization or the emergence of real political competition. While there were, at the time, rumours of intra-elite political conflict, they tended to focus on the potential for a Putin-Medvedev rift. Medvedev's acquiescence to Putin's announcement of his intention to run for a third term as President signalled an unwillingness on Medvedev's part to trigger an elite split in support of liberal elements rhetorically present in his modernization programme.

Electoral politics and public protest

Over the past several years, various opposition parties and movements (mostly those not represented in the Duma) have launched a range of campaigns against the regime, some involving public demonstrations, most not approved by the authorities, and ending in clashes between activists and law-enforcement officials. Survey data from the Public Opinion Foundation indicate that at the outset of the crisis there was general public scepticism or indifference to these sorts of protests and actions (Fond, 2007). For example, in 2007 two-thirds of Russians had never heard of the 'Marches of Discordants', the best organized civil actions of political protest. Only 9 per cent of respondents approved, 7 per cent disapproved, and 11 per cent of respondents said that they were indifferent to the protests. Most respondents were indifferent or negatively disposed to leaders of the movements as well (e.g., Gary Kasparov, Boris Nemtsov, Mikhail Kasyanov).

Organized protest movements did, however, garner greater public attention and participation in 2009 and 2010 than earlier. New anti-government movements, such as 'Strategy-31' emerged in 2009 (under the leadership of Eduard Limonov and Lyudmila Alekseeva); however, these protests had minimal impact and were largely limited to Moscow and St. Petersburg. More traditional civil actions took place under the aegis of the Communist Party of the Russian Federation (CPRF). On 31 January 2009 an all-Russia protest action against government anti-crisis policies took place in almost all regions (Schwirtz and Levy, 2009).

Further protests across the country were directed at specific policies of the government. Examples included actions against new import rules of used cars and spare parts from abroad, tax rates on transport and gasoline, reduced subsidies for public transport, and, in Moscow, poor traffic management and differential enforcement of traffic rules. Protest actions sometimes involved blocking public roads and approaches to airports (Levy, 2008). A new ecological cause emerged almost simultaneously with the crisis. Public protests against the building of a new highway between Moscow and St. Petersburg that cuts through a forest in the town of Khimki, near Moscow, resulted in violent collisions with law-enforcement forces. Later, this ecological movement took on political overtones involving radical political demands, such as Putin's resignation. This example indicates that protests emerging during this time period were not linked exclusively to the economic crisis, but were bolstered by other undercurrents of discontent.

Other public protests were elicited more directly by the effects of the economic crisis. A particularly important protest occurred in Pikalyovo (Leningrad oblast), discussed below. Overall, in 2009 over 200 mass protest actions were inspired in one way or another by the economic crisis. Demands included: payments of wage arrears, reinstatement of operational activity of factories, and improved work conditions. Among the most prominent public actions were protests and strikes by workers of Ivanovo textile mills (February 2009), of miners in Rostov oblast (April 2009), a hunger strike of workers of the Severomuysky tunnel (June 2009), and an all-Russia 'partial' strike of air-traffic controllers (April 2010). Political issues (such as demands for the resignation of regional or federal leaders) were rarely mentioned (an exception was the demands in Kaliningrad oblast for the removal of the Moscow-appointed governor Georgii Boos and for a return of gubernatorial elections).

Data from surveys conducted by the Public Opinion Foundation indicate that from March to May 2009 between 18 and 23 per cent of the workforce was affected by delays in wage payments; 16–23 per cent suffered pay cuts and 7–11 per cent suffered cutbacks in work hours (Fond, 2009a, p. 23). In an October 2010 survey, 35 per cent of respondents indicated that the 2008 crisis had affected their lives or those close to them in a significant way; 23 per cent responded that they still had not been able to overcome the impact (Fond, 2010, pp. 15–6). In short, the effects of the crisis were felt by Russian citizens to be reasonably widespread and long-lasting, and more so in large cities and extractive and industrial sectors.

These effects may have fed a protest mood in the country. According to a survey carried out in late March/early April 2009, 42 per cent of respondents who identified themselves as 'workers' (*rabochie*) indicated that they would consider participating in collective protest actions at the enterprise level. This sentiment was highest in the extractive and metallurgical sectors and in larger enterprises (Klimova, 2009, pp. 37–8). Among the population at large, the 'protest mood' (i.e., the per cent of respondents indicating that they would personally consider the possibility of participating in some kind of protest action) actually began to rise in December 2009, reaching a high of 45 per cent in February 2011 (Fond, 2011c, p. 18; Fond, 2009c, pp. 23–7). A June 2009 survey of the general population put economic issues among top motivations for potential protest (e.g., low pay, inflation, poor communal services), alongside general dissatisfaction with the authorities and corruption (Fond, 2009c). In October/November 2009 inflation, declining incomes and unemployment were top concerns (Fond, 2009d, p. 21). Public opinion assessments of the economic situation in the country were most negative in March 2009, gradually improved, and then took another negative turn in early 2011 (Fond, 2011a, p. 19). Despite these public concerns, until late 2011, popular protests showed little likelihood of spurring the type of systemic conflict that could contribute to real political change. In the immediate context of the economic crisis, the fact that protests did not become more widespread may have been, in part, due to pre-emptive actions by both the federal government and governors. However, it seems likely that economic worries, combined with a perception that the authorities were not using their power responsibly, served as backdrop to the public protests of late 2011 following the Duma elections.

In contrast to the predominance of economic worries in 2009, popular assessments of reasons for the much larger mass protests of December 2011 highlight political factors such as election fraud (Fond, 2011b, pp. 19–20). The economic crisis was likely a general contextual factor contributing to the rising dissatisfaction with United Russia and the political establishment. We can thus posit a likely *indirect* impact of the economic crisis on civil society activism. Protest moved from being specific and localized, with local responses in the direct crisis period, to involving a general critique of political relations, widely covered by the media in late 2011.

Electoral impacts

Regional electoral contests in 2009 and 2010 did not show evidence of a fundamental change in political relationships, although the share of the vote received by the CPRF did increase marginally, from an average of 13.6 per cent, in the two sets of regional elections in 2008 to 18.0 per cent in 2010. The latter was edging towards the figure reported for the party (19.2 per cent) in the 2011 Duma elections. Accordingly the share of the vote received by United Russia declined to an average of 53.5 per cent in 2010 from 68.9 per cent in the 2008 election.[3]

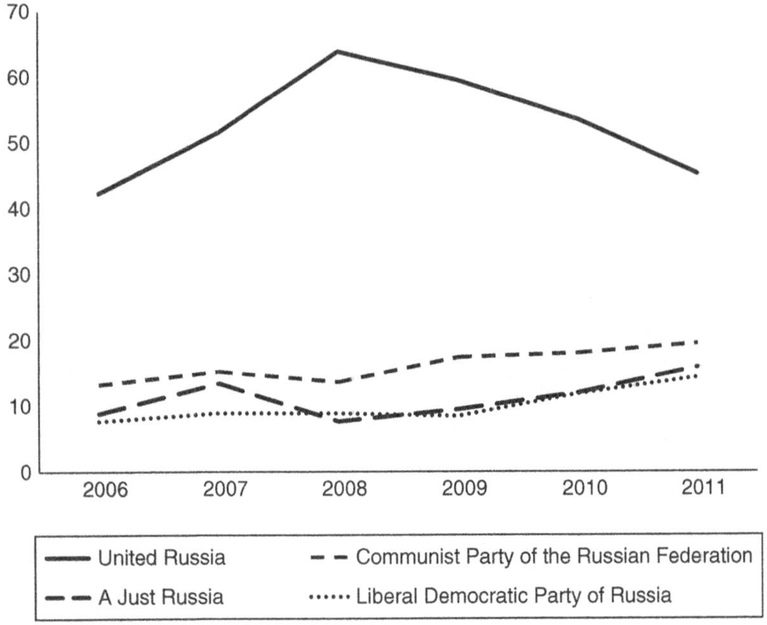

Figure 8.3 Aggregated results of four major Russian political parties during the regional elections

While overall there was no effective challenge to the dominant party, the trend line suggests a moderate trajectory of decline in support for United Russia from the beginning of the economic crisis (see Figure 8.3). Given the controlled nature of the electoral processes, these changes may be a quite significant indicator of bubbling popular discontent. Overall, the elections reasserted the overriding ability of United Russia to assure its continued electoral dominance and the inability of any of the opposing parties to launch a credible challenge. Nonetheless, the three other political parties represented in the Duma issued charges of widespread electoral fraud (gazeta.ru, 2009). On 14 October 2009 deputies of the CPRF, the Just Russia party and the Liberal Democratic Party abandoned a session of the State Duma as a sign of protest against the results of regional elections that took place in several regions of the federation and ended up with victory of the United Russia party. Leaders of these three parliamentary parties accused the leading party of infringement of electoral procedures and demanded that the president intervene (*Vesti*, 2009), and, in particular, asked that the election results be nullified. However after consultations with the president, deputies of all three parties resumed their work and withdrew these demands.

Only the CPRF has taken an active role in the most important mass protest actions. The Just Russia party has concentrated on the critique of anti-crisis conceptions of both the United Russia party and the CPRF. It launched a few protest campaigns in several regions of Russian Federation. The major slogans of those events were critiques of some governmental policies (such as the reform of housing and communal services) and of the United Russia party, as well as demands to counteract corruption. Such actions involved only a few activists and could not be considered as politically significant. Actions of the Liberal-Democratic Party were similar to those of 'A Just Russia' in terms of scope and agenda.

There is little indication that the public discontent that was sporadically evident in the streets in response to economic hardship was used by opposition parties as an effective tool of electoral mobilization. From 2008 to 2010 there was also little uncertainty at the regional level as to who was in charge, particularly as Medvedev held control over the gubernatorial reappointment process. According to Russian expert Rostislav Turovskii (interview, 2010), no opposition party constituted a real political alternative to the existing political elite. Anti-crisis measures allowed the regime to avoid significant and widespread mass protest actions and 'the society was attuned to the strategy of individual survival' (Turovskii interview, 2010). Political parties seemed unable to change this.

Popular protests and regional power

The economic crisis did, according to public opinion surveys, seem to adversely affect the reputation of governors in Russia's regions (Fond, 2009b, pp. 15–24), as the public expects governors to provide solutions to immediate economic problems; likewise, the Kremlin also placed the responsibility on governors to resolve economic problems in their own regions. The Pikalyovo crisis, mentioned above, posed the issue of gubernatorial responsibility in sharp form and provided a lesson for regional leaders across the country. Pikalyovo is a district town in Leningrad oblast where, in the Spring of 2009, civil unrest was directed at the regional government when a rupture of technological and supply links between the town's three interconnected factories resulted in massive dismissals of workers, with spin-off effects leading to a cut in the hot water supply. Public protests and a deterioration in the situation forced

Prime Minister Putin to personally intervene to pressure business leaders to sign agreements on a continuation of the supply of raw materials. The prime minister placed the blame on local officials for inadequate and unprofessional behaviour.

The crisis was successfully defused and did not trigger more widespread popular outpourings of discontent. The Kremlin followed a pragmatic approach, allowing the governor to correct the situation, rather than being 'punished' (DeBardeleben and Zherebtsov, 2010). Through Pikalyovo, the Kremlin leadership sent a clear message that central intervention to rescue local officials should not become the norm. During a teleconference with governors in June 2009, Medvedev reportedly demanded that governors solve such problems themselves. The Kremlin's pressure on governors was presumably driven by apprehension over a potential spread of mass disorders (the so-called Pikalyovo effect) (Skorokhodova, 2009).[4] The Pikalyovo example seems to have spurred governors to try and find solutions in the early stages of conflict. Thus, the governor of Kemerovo oblast, Aman Tuleev, took control of coal from the mines, in order to sell it to generate necessary revenue to pay delayed wage arrears (*Chestnoe slovo*, 2009). Other examples of regional leaders resolving local economic problems are also reported in Svetlogorsk (Primorskii krai) (Skorokhodova, 2009; Dvoinova, 2009), Irkutsk (Aliev, 2009), and Chelyabinsk (Moiseev, 2009). How did the governors achieve success in these situations? The dynamics are not clear, but likely they involved the use of so-called 'administrative resources', such as selective law enforcement (or threats thereof) (Ledeneva, 2006, pp. 48–52) or promises of future favours. In some regions, however, governors weren't able to avoid mass protests. In more complex cases, such as the troubled industrial giant AvtoVAZ (Samara oblast), direct federal intervention was required, as the size and importance of the economic interests involved are of national significance (*Vzgliad*, 2009). These diverse examples suggest that most instances of social protest were handled locally and were not linked to broader critiques of power relations.

The Kremlin strategy appeared to be to appeal to governors as part of an 'integrated executive structure'. Underlying this appeal is the President's critical resource – the power of appointment of governors – which so far seems to have constrained governors from using popular unrest as a resource to increase their autonomy. Compared to Putin's earlier approach, Medvedev took a more assertive policy of replacing governors, installing what DeBardeleben and Zherebstov (2010) refer to as a managerial patronage system, which combines requirements of managerial ability with political loyalty. In this way, Medvedev made clear that there was a stick in addition to a carrot. In a meeting with the leaders of the United Russia party in April 2009, Putin also criticized some unnamed governors, noting that some regions had experienced deterioration: 'not everywhere have governors taken an active role in the work of regional anti-crisis committees' (Preobrazhenskii, 2009). In approving a set of formal criteria to assess the effectiveness of gubernatorial governance, the Kremlin also implied that tighter evaluation of performance might be on the agenda. Some indications are that unemployment levels may be one such criterion, along with dozens of others (Khomiakov, 2009). The avoidance of overt expressions of social unrest might possibly be another. Given the dependence of governors on the centre, public protests seem to have stimulated a sense of shared interests between regional and central elites, rather than eliciting conflict.

Just as the federal centre appears to have placed responsibility on the governors for dealing with the economic crisis (Khomiakov, 2009) and evaluating their performance accordingly, some governors attempted to shift responsibility away from themselves either back to federal authorities or down to the municipal level (Starovoitov, 2009). Some clear tensions emerged between the federal centre and regions regarding the financing of regional budgets (see Kompalla and Nestmann, 2009, p. 14). One report indicates that as regions developed their budgets for 2009, most faced deficits of 10–12 per cent and were uncertain about levels of projected income (Bilevskaia, 2008). During a meeting between vice premier Viktor Zubkov and governors of the Northwest Federal Okrug in St. Petersburg in March 2009, the governors raised objections to certain aspects of federal policy on the grounds that anti-crisis funds were misdirected and not reaching their regions. Reportedly even Kremlin loyalist, Kaliningrad Governor Georgii Boos, raised strong objections that his region had been omitted in the distribution of funds from the centre to help support the auto industry; other governors criticized the process of distributing anti-crisis help as characterized by 'lobbyism' (Andrianov and Sapozhinikov, 2009).

The case of Governor Boos is of particular interest. He was one of the several 'governor-managers' parachuted by the Kremlin into particularly complicated or important regions (in this case the exclave of Kaliningrad oblast). Boos' dismissal by the Kremlin occurred in September 2010, in the face of many mass protest actions in the region. As noted above, Kaliningrad oblast was one of the few Russian regions where the current economic crisis took the shape of massive social protests, which included demands for resignation of the governor. Despite Boos' efforts to diminish negative effects of the mass protests, he proved unable to prevent the creation of the broad opposition coalition, 'Our Kaliningrad', supported by opposition political parties (CPRF, A Just Russia, and The Russian Patriots) (Riabushev, 2010). The resignation of Georgii Boos indicates the limits of presidential tolerance for faltering efforts of governors to deal with the crisis and to control popular discontent. Despite the governor's efforts to shift blame to the federal level, he seemed reluctant to mobilize popular discontent to increase the autonomy of the region.

Alexei Titkov (2009) argues that the growth of demands from regions to the federal centre will inevitably increase, creating a possibility that this could produce tensions among federal leaders. However, as long as the federal centre maintains a united position, regional leaders will likely continue to comply in order to receive benefits that come with loyalty, despite some verbal criticism directed at particular federal departments. Other commentators, for example Mikhail Rogozhnikov (2009), see the crisis as having the potential to further the development of federative relations in Russia. He argues that Medvedev's demand to the regions to resolve urgent problems without assistance was 'the first evidence of the rise of federalism' in Russia. In the face of possibly increasing conflict between levels of government, one commentator raised the possibility that this could even lead to separatism, if not handled properly by the centre (Minchenko, 2008).

Despite such speculations by Russian political commentators, in practice, however, thus far the positions taken by regional leaders do not seem to suggest a real impetus for change. Federal authority has not been overtly challenged, and, if anything, governors seem to have resisted an expansion of their jurisdiction out of fear that resources would be inadequate to fulfill the responsibilities given to them. Governors have neither attempted to mobilize the public nor have they created alliances that would undermine the legitimacy of federal efforts. In May 2012, in response to protests following the 2011–12 federal elections, a law reinstating a modified form of gubernatorial elections was passed; this may throw a new element into this equation.

Conclusion

There is only minimal evidence that the financial/economic crisis of 2008–09 put in place dynamics contributing either to political liberalization or a challenge to Russia's 'power vertical', as indicated in Table 8.2. To the extent that the crisis did contribute to public activation or reform

Table 8.2 Indicators of liberalizing dynamics in Russia, 2008–11

Type of indicator	Evidence of liberalizing potential of the indicator	Evidence of minimal liberalizing potential of the indicator	Implications for other dynamics
Elite conflict at the federal level	• Somewhat better performance of opposition in regional and 2011 Duma elections	• Personal power of Putin a focus of discussion • Elite does not publicly display essential divisions	• Leads to proposal to reinstate gubernatorial elections • Unclear whether this will provide an opening for self-assertion by regional elites
Civil society activism – public protests or actions	• Broad public critique of power relations follows Duma elections • Protests gain wide media coverage	• Local economic issues arise in the immediate crisis context • These are placated by local concessions • Link of protests to the economic crisis is inconsistent or unclear	• Public activism concentrated in larger cities • Regional elites apparently not mobilized • Repressive measures are generally non-violent
Conflict with or self-assertion by regional elites		• Conflict with regional elites is primarily over resources • Demands are generally deflated • Limited demands for expanded regional authority	• Regional demands do not spur central elite conflict or repressive measures by the centre

tendencies, the impact was mild and in some cases indirect. The Russian government responded to the crisis with a modest programme of economic modernization that involved neither an effective path to the diversification of Russia's resource-dependent economy nor a significant political dimension.[5] Public protests elicited by the crisis were sporadic and concessions generally assuaged public discontent and limited any contagion effect. The fact that the crisis had external origins may have reinforced public perceptions that Russia's leaders could only cope with the cards dealt to them by 'the West', generating a greater willingness to accept 'satisficing' concessions. While the crisis placed new demands on governors, regional dependence on the federal centre constrained their ability and will to institute meaningful reforms or demand increased political autonomy from the centre.

Only in regional electoral contests of 2009 and 2010 was there some evidence of marginal inroads into United Russia support, which, in retrospect, might be seen as a precursor of its further decline in the 2011 Duma election. Following Putin's announcement in October 2011 that he would run for president in 2012, the primary focus of popular demands was not, however, economic, but rather directed at corruption, lack of accountability, election fraud, and the leaders' arrogance in wielding of public power. While the role of economic factors in this trajectory was not the primary issue spurring public activism, it may have been supportive by creating a backdrop of public dissatisfaction with results that politicians were delivering.

The short duration of the acute phase of the crisis and the presence of a reserve fund to minimize immediate social impacts make this case only a limited test of the hypothesis that crisis could, under some circumstances, spur political liberalization. For now, political optimists may need to seek other stimuli for hope of a reversal of Russia's authoritarian trajectory. One such impetus might be a deeper and longer drop in energy prices, which could be a spin-off of a new recession in Europe; the events of late 2011, however, suggest that the collective activation of political cynicism through social media may be a more powerful motor. This suggests that politics, rather than economic factors, may be more important triggers for change.

Notes

1. For the economic impact of the crisis in Russia, see Shadrina and Vinhas de Souza (2010).

2. For the modernization plan and debate, and link to the economic crisis, see Pynnöniemi (2010).
3. Because only a portion of regions voted on regional legislatures in any given year, the year-to-year change is not a reliable indicator of a political trajectory but is suggestive.
4. Some protests did erupt, subsequent to Pikalyova, feeding this apprehension (see Skorokhodova (2009)).
5. Cooper, Bacon, and Monaghan (2009, p. 5) depict the political response as one of 'muddling through'.

Bibliography

Aleksashenko, S. (2009) 'Crisis 2008: Time to Make a Diagnosis', *Problems of Economic Transition* 51(9), 33–50, translated from *Voprosy ekonomiki* (November 2008), 33–50.

Aliev, A. (2009, 15 June) 'Tsellulozno-bumazhnoe reshenie', *Ekspert*, http://www.expert.ru/articles/2009/06/15/shuvalov-irkutsk-soveshanie/, accessed on 1 January 2012.

Anderson, G. (2009) 'Central Governments Lead Charge Against Financial Meltdowns', *Federations*, September/October, http://www.forumfed.org/en/products/magazine/vol8_num2/president.php, accessed on 1 April 2012.

Andrianov, K. and O. Sapozhkov (2009, 30 March) 'V otnosheniiakh gubernatorov i pravitel'stva nastupil krizis', *Kommersant-Daily* 55 (4110), http://www.kommersant.ru/Doc-rss/1146421, accessed on 1 December 2012.

Bilevskaia, E. (2008, 27 November) 'Dlia gubernatorov prigotovili test', *Nezavisimaia gazeta*, http://www.ng.ru/politics/2008-11-27/1_gubernator.html, accessed 1 January 2012.

Chestnoe slovo (2009, 14 June) 'Arest kak sposob zarplaty', http://www.chslovo.com/index.php?idst_p=1092, accessed on 1 January 2012.

Cooper, J., E. Bacon and A. Monaghan (2009) *'Muddling Down': The Economic Crisis in Russia and Its Political Impact* (NATO Research Report, September) (Rome: Research Division, NATO Defense College).

DeBardeleben, J. and M. Zherebtsov (2010) 'The Transition to Managerial Patronage in Russia's Regions' in V. Gel'man and C. Ross (eds), *The Politics of Sub-National Authoritarianism in Russia* (Aldershot: Ashgate), 85–105.

Dement'eva, S. and Iu. Chaikina (2008, 22 September) 'Neraspredelennye obeshchaniia', *Kommersant* 170 (3987), http://www.kommersant.ru/doc.aspx?DocsID=1029749, accessed on 1 January 2012.

Deryugin, A. (2009) 'Hit Late by the Slump – Russia Responds', *Federations*, September/October, 33–34.

Dvoinova, T. (2009) 'Volframovyi dolzhnik', *Nezavisimaya gazeta*, http://www.ng.ru/regions/2009-06-18/2_wolfram.html, accessed on 1 January 2012.

Europa (2010) *EU and Russia launch new Partnership for Modernization*, press release RAPID, Brussels, 1 June, http://europa.eu/rapid/pressReleasesAction.do?reference=IP/10/649, accessed on 1 January 2012.

Fond Obshchestvennoe Mnenie (Fond) (2007) 'Marshi nesoglasnykh', (*Marches of discordants*), 26 April, http://bd.fom.ru/report/map/d071721, accessed on 1 January 2012.

Fond Obshchestvennoe Mnenie (Fond) (2009a) 'Rabotaiushchie rossiiane v situatsii krizisa: vozdeistvie krizisa na pabotaiushchikh', *Dominanty* 20, 21 May, http://bd.fom.ru/pdf/d20_rabross.pdf, accessed on 1 January 2012.
Fond Obshchestvennoe Mnenie (Fond) (2009b) 'Reputatsiia gubernatorov v period ekonomicheskogo krizisa', *Dominanty* 20, 21 May, http://bd.fom.ru/pdf/d20_gub.pdf, accessed on 1 April 2012.
Fond Obshchestvennoe Mnenie (Fond) (2009c) 'Potestnye nastroeniia: tipologicheskie gruppy: doli v naselenii Rossii', *Dominanty* 27, 9 July, http://bd.fom.ru/pdf/d27protest.pdf, accessed on 1 April 2012.
Fond Obshchestvennoe Mnenie (Fond) (2009d) 'Sostoianie rossiiskoi ekonomiki: otsenki i prognozy', *Dominanty* 44, 5 November, http://bd.fom.ru/pdf/d44ekon.pdf, accessed on 1 January 2012.
Fond Obshchestvennoe Mnenie (Fond) (2010) 'Ekonomicheskii krizis 2008 goda i ego posledstviia', *Dominanty* 39, 10 October, http://bd.fom.ru/pdf/d39ekiep10.pdf, accessed on 1 January 2012.
Fond Obshchestvennoe Mnenie (Fond) (2011a) 'Sostoianie rossiiskoi ekonomiki', *Dominanty* 15, 14 April, http://bd.fom.ru/pdf/d15sre11.pdf, accessed on 1 January 2012.
Fond Obshchestvennoe Mnenie (Fond) (2011b) 'Miting na Bolotnoi ploshchadi', *Dominanty* 51, 22 December, http://bd.fom.ru/pdf/d51mnbp11.pdf, accessed on 1 January 2012.
Fond Obshchestvennoe Mnenie (Fond) (2011c) 'Uroven' protestnykh nastorenii,' *Dominanty* 52, 29 December, http://bd.fom.ru/pdf/d52ypn11.pdf, accessed on 1 January 2012.
gazeta.ru (2009, 14 October) 'KPRF, LDPR i "esery" pokinuli zasedanie Gosdumy', http://www.gazeta.ru/news/lastnews/2009/10/14/n_1413775.shtml, accessed on 1 January 2012.
Government of the Russian Federation (2009), 'Programma antikrizisnykh mer Pravitel'stva Rossiiskoi Federatsii na 2009 god', 20 March, http://www.rg.ru/2009/03/20/programma-antikrisis-dok.html, accessed on 4 October 2012).
Haggard, S. and R. Kaufman (1997) 'The Political Economy of Democratic Transitions', *Comparative Politics* 29(3), 263–83.
Hanson, P. (2007) 'The Russian Economic Puzzle: Going Forwards, Backwards or Sideways?' *International Affairs* 83(5), 869–89.
Inozemtsev, V. (2010) 'In Economic Terms, for Russia – 2010 Will Be a Lost Year', 2 February, interview by G. Ionita, http://gabrielaionita.wordpress.com/2010/02/02/vladislav-inozemtsev-%E2%80%9Din-economic-terms-for-russia-2010-will-be-a-lost-year%E2%80%9D/, accessed on 1 January 2012.
Khomiakov, V. (2009) 'Valerii Khomiakov: gubernatorov pytaiutsia sdelat' krainimi', interview by V. Popov, 5 May, http://club-rf.ru/expert/8385/, accessed on 1 January 2012.
Klimova, S. (2009) 'Ekonomicheskii krizis i rossiiskie rabochie', *Dominanty* (Fond Obshchestvennoe mnenie) 21, 2 May, http://bd.fom.ru/pdf/d21ek_kr.pdf, accessed on 1 January.
Kompalla, P. and T. Nestmann (2009) 'Die russischen Regionen: Moskau ist nicht alles', (Aktuelle Themen 465, 10 November) (Frankfurt am Main: Deutsche Bank Research).
Konishcheva T. (2008, 1 October) 'Banki deneg ne berut', *Rossiiskaia gazeta* 4762, http://www.rg.ru/2008/10/01/banki.html, accessed on 1 January 2012.

Ledeneva, A. (2006) *How Russia Really Works: The Informal Practices That Shaped Post-Soviet Politics and Business* (Ithaca and London: Cornell University Press).

Lenta.ru (2009, 25 September) 'Minfin uvelichil raskhody Rezervnogo fonda na pokrytie defitsita biudzheta', http://lenta.ru/news/2009/09/25/deficit/, accessed on 1 January 2012.

Levy, C. (2008, 21 December) 'Protests Erupt in Russia over Raising Car Tariffs', *New York Times*, http://www.nytimes.com/2008/12/22/world/europe/22russia.html, accessed on 1 January 2012.

Liasko, A. (1999) 'The Economic Crisis and Its Consequences for the Budgetary System of Russian Regions', *Problems of Economic Transition* 42(7), 6–22, translated from *Voprosy economiki* 3, 21–32

Luong, P. and E. Weinthal (2004) 'Contra Coercion: Russian Tax Reform, Exogenous Shocks, and Negotiated Institutional Change', *American Political Science Review* 98(1), 139–70.

Medvedev, D. (2009, 10 September) 'Rossiia vpered', *Gazeta.ru*, http://www.kremlin.ru/news/5413, accessed on 1 January 2012.

Minchenko, E. (2008, 2 December) 'Ne dopustit' separatizma', *Nezavisimaia gazeta*, http://www.ng.ru/ng_politics/2008-12-02/9_separatism.html, accessed on 1 January 2012.

Moiseev, D. (2009, 16 June) 'Pikalevskii sindrom na Iuzhnom Urale', *Nezavisimaia gazeta*, http://www.ng.ru/regions/2009-06-16/1_syndrome.html?mthree=4, accessed on 1 January 2012.

Osborn, A. and A. Cullison (2008, 19 December) 'Oil's Crash Stirs Unrest in Russia as Slump Hits Home', *Wall Street Journal*.

Petrov, R. and N. Shklyar (1999) 'Russian Regions after the Crisis: Coping with Economic Troubles Governors Reap the Benefits', *Demokratizatsiya* 7(4), 527–43.

Preobrazhenskii, I. (2009) 'Gubernatory otvetiat za krizis', *Rosbalt Information Agency*, 4 March, http://www.rosbalt.ru/2009/04/03/631244.html, accessed on 1 January 2012.

Pynnöniemi, K. (2010) *Russia's Modernization Reloaded: Political Constraints in Economic Development* (Briefing Paper 67, 16 November) (Helsinki: The Finnish Institute for International Affairs).

Riabushev, A. (2010, 3 April) 'Vsem mirom protiv "Edinoi Rossii"', *Nezavisimaia gazeta*, http://www.ng.ru/politics/2010-03-04/2_meetings.html?insidedoc, accessed on 1 January 2012.

Rodin, I. (2007, 6 August) 'Neponiatnyi al'ians', *Nezavisimaia gazeta*, http://www.ng.ru/politics/2007-06-08/1_aliance.html, accessed on 1 January 2012.

Rogozhnikov, M. (2009, 11 June) 'Federalizatsiia ponevole', *Ekspert* 24 (662), http://www.expert.ru/printissues/expert/2009/24/federalizaciya_ponevole/, accessed on 1 January 2012.

Russian Federation, Government of (2009) 'Programma anticrizisnykh mer Pravitel'stva Rossiiskoi Federatsiia na 2009 god', *Rossiiskaia gazeta*, http://www.rg.ru/2009/03/20/programma-antikrisis-dok.html, accessed on 1 January 2012.

Schwirtz, M. and C. Levy (2009, 31 January) 'As Economy Sinks, Russian Protest', *New York Times*, http://www.nytimes.com/2009/02/01/world/europe/01russia.html, accessed 1 January 2012.

Sergeev, M. (2008, 10 October) 'Biznes ne dovolen pravitelstvom', *Nezavisimaia gazeta*, http://www.ng.ru/economics/2008-10-10/4_rspp.html, accessed on 1 January 2012.

Shadrina, E. and L. Vinhas de Souza (2010) 'Russia and the "Great Recession"', *International Affairs* (Moscow) 45(2), 113–29.

Skorokhodova, A. (2009, 19 June) ' "Ekho Pikayovo" pokatilos po strane', 19 June, *Moi raion onlain*, http://www.mr7.ru/articles/14348/, accessed on 1 January 2012.

Starovoitov, S. (2009, 4 May) 'Krizis – eto EGE dlia gubernatorov', *Zhurnal rukovodetelia*, http://www.journal-volgograd.ru/person.html?nid=14, accessed on 12 January 2012.

Titkov, A. (2009) 'Lapochki i umnichki', interview by Artur Piatnitskii, *Nezavisimaia gazeta*, 27 January, http://www.ng.ru/scenario/2009-01-27/10_umnichki.html, accessed on 1 January 2012.

Turovskii, R. (2010), Interview by author (MZ), Moscow, 23 December.

Vesti (2009, October 14) 'Demarsh oppozitsii v Gosdume', http://www.vesti.ru/doc.html?id=320460, accessed on 1 January 2012.

Vzgliad: Delovaia gazeta (2009, 30 October) 'Putin: vlasti vydeliaiut na sotsob"ekty AvtoVAZa 1 milliard rublei', http://www.vz.ru/news/2009/10/30/343701.print.html, accessed on 1 January 2012.

9

Economic Relations between the European Union and Russia: Before and after the Crisis

Vladislav Inozemtsev and Ekaterina Kuznetsova

Although the economic and financial crisis has profoundly affected every European country, national responses to the new challenge of establishing a more effective regulatory regime and resuming economic growth highlighted a sharp divide in economic approaches between two major players on the European continent – the European Union (EU) and the Russian Federation. These differences could not help, but influence bilateral economic relations. Which direction is economic cooperation between the two partners drifting after the crisis? This chapter examines how efforts to adjust economic structures in both Europe and Russia are likely to influence trade, investment and financial services, and perspectives for the EU–Russian strategic partnership.

Pre-crisis situation

The EU and Russia are the two largest European economies, complementary to one another and destined for close cooperation. In 2008, when the financial crisis was just beginning, bilateral trade between Russia and the EU peaked at US$382.94 billion, making the EU Russia's largest trading partner (accounting for 56.7 per cent of Russia's exports and 43.7 per cent of its imports) (Federal Customs Service, 2009); Russia was the third-largest (6 per cent of exports and 9.6 per cent of imports) trading partner of united Europe. Even more significant was the share of European foreign direct investment (FDI) in the Russian economy: by the end of 2008 around 73.4 per cent of FDI accumulated by the Russian Federation was of European origin, and EU banks and financial institutions provided Russian financial and non-financial corporations with more than €360 billion in loans (Ministry for Economic Development, 2010). Due to these close ties between European economies and the Russian economy, the financial crisis that broke out in 2008 in the United States, and then spread to Europe, did not leave Russia untouched (although the Russian economy itself exhibited many preconditions for it to occur sooner or later as well).

The vulnerability of Russia to the crisis is primarily due to the nature of the Russian and EU economies. Russia and the EU exemplify two opposite economic strategies: while Russia is steadily securing its role as a natural resources supplier, the EU is moving along the path of post-industrialism. Russia today supplies Europe with raw materials and the products of their primary processing. Oil, gasoline, gasoil, and natural gas alone in 2010 accounted for 74.6 per cent of Russia's exports to the EU. Europe's exports to Russia mostly represent a highly competitive industrial sector and include automobiles, industrial equipment, and consumer goods (86.5 per cent of Russia's imports from EU countries) (Eurostat, 2011). Therefore, the trading relationship between Russia and the EU can be labelled quasi-colonial. One must consider this peculiarity when assessing the consequences of the 2008–09 economic crisis for the future patterns of economic and political cooperation between Russia and the EU.

Out of the wide spectrum of bilateral relations, Russian–European economic ties, established in the 1990s and carefully nurtured by the Kremlin ever since, are traditionally considered in Russia as the basis for deeper cooperation or partnership. In the years prior to the 2008–09 recession, Russia confirmed its status of main energy supplier to Europe. In 2007, Russian oil and gas controlled by large state-owned companies covered 26.2 and 23.4 per cent of EU needs, respectively (*Energy Dialogue*, 2009, pp. 4–5). This energy linkage contributed to the introduction of pragmatic thinking into EU–Russia relations. As a result, real cooperation was primarily built around a handful of giant infrastructure projects in the sphere of energy, notably the Nord Stream gas pipeline, the development of the Sakhalin off-shore gas fields, and the development of a consortium for the exploration of the Shtokman gas deposit. This solid energy nexus nevertheless helped to create a favourable environment for cooperation in the 'real economy', a trend manifested in several ways. Retail, automotive, food processing, insurance companies, and banks from Europe flooded Russia's non-saturated market and obtained a considerable share of it; Russian industrial companies extensively borrowed from European financial institutions, and the volume of bilateral trade was constantly growing. The largest part of Europe's

FDI in Russia was channelled into four sectors – oil extraction, banking and finance, retail trade, and production of food and consumer goods. (One notable exception is the automotive industry; factories built by European automakers manufactured 1.04 out of 1.71 million passenger cars assembled in Russia in 2011, making up 60.8 per cent of all domestic output, Rambler News Service, 2012.) The EU has increasingly regarded Russia as an energy supplier, a broad market for European goods, and a country where European companies are able to produce goods aimed at local consumers.

Crisis realities

Given the above patterns, the damage done to Russia–EU bilateral economic relations during the economic crisis has proven to be selective, with three sectors in particular suffering the most severely: the gas market, investments, and trade relations.

The economic crisis has challenged the position of the main Russian exporting company, Gazprom, in the European market. Given that virtually all Russian gas (96.4 per cent in 2009) is exported through the pipeline system, Gazprom is committed to long-term contracts and fixed prices, which European customers view as unfair. (In the first half of 2010 average prices of Gazprom supplies to EU countries stood at US$289 per thousand cubic metres of gas, while the average spot prices in the United Kingdom during the same period were as low as US$208 per thousand cubic metres, and in the US Henry Hub spot prices in July hit US$156 [BP, 2011, p. 27].) However, Gazprom only has a limited capacity to cut prices, since its costs have grown rapidly due to inefficient management, the servicing of the company's US$72 billion debt to foreign banks, and the maintenance of a huge mass of non-core assets. As a result, in 2009 Gazprom sales to the EU decreased by 11.9 per cent, and for 2007–09 its share on the European gas market declined from 23.8 to 18.9 per cent (seized predominantly by liquefied natural gas [LNG] supplied by Qatar and pipeline gas supplies from StatoilHydro of Norway) (Inozemtsev, 2010, p. 124). By 2010, Gazprom managed to recover part of these losses in the European market, mostly due to the upsurge in oil prices related to the worldwide economic recovery, the domino effect of regime changes in Northern Africa, and instability in the Middle East. The ongoing economic recovery, combined with the possibility of delivery cuts by other important suppliers (Libya, Algeria, Bahrain), revived the interest of European gas and oil companies in the big resource extracting projects of Russian state-owned companies.

In 2011, BP approved the cross exchange of shares with the Russian national oil company Rosneft with a view to becoming a partner in the Rosneft Arctic projects. However, the deal was blocked by the Russian shareholders of TNK-BP, the joint venture of BP and the Russian consortium AAR, and was finally abandoned in Summer 2011. At the same time, France's oil and gas group, Total, entered the Russian gas market through the acquisition of a 12.5 per cent stake in the Novatek gas company (a company that seven years earlier was still owned by its founders and was considered a 'strategic asset' not eligible for a sell-off to foreigners, but was later exempted from the list after a considerable stake was acquired by offshore firms controlled by Gennady Timchenko, the owner of the oil-trading company Gunvor and a close friend of Prime Minister Vladimir Putin).

Investments in Russia were made in the hope of further increases in domestic prices, which were much higher than anywhere in the world for non-ferrous metals, steel, aluminium, construction materials, and many consumer goods, allowing entrepreneurs high-profit margins. Therefore, the credit bubble burst hit hard and almost completely dried up new investment in the first half of 2009, which led to a serious decrease in bilateral trade, since the lion's share of EU exports to Russia consisted of machinery, equipment, and industrial products. Imports of machinery and equipment (including passenger cars and civil aircraft) from the EU fell by 51 per cent in 2009, compared with 2008, and the growth in 2010 compensated for less than a half of this reduction (Federal Customs Service, 2011). At the same time, Russian consumers were hit hard by the crisis, which affected above all the country's emerging middle class. As a result, imports of goods from Europe, mostly passenger cars, furniture, clothing, and luxury goods decreased by 35.4 per cent in 2009 (Federal Customs Service, 2009).

The economic crisis levelled a serious blow to the 'real sector' of EU–Russian economic relations, at the same time leaving large projects with strong political backing almost unaffected. While the competition between different energy suppliers to Europe was sharpened due to the decrease of oil and gas prices, Russia intensified its lobbying efforts to draw in new partners to its resource extraction and transportation projects. Budget cuts that were unavoidable, given the situation of shrinking revenues, did not affect these plans. 'Strategic' projects, such as the construction of the Nord Stream underwater gas pipeline in the Baltic Sea heading to Germany and the South Stream underwater pipeline via the Black Sea to the Balkans and Italy, continued to dominate the political and economic agenda. The depth of cooperation is clearly evidenced in the ownership structure: Germany's Wintershall and E.ON Ruhrgas each hold 15.5 per cent of Nord Stream's capital, and Dutch Gasunie and French GDF Suez have 9 per cent each (Nord Stream, n.d.); Total of France and Statoil of Norway own 25 and 24 per cent, respectively, in Shtokman Development AG (Shtokman, 2012). However, these facts are less an indicator of European companies' interest than they are of Russia's need for new technologies (such as underwater drilling) crucial to the success of these projects.

During the crisis years, the Russian government introduced several measures that were aimed at economic recovery, but primarily affected Russian companies. It ordered an US$800 million aid package to the national automaker, AvtoVAZ, and initiated a massive 'cash-for-clunkers' scheme that included – at least in its first stage – only Russian automakers, since the price of new cars that could be bought under the programme was limited to 350,000 roubles (around US$11,000 at the time). The new regulations put into force were considered by Europeans and Americans as purely protectionist. In the midst of the crisis, on 9 June 2009, Prime Minister Vladimir Putin declared that Russia was, effectively, walking out of World Trade Organization (WTO) accession talks, announcing that the country only wanted to join the organization as a part of a broader Customs Union with Belarus and Kazakhstan. While President Medvedev resumed the talks shortly after the announcement, these and many other measures slowed down the intensity of the economic dialogue between the EU and Russia, resulting in a massive capital flight from the Russian Federation (as much as US$129.9 billion in 2008, US$52.4 billion in 2009, US$38.3 billion in 2010), which accelerated to US$84.4 billion in 2011 (Central Bank of the Russian Federation, 2011).

Partnership for nothing

In the middle of the economic crisis, Russia and the EU unexpectedly announced a new joint diplomatic initiative. An ambitious Partnership for Modernisation, conceived of as a new flexible framework able to integrate the achievements of previous stages of integration, was initially regarded as an emergency exit out of the sclerosis and estrangement caused by the war in South Ossetia and disagreements over energy issues. The new initiative was free of the vagueness and unrealistic goals of earlier programmes and was aimed at cooperation in a relatively limited number of areas, in contrast, for example, to the Road Maps of 2005. More particularly, the Partnership for Modernisation looked towards cooperation in areas such as bilateral investment, innovation, assistance to small- and medium-sized enterprises, and rapprochement of technical regulations and standards.

Both the timing and the economic focus of the new initiative clearly indicate that the Partnership for Modernisation stemmed out of the economic crisis that severely plagued the two sides and raised dark expectations about the future. Major official publications on the economic situation and the prospects for Russia that appeared in early 2009 had identified the crisis as one of the main factors that threatened the long-term development of Russia and pressed for efficient new strategies. Thus, the Strategy of Foreign Economic Activity of Russia, published in December 2008, anticipated the tightening of competition, a restructuring of the global economy, the acceleration of technological development of the world economy, and a number of other crisis determined shifts. No doubt, sharp decreases in oil prices in 2008–09, the rise of competition on the global energy market, capital flight, investment shortages, aging and deterioration of the Russian industrial base, and the poor stance of the research and development (R&D) sector underscored the urgency of modernization. At this stage of the crisis and at that level of awareness about the future, the EU emerged as a natural partner and source for the economic modernization of Russia.

However, in addition to the crisis another important factor was playing a role. From the start of his term, President Medvedev, who succeeded Vladimir Putin in 2008, adopted a more cooperative approach towards the EU. Clearly, the war in Georgia in August 2008 changed that direction. It has to be noted, however, that the Partnership for Modernisation became a third major EU-oriented diplomatic initiative of President Medvedev in only a year and a half, along with his proposal for a new architecture for Euro-Atlantic security and a new energy charter. Already in 2008, President Medvedev had reiterated that the biggest challenge Russia faced was to overcome its enormous oil dependence. To achieve that, a large-scale modernization programme was launched. However, the lag in technological development and the general decline of industry, exacerbated by lack of investment, poor management techniques, and outdated infrastructure, finally led the authorities to comprehend the necessity of striking international alliances with more economically advanced partners. International partnerships for modernization were regarded as a tool to achieve domestic goals. Therefore, the development of economic cooperation with the EU within the Partnership for Modernisation should be analysed within a broader context of developments inside the country, notably the modernization of the

Russian economy that Medvedev declared as his goal in 2008. The Concept of Foreign Policy, the Strategy of Foreign Economic Activity, and later the Strategy of Innovative Development of Russia were all adopted under President Medvedev and reiterated the crucial importance of closer economic cooperation with Europe.

The first draft of the EU–Russian Partnership for Modernisation predictably took a blurred form with distant and unrealistic goals. The first paper was produced at the beginning of 2010 and was bold enough to anticipate the first visible results by the end of 2010. The Partnership for Modernisation was erroneously considered in Brussels as an invitation to table European priorities. So the European proposal listed among its priorities the creation of a greener economy, which is hardly relevant for a country with a level of energy consumption twice as high as in the United States, and 2.8 and 3.1 times as high as the levels in France and Italy, respectively. Another EU priority was the balanced development of the Russian economy, which is notorious for its distortions. At the same time, the EU insisted on political reforms as a prerequisite for a better functioning economic system, a taboo among Russia's ruling class. The European plan also proposed to enhance the dialogue with civil society and ensure the rule of law. Thus, the first draft lacked pragmatism insofar as it advanced an economic agenda hardly compatible with the priorities of Russia.

During the first half of 2010, the main priorities set up in the Partnership were amended. More issues were embraced such as expanding investment opportunities, promoting small- and medium-sized enterprises, promoting alignment of technical regulations and standards, enforcement of intellectual property rights, improving transport links, promoting energy efficiency, enhancing cooperation in innovation, and cooperation in R&D (Goltz et al., 2010, p. 19). However, it was not an easy task to trace these priorities to concrete measures.

A rolling work plan (Delegation, 2011) that followed the signing of the memorandum of understanding in May 2010 and was supposed to feature main events or measures to be implemented could have been very useful in order to transform abstract ideas into a detailed plan of practical action. However, it only reconfigured and reproduced the list of key areas of cooperation: widening of investment opportunities, liberalization of trade and deepening of bilateral trade relations, cooperation in innovation and research, the rule of law, improvement of the investment and social climate, and, finally, contributions to people-to-people contacts; there was no draft of a 'road map' to achieve these goals.

Simultaneously, slowdowns and delays started occurring in Russia, primarily due to three reasons. First, Russia had survived the economic crisis more easily than many domestic experts had expected in 2008. The volume of exports in 2011 returned to the pre-crisis level and even exceeded it; disposable income in 2011 was only 1 per cent short of the 2008 level, and more cars and houses were sold in 2011 than ever before. All of this was due to the record oil prices, which on average reached US$107.6 per barrel in 2011, the highest level ever registered. Second, with the sharpening of political struggle in the lead up to the watershed presidential election of 2012, it became more difficult to bridge the divisions within the society over modernization issues. Third, the debt crisis in Europe added to doubts about the feasibility and timeliness of deeper economic cooperation.

As a result, Russia walked out of negotiations to join the EU Seventh Framework Program of scientific research and innovation. In late 2009, Russia abandoned the regime of temporary application of the Energy Charter that had been the only mechanism of foreign investment protection, and the Customs Union with Belarus and Kazakhstan caused confusion over Russia's WTO accession. (Russia finally joined the WTO in December 2011.)

Finally, the most practical initiatives listed in the plan fell to endless 'dialogues', 'exchanges of opinion', 'cooperation', and 'preparatory work on road maps'. Other ideas seemed rather premature, for example, a fast-train railway linking Russia and the EU or the common elaboration of energy saving monitoring methods, when Russia lacks aggregated statistics on energy spending.

Despite the fact that the Partnership for Modernisation was put at the top of the agenda at three Russia–EU summits in a row (in 2009, and twice in 2010), it did not gain an autonomous status, but was rather considered as an initiative able to bring added value to the already existent institutional framework that includes four EU–Russia Common Spaces. Sectoral dialogues were determined as key implementation instruments of the new partnership.

To put it bluntly, little has changed in the Russia–EU economic relationship since the appearance of the Partnership for Modernisation. The most tangible effect of the Partnership was ideological in nature. Considering the absence of consensus about modernization in Russian society and sceptical expectations about the possibility of economic modernization without political reform (Goltz et al., 2010), the support from the EU was expected to add legitimacy to the new and painfully promoted modernization agenda inside the country. However, the Partnership appeared to be manifestly biased since it tends to promote the European agenda for Russia's modernization with the instruments hardly acceptable for the Russian authorities.

Russia's agenda: a strike back

In the two years prior to the announcement of Putin's intention to run for a third term as president, Russia's recovery strategy was marked by a hidden competition between the two leading Russian political personalities. The approach advanced by President Dmitry Medvedev centred on the modernization of the Russian economy by putting it on a new technological footing (Medvedev, 2009). Prime Minister Vladimir Putin, on the other hand, primarily perceived Russia as an 'energy superpower' and tended to limit cooperation with the EU down to few energy issues (Putin, 2005). These two agendas imply totally different partnerships and cooperation patterns with the EU. The apex of the modernization discussion coincided with the time of the economic crisis and the associated uncertainty about Russian economic prospects. The new awareness brought by the economic crisis of 2008 led to the launch of Medvedev's modernization programme in Russia, but it was subsequently aborted for political reasons. Likewise, the Partnership for Modernisation was doomed to fail after the defeat of Medvedev's vision for modernization inside the country. Furthermore, recent developments in the world economy are also pushing the modernization agenda into the background, since the rise of oil and gas revenues means that the Russian ruling elite is disinclined to undertake painful reforms able to break the 'oil curse', given their proficiency in redistributing natural resource rents. No surprise that after a short interruption, the isolationist agenda advanced by Putin is back on stage, a tendency that has been gaining momentum since the announcement of Vladimir Putin's political comeback.

Russia lost another opportunity to move forward with closer cooperation with Europe when it distanced itself from the EU during the debt crisis. There was no substantive reaction to the problems in the Eurozone, and no assistance or loans were offered or support provided to the struggling EU. In the beginning of the debt crisis in Europe, financial relief to Iceland was discussed by the Russian government, but the idea was finally abandoned due to the budget deficit. Cyprus was luckier. Despite the downgrade of Cyprus' credit rating into junk territory, Russia in December 2011 agreed to lend €2.5 billion to the country, allegedly because a high number of Russian offshore companies are registered on the island (see RBC, 2012).

Without properly functioning institutions, Russian modernization has very slim chances of success. Furthermore, institutional and political modernization can only occur with momentum from inside the country. The political awakening of Russian civil society after the rigged elections of December 2011 triggered the announcement of massive political reforms that were inconceivable earlier. Putin's announcement about the reinstitution of regional gubernatorial elections and the liberalization of electoral procedures came shortly after people took to the streets of Moscow and other big cities in December 2011 protesting against electoral fraud. However, even political reforms such as these will not be enough to win the modernization race. While modernization depends on the political situation in the country, it also requires a basic infrastructure able to accommodate investors, innovations, and researchers. For this type of modernization, at least three basic elements are missing in Russia – an appropriate transport and logistics infrastructure, investments, and access to international markets.

The defeat of Medvedev's modernization agenda means that Russia will have to meet the challenge of economic modernization in far less hospitable conditions. First, Russia is notorious for its poor transportation infrastructure. Since the collapse of the Soviet Union, the length of Russia's road network has been shrinking and the intensity of the transport network has been decreasing. Ground transportation speed stood at 290 kilometres a day on average in 2010 against 680 kilometres for the EU countries (Inozemtsev, 2009, pp. 84–5). Transportation costs accounted for 17 per cent of the final costs compared to 5–7 per cent in the EU. Russia has only 57 kilometres of paved roads for every 1000 square kilometres while France has 1604 and Germany 1803. The situation is particularly difficult in the electrical power industry and housing services and utilities. A rise in domestic prices has also occurred in recent years. Gasoline has gone up sixfold from 2000 to 2010; the price for electrical power has risen ninefold and gas elevenfold. However, the increase of prices has led neither to an increase of overall production capacity nor to a hike in market competition.

Cooperation between Russia and the EU in this area could play a crucial role for Russia and bring sizable benefits to Europeans. Today a two-lane paved road in Russia costs US$11.4 million per kilometre when the cost is US$3.2 million in Western Europe and US$2.2 million in Central and Eastern Europe. If European contractors had the opportunity to tender on an equal footing with Russian companies for the construction of new roads or railways and were given the right to operate them and yield them to the government later, the Russian authorities would not have to use public funds for these purposes. The same is also relevant for high-speed railways, since Russia does not have experience in laying such tracks. The thirst for investment in electrical power, gas, and water distribution systems is estimated at US$40 billion a year. Cooperation in rebuilding the infrastructure of Russia could become one of the driving forces of Russian–European economic cooperation.

Second, year after year Russian politicians and top officials reiterate that Russia is highly interested in attracting investment from Europe. The need for such investment is indeed large, since the major part of Russian fixed assets is getting old (with an average age of 16.8 years as of January 2010), and the infrastructure remains poor. Government experts admitted in 2010 that the 112 trillion roubles (US$4 trillion) the Russian government is expected to allocate for industrial modernization up to the year 2020 will only help to halt the deterioration of the current situation, and will by no means guarantee an industrial revival (Zaiko, 2010).

The major problem of FDI into Russia is that it does not engender the modernization of the secondary sector of the Russian economy. Almost 80 per cent of all investments go to mineral production, the real estate market, trade, and financial services. In March 2011, President Medvedev recognized that the investment climate in Russia is bad – mainly because access for foreign investors to the most lucrative spheres of the economy is infrequent, due to restricted competition (Medvedev, 2011). In other words, private firms may invest in a very limited number of spheres, while others are banned. For years, many Russian enterprises and whole industries were declared closed to European investors, due to their 'strategic' nature. Even after President Medvedev limited the number from 208 to 41 in 2010, the situation didn't improve much. In addition, European investors are reluctant to invest directly in the Russian economy: the volume of all FDI, most of which comes from Europe, dropped from US$15.9 billion in the crisis year of 2009 to US$13.8 billion in 2010, when the country, according to government statements, was rapidly recovering from the economic meltdown. The situation looks grimmer if one considers the fact that out of US$564 billion of foreign investment accumulated in Russia by the end of 2010, US$458 billion, or 81 per cent, represented short-term loans to banks and non-financial institutions (Central Bank of the Russian Federation, 2010). The Russian economy needs a great deal of additional investment, partly because many state-owned enterprises invest their money inefficiently, drying up domestic savings.

The crisis might have been able to open an entirely new chapter in EU–Russia investment relationships if the Russian government had not bailed out the country's biggest companies, which were highly indebted to European banks. By the end of 2008, UC Rusal, JSC Metalloinvest, Evraz Group, and several other giant Russian companies were unable to repay a massive US$24 billion of maturing debt, secured by a considerable part of their shares (Inozemtsev and Krichevski, 2009). For example, a consortium of European banks led by Société Générale was close to acquiring a 25 per cent stake in Norilsk Nickel, the world's largest nickel and platinum producer, for just a US$4.5 billion loan. Having bailed out Rusal and other companies, the Russian government *de facto* approved and legitimized the irresponsible business strategy adopted by national flagships. The opportunity to allow for strategic European investment, to bring the oligarchs to account, and, finally, to improve the investment climate and Russia's image abroad was therefore wasted. But, the Russian government was quick enough to provide emergency relief to the oligarchs, allowing European banks to withdraw their funds from Russia.

There are other serious obstacles in the way of investment flows, such as the lack of respect for the rule of law, the interference of the state in the economy, ever-changing laws and rules, old fashioned bureaucracy, and widespread corruption. At the same time it must be mentioned that many Russian civil servants possess their own businesses, which causes a conflict of interests damaging the overall quality of public management.

Third, Russian policy makers speculate about the alleged denial of access for Russian companies to the European market. Discussing bilateral investment issues, Russian officials often hint at, although never directly link, the access of European companies to the Russian market with the liberalization of the Russian companies' access to the European market (Ministry for Economic Development, 2008, pp. 236–7). No doubt, mutual investments require reciprocity. However, reciprocity is often understood in Russia as an exemption from the rules and norms adopted by the EU within its sphere of competence. For instance, in 2007, Vladimir Putin, then president, proposed to German Chancellor Angela Merkel a 37-year long supply contract for natural gas, in exchange for an exemption for Gazprom from the EU's 'third energy package'. Ever since then, Putin has been warning Europeans that the consequences of reform in the European energy sector may endanger the EU's energy security. This issue re-emerged most recently during Putin's visit to Brussels in February 2011. Long before that, however, Putin had criticized the Energy Charter that was threatening Gazprom's operations in Europe and, in 2009, finally rejected ratification of the Energy Charter Treaty that Russia had previously signed. Energy sector reform in the EU is widely viewed in Russia as a protectionist measure targeting Russian interests. Russia wants to invest in EU Member States, while neglecting their rules. In Spring 2009, the Russian oil company Surgutneftegaz, which is widely believed to be partly owned either by Putin himself or by his closest friends, bought a 21.2 per cent stake in the Hungarian gas and oil distributor MOL for €1.4 billion, but was forced to sell in May 2011 since the company declined to declare its beneficiary owners that was obligatory by European law (*News.ru*, 2011). To conclude, Russian acquisitions in Europe are limited to a number of oil-processing facilities, retail trade chains, construction companies, a minor British automaker, several newspapers and a lot of real estate.

The Russian leadership clearly prefers giant projects to everyday tasks. While modernization directly depends on competitive and highly profitable markets, small- and medium-sized businesses account for only 15 per cent of Russia's gross domestic product (GDP), and there are few options for foreign investors to enter this sector. Foreign investors usually receive a lukewarm welcome unless they invest in joint gas or oil extracting ventures. Only big businesses with strong government support are welcome in Russia. This tendency was clear during Putin's years in power, when he stood behind the launch of two energy megaprojects, Nord Stream and South Stream. Both projects, valued at US$12 and US$16 billion, respectively, are now in progress. Putin is strongly focused on natural gas issues: a simple calculation shows that in his reported talks with high-level foreign officials held in Moscow or abroad during the year 2009, 86 per cent of meetings addressed gas related issues, while natural gas accounted for only 13.1 per cent of Russia's exports that year and the gas industry as a whole for 4.2 per cent of the country's GDP. During these talks, conditions of price and supply were Putin's primary concern, including efforts to secure the possibility for Gazprom to buy European distribution companies. Since the so-called Third Package of EU energy policy demands the 'unbundling' of energy production and distribution, this outcome seems unlikely. President Putin's EU policy from 2002 to 2008 was based on building linkages and enhancing ties with leaders of particular European states, rather than with the EU as a whole. The proposed South Stream pipeline project directly challenges Nabucco (an EU-sponsored international project of building a gas pipeline enabling the transport of Iranian and

Turkmenistani gas to Europe via Turkey), which is officially supported by pan-European institutions, but is backed by a number of national leaders, especially former Prime Minister Silvio Berlusconi of Italy. Similarly Nord Stream focuses on the German political and business community, with whom Moscow developed a lasting relationship.

Conclusion

The last four years show that Russia and the EU are – and will remain, in spite of the crisis – natural economic partners. Russia supplies Europe with hydrocarbons and other primary commodities and buys from it finished industrial and high-end consumer goods. Europe will for a long time remain the primary destination for Russian exports, as well as its major source of industrial goods, financial products, and industrial investment. The 2008/09 economic crisis changed little in EU–Russian economic relations: the volume of trade in 2011 was even larger than in 2008, due both to record oil prices and to the growing demand in Russia for European industrial goods, especially cars and equipment. No major joint ventures were launched, and the achievements of those already under way are not too inspiring. From the crisis, Russia re-emerged as a 'commodity appendix' to the EU with no hope of change any time soon.

At the same time, the crisis brought political changes to the game. In 2008–09, the Russian political elite took fright at the possible consequences of the crisis, and even more at the grim prospects for a technologically lagging Russian economy in the accelerating global economy. While the United States, China, and the EU announced massive programmes of technological renovation and channelled billions of dollars into support and development of high-tech industries, Russia tried to follow suit and launched the programme of economic modernization. Even more so, for the first time ever Russia linked its foreign policy to the goals of the country's economic development. In Russia–EU relations this resulted in the Partnership for Modernisation, adopted in 2010. But since the crisis in Russia loosened its grip (the severity of the crisis in Russia was eased by huge reserves accumulated in 2005–08 and the rebound of oil prices), ideas of 'political stability' finally prevailed over the winds of change. At the same time, growing divisions between the EU and Russia on foreign policy issues (e.g., Libya, Syria, and Iran) and the turn of Russia towards the post-Soviet space added to the popularity of Vladimir Putin, who finally decided to run for a third presidential term in 2012. During a new Putin presidency, Russia's strategy towards the EU will likely return to the pre-Medvedev agenda.

The only true driver of change is Russian society, which seems to be awakening after a decade of indifference and silence. Nevertheless, today no one can be certain about changes that the regime change might bring to Russia–EU relations. However, one thing is clear; with Putin as president, Russia is unlikely to turn back from an authoritarian path and is more likely to tighten links with its even more authoritarian neighbours in the Eurasian Union. In this case, the development of Russia–EU relations will be reduced to economic issues, with little or no political cooperation. A different EU-Russia agenda is only possible if political changes happen inside Russia, changes that will need to bring democracy and accountability.

Bibliography

BP (2011) *BP Statistical Review of World Energy*, June, 2011, http://www.bp.com/sectiongenericarticle800.do?categoryId= 9037128&contentId= 7068555, accessed on 3 February 2012.

Central Bank of the Russian Federation (2010) *International Investment Position of Russia for 2000–2010: External Assets and Liabilities at End of Period*, updated 6 July 2011 http://www.cbr.ru/eng/statistics/print.aspx?file= credit_statistics/iip_rf_e.htm&pid= svs&sid= mip, accessed on 13 April 2012.

Central Bank of the Russian Federation (2011) 'Chistyi vvoz/vyvoz kapitala chastnym sektorom v 1994–2011 godakh i I kvartale 2012 goda http://www.cbr.ru/statistics/print.aspx?file= credit_statistics/capital.htm&pid= svs&sid= cvvk, accessed on 22 November 2011.

Delegation of the European Union to Russia (2011) *Partnership for Modernisation Facility*, http://eeas.europa.eu/delegations/russia/eu_russia/tech_financial_cooperation/partnership_modernisation_facility/index_en.htm, accessed on 13 April 2012.

Energy Dialogue EU-Russia: the Tenth Progress Report (2009) report presented by Andris Piebalgs and Sergey Shmatko, Moscow, November, http://www.russianmission.eu/userfiles/file/energy_dialogue_10_progress_report_2009_english.pdf, accessed on 13 April 2012.

Eurostat (2011) 'EU-Russia Summit: Partial Recovery of Trade in Goods between EU27 and Russia in 2010', 9 June, http://eeas.europa.eu/delegations/russia/documents/news/20110609_02_en.pdf, accessed on 13 April 2012.

Federal Customs Service (2009) *Vneshniaia torgovlia Rossiiskoi Federatsii po osnovnym stranam ianvar'-dekabr' 2008* g., 4 February, http://www.customs.ru/index.php?option= com_newsfts&view= category&id= 125&Itemid= 1976&limitstart= 30, accessed on 26 March 2012.

Federal Customs Service (2011) *Vneshniaia torgovlia Rossiiskoi Federatsii po osnovnym stranam za ianvar'-dekabr 2011 g.*, February 8, http://www.customs.ru/index.php?option= com_newsfts&view= category&id= 125&Itemid= 1976, accessed on 13 April 2012.

Goltz, A. et al. (2010) *Russia in the 21st Century: Vision for the Future*, Abridged Report, (Moscow: Institute of Contemporary Development, January), http://www.insor-russia.ru/files/INSOR%20Russia%20in%20the%2021st%20century_ENG.pdf, accessed on 13 April 2012.

Inozemtsev, V. (ed.) (2009) *Prinuzhdenie k innovatsiam: strategiia dlia Rossii* (Moscow: Centre for Post-Industrial Studies).

Inozemtsev, V. (2010) 'Gazovyi Front', *Vokrug sveta Magazine*, 12 (2843), 124.

Inozemtsev, V. and N. Krichevskii (2009) 'Postpikalevskaia Rossiia: Plan spaseniia oligarkhov', *Vedomosti* no. 155, August 20.

Medvedev, D. (2009, 10 September) 'Rossiia vpered', *Gazeta.ru*, http://www.kremlin.ru/news/5413, accessed on 1 January 2012.

Medvedev, D. (2011) 'Zasedanie Komissii po modernizatsii i tekhnologicheskomy rasvitiiu ekonomiki Rossii', Magnitogorsk, 30 March, http://www.kremlin.ru/transcripts/10777, accessed 21 November 2011.

Ministry for Economic Development (2008) *Kontseptsiia dolgosrochnogo sotsial'no-ekonomicheskogo razvitiia Rossii do 2020 goda* (Moscow: Ministry for Economic Development, 17 November).

Ministry for Economic Development (2010) 'Statistika vneshnei torgovli i investitsii Rossii-ES,' *Monthly Bulletin for Russia-EU Trade Statistics*, November (Moscow: Ministry for Economic Development).

News.ru (2011, 25 May) ' "Surgutneftgaz" prodal edinstvennyi zarubezhnyi aktiv – v vengerskom kontserne MOL', http://www.newsru.com/finance/25may2011/mol.html, accessed on 22 March 2012.

Nord Stream (n.d.) 'O proekte', http://www.nord-stream.com/ru/o-proekte/, accessed on 26 March 2012.

Piebalgs, A. and S. Shmatko (2009) *Energy Dialogue EU-Russia: The Tenth Progress Report* Moscow, November, http://www.russianmission.eu/userfiles/file/energy_dialogue_10_progress_report_2009_english.pdf, accessed on 13 April 2012.

Putin, V. (2005) 'Vladimir Putin reshil vyvesti Rossiiu v lidery mirovoi energetiki', Address to the Security Council of the Russian Federation, 22 December http://www.newsru.com/russia/22dec2005/energy.html, accessed 13 April 2012.

Rambler News Service (2012, 10 January) 'PwC: Obzor rynka legkovykh avtomobilei v Rossii. Prognozy', http://news.rambler.ru/12492482/, accessed on 22 March 2012.

RBC (2012), 'Kipr poluchil vtoroi transh rossiiskogo kredita', 26 January http://top.rbc.ru/economics/26/01/2012/634953.shtml, accessed on 20 March 2012.

Shtokman (2012) 'About the Company', http://www.shtokman.ru/en/about/, accessed on 26 March 2012.

Zaiko, A. (2010) 'Strategiia "maloi Rossii"', *Ekspert*, 39 (723), 124–28.

10
The 2008–09 Economic Crisis: Consequences in Central and Eastern Europe*

Piotr Dutkiewicz and Grzegorz Gorzelak

In 2008, less than 20 years since most former communist countries of Central and Eastern Europe (CEE) embarked on a major process of political transformation and economic restructuring, Europe was hit by the global economic crisis. The post-communist countries were not spared by the economic turmoil. On the contrary, some of them paid a high price for their close integration into the global economy (thus 'importing' a similar disease as the developed 'others'); some paid for their own policy mistakes, which exacerbated the depth of the problem and in many cases these processes were combined. It was the second recession of the post-Soviet period, with the first, between 1989 and 1994, a massive transformational recession caused by radical changes in the entire economic system, from planned to market economies; the second recession, in 2008–09, had different roots, and thus the policy reaction to it was also different.[1]

The goal of this chapter is threefold. By examining a large body of comparative data collected by the Centre for European Regional and Local Studies (EUROREG, Warsaw), covering the period 2008–10, the chapter (1) provides a taxonomy of CEE economies before the crisis; (2) examines how the taxonomy changed under the influence of the 2008–09 crisis; and (3) provides an analysis of how and why various

*This chapter represents an updated version of a chapter published previously as: Piotr Dutkiewicz and Grzegorz Gorzelak, 'Central and Eastern Europe: Shapes of Transformation, Crisis, and Possible Futures', in Craig Calhoun and Georgi Derluguian (eds), *Aftermath: A new Global Economic Order* (New York, London: New York University Press, 2011), 181–207.

governments in the region reacted to the crisis in a differentiated manner, with the effect of either easing or deepening the recession.

Central and East European countries: a pre-crisis economic taxonomy (1989–2007)

To begin with, the term Central and East European countries (CEECs) is itself a contested notion and – for some – even an 'elusive' one (Davies, 1997, p. 13). What united most of the CEECs in 1989–91 was an ongoing state of underdevelopment in comparison to the European core. Thus, the grand transformation that began in 1989–91 not only had to overcome the historical, long-term backwardness of the region but also needed to deal with the mostly negative economic legacies of the more recent communist period. Economically speaking, there were both similarities and wide disparities between the different CEECs at the start of the transformation. The similarities were basically constructed by the general developmental model based on a so-called planned economy, which shaped their economic and social systems in previous decades.[2] The differences between the CEECs were based on the ways in which the economic 'model' was culturally and institutionally 'reshaped' during the implementation process to reflect the specific social and political environment prevailing in each country. The above, combined with the differentiated 'initial environment of transformation' (including the level of political will to implement change, levels of social support for different speeds of change, and different types of economic policies that were implemented) resulted in the nationally diverse patterns of economic growth that the region has seen over the past 20 years.

Generally, we can detect a clear pattern in the transformational processes in the CEECs in the immediate post-communist period. All of them followed a J-curve pattern (Bradshaw and Stenning, 2000), in which the first phase of restructuring was marked by a decline in overall output (in some cases, such as Russia or Ukraine, a dramatic decline of nearly 50 per cent of gross domestic product [GDP]).[3] The second phase was marked by differing speeds of recovery in the new, capitalist market environment. The speed of the recovery mostly depended on a complex combination of some initial conditions (economic, social, and political), type of economic policies that were implemented (ranging from 'shock' to 'slow-gradual' reforms) and state institutional capacity for their implementation. The third phase (2008–09) was highlighted by the 2008 global financial crisis during which almost all CEECs (except Poland) noted a modest-to-severe decline in GDP.

Some analysts compare the transformational recession of the post-communist period to the Great Depression of the 1930s (Buckley and Mini, 2000). Indeed, particularly in the post-Soviet republics and Russia itself, the scale of the decline in production is roughly comparable to the losses of the Great Depression – an approximate 30 per cent drop in 1929–32 with the output restored by the late 1930s. However, prior to the 1990s the world had never before seen output drop by 50 per cent or more, nor seen a major drop that would take 15–20 years to overcome. Examples of deeper and even more prolonged declines in production can be found in certain countries, but only in times of war, epidemics, or natural disasters, never as a result of government-based economic policy. Nonetheless, it is probably prudent to say that sudden exposure to an open market economy was largely a successful strategy (Gorzelak and Smętkowski, 2010). Notwithstanding, a heavy social price was paid for such growth, such as temporarily lowering the standard of living, growing social disparities, and shattering welfare provisions (Kolodko, 2000).

The Russian case seems to stand alone and does not fit into the above generalization, as reforms of the early 1990s were revolutionarily deep (so as to position Russia as a regional and world leader), but they did not lead to a successful transformation. Quite on the contrary, in the 1990s the Russian state lost its capacity to govern and could not manage the tremendous burden of transformational change. The state, facing internal and external pressures, almost withdrew from its basic functions (protection of its citizens, provision of health care, securing legally bounded transactions, monetary oversight). The situation only started to improve – in GDP terms – in the early 2000s. However, this was mostly due to the price increase of the state's main export commodities, and not due to an improvement in the overall economic efficiency or the success of structural change.

The comparison of Russia with the rest of the CEECs provides an important foundation for clarifying the main causes of success in a given country, whether they are the radicalism/speed of the implemented policies or supportive socio-economic conditions at the beginning of the transformation. The state has been one of the key actors/factors with a strong impact on the overall speed, depth, and efficiency of transformation. In other words, the state might be a strong corrective variable that could play an important (positive or negative) role in the speed of the economic recovery, particularly when it comes to the efficiency of its institutions, quality of its policies and the ability to implement them. Thus, it seems that the transformational recession was brought on not so much by market liberalization, as by the virtual collapse of the Russian state.[4] That is, in countries that were most successful in keeping government revenues and spending from plunging drastically (as was the case in most CEECs), the decline in production and associated social costs was less substantial. The Russian example shows that both a weak-state and a low-state capacity to implement policies were the main contributing factors to unsuccessful transformation.

At the beginning of the current crisis, the CEECs in the worst situation were those that seemed to have paid the heaviest social and economic price of the first years of post-Soviet transformation 'for nothing' (i.e., they did not effectively restructure and modernize their economies). Ukraine is a case in point, since the social sacrifices and deep decline of overall production in 1991–95 did not lead to a sufficient restructuring and modernization of the economy (Hellman, Jones and Kaufmann, 2000, pp. 8–11).

The performance of CEECs at the end of 2007 can be grouped in four different categories, creating the following 'performance grid' shown in Table 1.1:

1. *The Leaders*: Estonia (but only until 2007), Poland, Slovakia, Slovenia and, surprisingly, Belarus (Popov, 2009).[5] These countries managed to surpass the 1989 level of GDP by 50 per cent or more.
2. *The Strong Followers*: Hungary, Czech Republic, Lithuania, and Latvia. By 2007, these countries were able to exceed the 1989 GDP level by more than one-third.
3. *The Stragglers*: Romania, Russia, and Bulgaria. This group was not able to overcome 120 per cent of the 1989 GDP levels, due to a very deep decline at the beginning of the transformation period and/or an unstable pace of growth afterwards; in case of the two Balkan states this was caused by 'shaky' reforms.
4. *The Loser(s)*: Ukraine stands as a lonely loser, being a country with the most acute problems related to a lack of meaningful economic reforms since independence. We should note, however, that after a long period of decline (1991–2001), Ukraine enjoyed a phase of fast growth (2002–07), which was due to the increased demand for traditional industrial products (such as steel), but this did not change the overall lagging economic position of Ukraine.

Among countries in the third group, Russia stands out as a unique case, since its recovery and strong growth stemmed from high prices for oil and gas, which accounted for two-thirds of Russian exports (see,

Table 10.1 Economic transformation grid (prior to the crisis)

1. Leaders	Belarus* (note of caution about value of available data), Estonia, Poland, Slovenia, Slovakia
2. Strong followers	Czech Republic, Hungary, Latvia, Lithuania
3. Stragglers	Bulgaria, Romania, Russia
4. Loser	Ukraine

*Based on official statistical data that, according to some economists, may not be reliable.

for example, Gaidar, 2007; Popov, 2009; Dutkiewicz and Popov, 2009). Russia, therefore, is in quite a peculiar position, having strong oil-/gas-based growth for the last eight years (2000–08), having huge financial reserves (the highest in the region), but still not able to reach the GDP levels of its smaller neighbours. As Vladimir Popov (2011, p. 41) has observed: 'From 1999–08 the Russian economy was recovering at the rate of about 7 per cent a year and barely reached the pre-recession peak of 1989. Now even with some luck, pre-recession GDP won't be surpassed until 2010–12. In sum, therefore, for two decades there has been no increase in output'.

The economic crisis of 2008–09 and Central and Eastern Europe

The CEECs were obviously not spared from the economic turmoil of 2008–09. The crisis hit them, however, with differential speed and depth. In general, the difference of GDP dynamics between the strongest and weakest performers in the group during the crisis of 2008–09 was almost 20 percentage points, and the differences in unemployment rates around 11 percentage points, as indicated in Table 10.2.

Generally, the crisis affected all CEECs negatively. Surprisingly, Poland is a sole exception to the rule. At the beginning of 2010, it was the only CEEC that recorded positive economic growth. Polish GDP did not decline during 2008–09, and in 2009 Poland's GDP growth was 1.8 per cent[6] and both consumption and fixed capital formation were growing. Inflation was low, and unemployment was only slowly growing. Unfortunately, domestic spending did not decrease. The total output of the construction sector increased by 3.6 per cent, thanks mainly to major infrastructural projects co-financed by the European Union (EU). At the same time, there were also some less positive indicators. A decline of 7.4 per cent was observed in industrial output during the first seven

Table 10.2 Basic economic indicators in Central and Eastern Europe, 2007–09

	GDP growth Per cent change from previous year			Unemployment In per cent			Public finance deficit In percent		
	2007	2009	% points change	2007	2009	% points change	2007	2009	% points change
Bulgaria	6.4	–5.5	–11.7	6.9	6.8	–0.1	1.1	–3.9	–5.0
Czech Rep.	6.1	–4.1	–10.2	5.3	6.7	1.4	–0.7	–5.9	–5.2
Estonia	6.9	–13.9	–20.8	4.7	13.7	9.0	2.6	–1.7	–4.3
Hungary	0.1	–6.8	–6.9	7.4	10.0	2.6	–4.9	–3.9	1.0
Latvia	10.0	–18.0	–28.0	6.0	17.1	11.1	–0.3	–9.0	–8.7
Lithuania	9.8	–14.7	–24.5	4.3	13.7	9.4	–1.0	–8.9	–7.9
Poland	6.8	1.6	–5.2	9.6	8.2	–1.4	–1.9	–7.1	–5.2
Romania	6.0	–8.5	–14.5	6.4	6.9	0.5	–2.5	–8.3	–5.8
Russia	8.5	–7.8	–16.3	6.1	8.2	2.1		–5.9	
Slovakia	10.5	–4.9	–15.4	11.0	12.1	1.1	–1.9	–6.8	–4.9
Slovenia	6.9	–8.0	–14.9	4.8	5.9	2.5	0.0	–5.5	–5.5
Ukraine	7.9	–14.8	–22.9	6.4	8.8	2.4		–11.5	

Sources: World Bank: http://data.worldbank.org/indicator/NY.GDP.MKTP.KD.ZG; World Bank, http://data.worldbank.org/indicator/SL.UEM.TOTL.ZS; EUROSTAT: http://epp.eurostat.ec.europa.eu/cache/ITY_PUBLIC/2-22042010-BP/EN/2-22042010-BP-EN.PDF.

months of 2009. The banking sector noted a decline in profits. Twenty-two out of 70 banks operating in Poland noted net losses during the first quarter of 2009, but none of them lost solvency. Public finance also became exposed to tensions and the budgetary deficit had to be increased by one-third. In 2009, the deficit of public finance was higher than expected and reached 7.1 per cent of GDP. Foreign trade slowed down considerably. Exports in the first half of 2009 reached only two-thirds of exports during the first six months of 2008 and imports only 60 per cent (which allowed for a decrease in the negative balance of foreign trade). Losses, in the opinion of many experts, were compensated for by the growth of domestic demand (Gorzelak and Bachtler, 2009). Thus, until the end of 2009, the economic, social, and political situation in Poland was tense, but stable.

Slovenia and Slovakia have also maintained themselves in the group of economic 'leaders' among CEECs, in spite of a temporary decline in GDP. However, these economies still seem strong, with healthy public finances. Estonia – hopefully temporarily – moved to the category of the 'followers', as the country was not able to cope with the crisis with the same effectiveness as neighbouring states in the 'leaders' group. A closer examination of each case can substantiate this analysis.

Slovenia faced a significant reduction of its GDP in 2009 (by 8 per cent). Due to high integration with international trade flows (exports represented 69.5 per cent of GDP before the crisis) Slovenia was heavily exposed to the effects of the crisis, as its exports of goods and services declined by 20.8 per cent in real terms in the first half of 2009. Also in the first half of 2009, gross fixed capital formation dropped by 25 per cent compared to the previous year, due to lower investments in buildings/infrastructure and machinery/equipment. A high level of uncertainty led to an increase in the unemployment rate. As a result, private consumption dropped for the first time in nine years. Apart from an improved trade balance, due to a fall in imports (which declined even more than exports in the first half of the year, by 24.6 per cent), government consumption was the only GDP aggregate to increase in real terms.

Slovakia's prudent budgetary regime in the few years before the introduction of the euro in 2009 substantially limited risks in the public sphere and finance. Nevertheless, the Slovak economy is small, very open, and industry/export-oriented; it thus became quite vulnerable to the crisis. Strong dependency on exports was combined with acceptance of the euro, which brought advantages, as well as risks. The Slovak banking sector, with its conservative lending policies, coupled with the very conservative behaviour of its clients (with preferential cash transactions), did not suffer too much, but did see profits decrease compared to 2008. The decrease in exports was 25.1 per cent for the first three quarters of 2009. High dependence on exports to other countries has resulted in a serious crisis in the Slovak economy, which in fact inherited its metal (now especially US Steel Slovakia) and heavy chemicals as traditional national industries. As a result of the slowdown in demand abroad, Slovakia faced a substantial drop in its industrial production. This, in turn, resulted in fast-growing unemployment in that sector; notably, however, the construction sector managed to record some growth. Other sectors, such as travel and retail, were also seriously injured (almost 20 per cent on average by 2009). Overall – despite the slowdown – the Slovak economy is still strong by comparison with other CEECs.

Estonia was another victim of the crisis, seeing its GDP decrease significantly (by almost 14 per cent in 2009) as industrial production decreased by almost 30 per cent in virtually all industries (with the exception of shipbuilding). The main reason for the decline was insufficient demand in both domestic and external markets. The unemployment rate rose to 13.7 per cent by the end of 2009 (by comparison it was below 5 per cent in the previous year). The almost entirely foreign-owned banking system suffered significant losses, and within one year, Estonia was no longer the darling of investors. In our classification, it slipped a notch to the category of 'strong followers' (with good prospects for a steady recovery) (see Table 10.3).

The next group of 'strong followers' (Hungary, Czech Republic, Latvia and Lithuania, prior to the crisis) were struggling during 2008–09 with

Table 10.3 Economic transformation grid (during the crisis through 2009)

Super-leader*	**Poland**
1. Leaders	Slovakia, Slovenia, Belarus**
2. Strong Followers	Estonia, Czech Republic
3. Stragglers	Bulgaria, Hungary Lithuania, Latvia, Russia, Romania
4. Loser	Ukraine

*Due to problems such as high deficit of public finance and low innovation capacity, this position may not be sustainable in the long term.
**Based on official statistical data that, according to some economists, may not be reliable. (See for instance: Ioffe, 2004, p. 90.)

sharp declines in GDP and industrial production, leading Hungary, Latvia, and Lithuania to slip into the category of 'stragglers'. Moderate GDP decline in the Czech Republic (4.1 per cent in 2009) can be compared to countries that in the crisis period are categorized as 'stragglers': Hungary's 6.8 per cent, Romania's 8.5 per cent, and Latvia's downfall of 18 per cent. Lithuania, on the other hand, although suffering the highest decline in the region in the second quarter of 2009 (22 per cent), recovered quickly in the third and fourth quarters, recording the quickest recovery of GDP in the region (however, with an overall decline of almost 15 per cent). Hungary has since been bailed out by an International Monetary Fund (IMF) rescue package of €20 billion and its international borrowing rating has slipped since then.

Some key economic indicators illustrate the level of the recession in that category. Czech industrial output fell 23 per cent (2009), in Hungary it reached 25 per cent and in Latvia 16 per cent. In some industries the level of decline was dramatic. For instance, the Czech metallurgy industry saw a decline of 42.5 per cent (2009) and the car industry lost 17 per cent (2009); the Lithuanian construction industry lost 48 per cent (in the second quarter of 2009).

Latvia is one of the most dramatic examples of the effects of the economic crisis. Some economists attributed this to a combination of negative factors, such as: too rapid growth of domestic demand, mainly due to taking loans from foreign banks; prolonged low interest rates, and a real estate boom supported by cheap credit; a weak regulatory system; and strong positive growth expectations of foreign investors (Muravska, 2010). More specifically in Latvia, as a new EU Member State, foreign direct investment (FDI) and export-led growth was based over many years on cheap labour. Latvia's service and construction sectors grew rapidly during 2000–08, but manufacturing was left lagging behind. Strong domestic demand and a disproportionate current accounts balance, pushed inflation beyond the 10 per cent threshold.[7] The recession started in the first half of 2008 (European Commission, 2009). The economic downturn originated in the reversal of the domestic real estate boom, worsened rapidly, and affected GDP growth rates, which dropped to 4.6 per cent in 2008. The hardest downturn was in retail trade, real estate, and construction. Large domestic consumption, as the result of a liberal credit policy by banks (a majority of them Scandinavian crediting institutions) in Latvia, was one of the reasons for a lending boom in the country, as foreign currency loans dominated. The catalyst for the rapid economic downturn was the announced insolvency in November 2008 of the second-largest bank by total assets, and the only Latvian commercial bank – Parex Bank. Despite nationalization of the bank, rapid capital outflows continued, and the government introduced deposit withdrawal restrictions. Consequently, in one year (before December 2008) non-resident deposits, in general, decreased by 19.2 per cent in Latvia.[8] More broadly, the global financial turmoil put a blockage on credit channels, and investment flows into Latvia drained off. FDI, according to the Central Statistical Bureau, amounted to 16.5 million of Latvian Lats (LVL) in the first quarter of 2009, down almost 94 per cent from 260.8 LVL million, in the first quarter of 2008 (Muravska, 2010). Based on these declines, Latvia joined Romania, Bulgaria, and Russia in the 'stragglers' category.

In the 'pre-crisis' taxonomy, Bulgaria was placed among 'stragglers' as its economy (despite some noticeable recovery for a few years (2005–07)) was still showing considerable weakness. According to the World Bank Country Brief of 2010, the economic crisis had some severe consequences, as Bulgaria's GDP declined by 5.5 per cent in 2009 (World Bank, 2010). As the World Bank noted:

> Manufacturing and construction were hit hard by falling demand and tightening credit conditions. Exports declined by 10.8 percent in 2009 compared to 2008 with imports declining even faster in response to rapidly shrinking domestic demand. Unemployment rose to 7.9 percent in the last quarter of 2009 from a record low of 5.0 percent in the same quarter of 2008.
>
> (World Bank, 2010)

However, manufacturing was the most flexible sector to cope with the turmoil. The finance, credit, and insurance sector, as well as real estate and business services, were the only industries to escape the crisis that placed Bulgaria in our 'crisis taxonomy' in the position of 'straggler'.

For Romania, macroeconomic imbalances that accumulated over 2006–08 were reflected in high increases in private sector foreign-currency debt and large current-account deficits. Therefore, the downturn in activity after the fourth quarter of 2008 was severe: trade data and industrial output, and, after a lag, retail sales, all declined sharply. But outcomes could have been even worse. As a result of a combination of massive financial support from the IMF, the EU, and timely policy interventions, Romania has so far avoided a major crisis and macroeconomic meltdown. The root cause of the impact in Romania is believed to be the unsustainable economic growth before 2008, based mainly on the consumption of imported goods, financed by foreign resources. As the Romanian economic analyst Ilie Serbanescu has pointed out:

> The economic growth we recorded between 2004–2008 only boosted sectors of lesser importance to the economy, such as real-estate, automotive sales and home appliance sales. The economy could not be fed, and once foreign financing stopped for these sectors, they began to collapse. Downturns of 60–70 per cent could not be blamed on the crisis, as they were the result of anomalies that existed before the crisis began.
>
> (as quoted by: Goschin and Constantin, 2010)

Pre-recession high consumption was stimulated by the flat tax of 16 per cent introduced in 2005 (significantly increasing the disposable income, especially for the upper middle class) and was also favoured by large amounts of money sent by the Romanians working abroad, reaching a peak of €5.1 billion, or 4 per cent of the GDP in 2008. All this had fuelled an excessive demand for imports, putting trading balances at a significant deficit. The current accounts crisis was converted in 2008 into a public finance crisis, as the structure of the foreign debt was changed from private to public. Total external debt was up from 54 per cent of GDP in 2008 to an estimated 71 per cent in 2010, while total public debt increased from 20 per cent of GDP in 2008 to 30 per cent in 2009, and an estimated 34 per cent in 2010 (Voinea, 2009).

By now, the category of 'stragglers' in our 'economic crisis performance matrix' has grown. Russia, however, seems poised to recover quickly based on rising oil and gas prices, creating strong upward momentum that may see it joining the 'Strong Followers' category by the end of 2011. However, there are some structural problems well described by many Russian economists that might make a speedy Russian recovery uncertain. Vladimir Popov, for instance, is warning that

> the weakness of the Russian economy – an overvalued exchange rate, a poorly diversified industrial and export structure, low spending for investment and public goods, and high income inequalities – were partially concealed by high oil and gas prices in 2003–08, but were revealed in 2008–09, as world fuel oil prices fell. No wonder, the reduction of output in Russia (GDP fell by 8 percent in 2009) was greater than in all countries of similar or larger size.
>
> (Popov, 2011, p. 62)

The 'lonely loser' from the initial pre-crisis matrix – Ukraine – remains there, as the industrial output of Ukraine in the period January–August 2009 shrank by 29.6 per cent, compared with the same period in 2008. The fall in Ukraine's industrial output slowed to 26.7 per cent in July 2009, compared to July 2008; similarly, the decline was 27.5 per cent in June, and 31.8 per cent in April and May 2009 (compared to the same months in 2008). The Ukrainian economy contracted by almost 15 per cent in 2009, among the worst economic performances in the world. Thus, it remains in the 'loser' category even after being given a lifejacket in the form of an IMF loan of $400 million in September 2009 and (after electing a new president in February 2010) negotiating lower prices on Russian gas.[9]

Comparing Table 10.1 (pre-crisis) and Table 10.3 (crisis), the initial (pre-crisis) taxonomy was not dramatically reshaped by the crisis, but nevertheless there were some noticeable changes. The Polish economy already belonged to the 'leader' category before the crisis. At the beginning of 2010, Poland was still the only country that had not only maintained this position during and after the crisis but had also distinguished itself by being a clear and sole 'winner', as the only country in the EU with positive growth in 2009, and – importantly – without any deeper social dislocations. Some experts point out that despite its relative success in dealing with the crisis, the Polish economy faces many serious problems, including weak management of public finances, a still insufficiently reformed pension system and weak innovation (Żuber, 2010). These weaknesses were, however, not strong enough to significantly contribute to the deepening of the crisis. There are four explanations for Poland's relatively strong performance.

The first, and most general, explanation relates to Poland's limited integration into the global financial system. This, combined a certain level of 'traditionalism' among key banks managers and the fact that the foreign-owned banks in Poland were the branches chartered under Polish law (thus preventing the mother banks from withdrawing capital), shielded Poland from the full brunt of the crisis. Second, the size of the domestic market – the largest among CEECs – coupled with the influx of quite sizeable remittances from the almost one million Poles working abroad cushioned the impact of the crisis. Third, an influx of EU funds for the financing of infrastructure investments and other regional projects was also an important stabilizing factor. Finally, the flexibility afforded by a national currency (Poland did not join the Eurozone) permitted for a quite rapid depreciation of the currency; between October 2008 and April 2009 the Polish Zloty lost more than 60 per cent of its value to the dollar and 50 per cent to the euro. Thus, Polish exports retained their competitiveness and Poland avoided the fate of Slovakia, which adopted the euro with an overvalued national currency, and lost a great deal of its international competitiveness. A similar situation was faced by the Baltic republics and Bulgaria, which pegged their currencies to the euro. This is a complex issue, and should be considered in varying time frames. In the short run, the inability to devalue currency may lead to lower export competitiveness, while in the long term the monetary stability provided by the euro could increase the country's credibility. All these considerations have become unclear due to the unpredictable future of the Eurozone and the euro itself.

Is there, however, a universal lesson to be learned from the Polish example? Probably not. One should distinguish between the pace of overcoming the crisis and the capacity for growth after the crisis ends. In many cases these are contradictory abilities, since short-term anti-crisis measures may have an adverse effect on the competitiveness of a given economy in the long run. This may be the case for Poland, where export competitiveness is based mostly on low and medium technologically advanced products, with the national economy displaying a low capability for innovation and a growing burden of deficit of public finance.

How then can we explain some noticeable shifts in the economic performance of other CEECs before and during the crisis? The causes for the shifts fall into two general categories: external and internal. The external causes of the CEECs' crisis are mainly located in the process of 'importing the global crisis' to the domestic context. First, the dependence on *shrinking exports* hit those CEECs that, during their post-1989 transformation, were focused on export-oriented developmental strategies. This is true both for the small economies (Slovakia, the Czech Republic, Hungary) and for the biggest of the group, Russia. Despite sectoral differences in all 12 cases, shrinking external demand may have been a serious negative factor leading to a decrease in production.

The second and the most important factor was the *volatility of foreign banks* that were established in CEECs. This situation was most typical for the Baltic republics (especially Latvia and Estonia), where banks are almost entirely owned by the banks of the Nordic countries and Germany. In these cases, the difficulties of the 'master banks' were immediately translated into severe problems for their subsidiaries, which in turn led to the rapid decrease of approved loans and thus worsened the situation of local firms. Third, *the rapid decrease of FDI*, which happened without exception in all CEECs, led to a slowdown of economic processes and decreases in the balance of current accounts. Similarly, withdrawal of speculative capital increased the pressure on denomination of local currencies and/or worsened the balance of current accounts.

It is hard to measure the level of the impact of the 'external' versus 'internal' causes of the depth of the crisis, because in the real economy they are more often than not firmly – if not indistinguishably – intertwined. For analytical purposes, however, five categories of internal causes can be distinguished. The first is a strong dependence on *industrial specialization* in a narrow range of commodity groups (such as auto manufacturing, household appliances, raw materials, and the energy sector). During 2007–09 these were the most sensitive industries; a virtual collapse of demand for new cars in 2008 led to a dramatic drop in production in countries such as Slovakia and Poland; similarly, shrinking demand for raw materials negatively influenced the performance of the Russian economy with its heavy dependence on exports.

Second is *the growth of wages outpacing productivity*. This factor was especially pronounced in Latvia and Estonia, which enjoyed fast rates of growth after 2000 (especially marked by the EU accession in 2004). A combination of an almost 'uncontrolled spiral' of higher income, higher demand, cheap credit, and unshaken trust in a prosperous future – combined with the currency being pegged to the euro – led to a decline of international competitiveness just as fiscal policy tools were removed from their control. This process was exposed by the crisis and accelerated the highest GDP decline among CEECs.

Third – quite common to all CEECs, but particularly damaging to Hungary, Latvia, and Estonia – was a *credit bubble*, partly stemming from rapid investment in real estate and often denominated in foreign currencies (Gorzelak, 2010, pp. 106–26). The fourth factor was an *overvalued national currency* (as a result of pegging national currencies to the euro in Bulgaria and the Baltic republics), or entering the Eurozone just before the crisis with an overvalued national currency (as in Slovakia). An imbalance in public finances before the crisis was one of the key factors for making the crisis worse in the CEECs (the most dramatic example being Hungary). The final factor, and the most contentious, is *institutional inefficiency* as a contributor to or accelerator of the crisis. In a classic reading of the development theory, an inefficient institutional system should be one of the causes of poor adaptation to a deteriorating international situation. It is a paradoxical and counterintuitive surprise that this factor seemed to have the opposite effect in the CEECs; relatively poor and inefficient institutional settings appeared to have been negatively correlated with performance during the crisis. In countries that seemed to enjoy transparent and modern institutions (like Estonia) the crisis was much deeper than in the countries of traditionally 'soft' institutional settings like Poland and, especially, Bulgaria, notorious for its widespread corruption, and where the crisis decline in 2009 was not all that deep. It seems that in a crisis situation the 'additional flexibility' provided by national institutions with bending and murky rules, combined with (what seems to be an important, but hard to measure) 'grey economy' sector, served as a sort of the shock absorber that cushioned – at least temporarily – some of the symptoms of the crisis. Indeed, this suggests that what 'slows' the system (and makes it less effective) during the normal capitalist cycle may have proven to be a positive factor in the time of crisis, as it allowed for rapid institutional flexibility and revealed the spare capacity of the system – an interesting *glossa* to development theory.

Anti-crisis policy measures in Central and East European countries (2009–10)

The magnitude of world economic decline clearly created a nervous reaction in the CEECs, as they found that they were not immune to global trends; quite the opposite, those countries that were more integrated into the global economy suffered the most. Their reaction was to analyse key economic measures and adjust their own policies. Three of those policies were applied across all the CEECs.

The first policy was to pump public money into the economy in order to stimulate domestic demand and ease the fiscal strain on the banking system. This was accompanied by job-preserving fiscal incentives, such as organizing large-scale public infrastructural projects. Over the long term, however, such initiatives could feed inflation. A second strategy was a series of attempts to restore the balance of public finance through a classic bundle of austerity measures, such as reducing employment and/or salaries in public administration and scrapping some investment projects financed from public budgets. In some cases (e.g., in Hungary and Poland) applying these instruments was the condition for obtaining assistance from international financial institutions, such as the IMF. In the case of Slovakia, the banking sector underwent more than a 10 per cent reduction in employment; in Hungary fiscal policy was tightened, bringing budget deficits below 4 per cent of GDP since 2008. The Czech Republic introduced a whole range of measures to cope with unbalanced public finances, such as increase in indirect taxation (increase of lower band tax of value added tax from 10 to 11–12 per cent), cutting the public sector by 10 per cent, cuts to social benefits, and the reduction of the eligibility for social services; in Romania the government decided to cut public sector wages for 1.4 million public servants by 25 per cent (from July 2010), while all pensions were frozen.

The third set of measures was oriented towards the more distant future, aimed at increasing long-term economic competitiveness. Increased spending on applied research and development (R&D) and assistance for investing in new technologies undertaken by private companies are the best examples of such a strategy. While mainly applied in the United States and China, both during and post-crisis, these measures were also put into effect in some CEECs, for example, in Slovenia and Bulgaria. For instance, Bulgaria presented a new strategy for economic growth with a focus on the development of high-tech sectors and the promotion of investment and innovation as a basis for improving the competitiveness of research-industrial clusters to be developed with the support of the government (World Bank, 2010).

A range of policies was applied by CEECs in 2009 to counter the immediate effects of the crisis. In most cases all three approaches were applied simultaneously. Slovenia seems to be the country with the most consistent stimulus package that was directed not only towards quantitative dimensions of the current domestic demand but also to future technological advancement and to the innovation of the national economy. The Baltic states, with cuts in almost every facet of government spending and also in the social sphere, represent the opposite strategy to the 'stimulus'-based one. Most of the other countries seem to apply both types of instruments – cuts, on the one hand, and on the other stimulating the business sphere, most often by state's guarantees to banks and other financial institutions.

The relatively poor countries of CEE did not have the resources – or courage – to implement massive financial incentive packages, like the ones undertaken in the United States and in some Western European countries. They seem to have coped with the financial crisis in a more prudent way, trying to keep the deficit in public finances under control (though in some cases it has soared – e.g., over 7 per cent in Poland).

So what will be the CEECs' situation after the recent phase of the crisis is over? One may presume that they will not lose their competitiveness and that in some ways the crisis will not only have short-term negative effects, but that it may even bring about some positive results, namely through an important 'cleansing' role, involving the elimination of less competitive business entities. The crisis also may have an educational role, especially in the CEECs, where the citizens are still attached to the sheltering role of the state.

Conclusion

Crises have reinforced the diversity of the development experience of the CEECs. It can be said that CEECs have lost their collective identity; they have become an integral part of the European space, thereby making Hungary closer (in an economic sense) to Portugal and Latvia closer to Greece, than they are to one another. While the crisis underlined some global trends, it also demonstrated the presence of local economic variants; the most lethal combination was the parallel presence of foreign ownership of banks, wages that grew faster than productivity, an overvalued currency, a credit/housing bubble, and a low institutional capacity of the state to react by implementing anti-crisis policies. This combination struck the Baltic republics (mainly Latvia and Estonia), though some of these factors can also be detected (on a much smaller scale) in other countries. As a result of high specialization in the exportation of products of low innovation, especially when coupled with an overvalued currency attached to the euro, or the euro itself, some countries became very vulnerable and recorded serious economic decline (as in the case of Slovakia).[10] There is also a strong correlation between the initial (pre-crisis) economic conditions and the CEECs' ability to cope with the crisis.

Placing the CEECs in the context of other EU countries, one of the most interesting findings is that the consequences of the crisis of 2008–09 were shallower in the CEECs (with the exception of Latvia and Hungary) than in the core developed economies of the EU. This can be attributed to certain deficiencies in institutional development in the region, namely, weak financial institutions combined with a rather conservative banking systems and conservative citizens' approach to borrowing/lending practices. These factors made the CEECs less exposed to the crisis in the financial sector.

For CEECs the global crisis of late 2008–09 was not the only major slump during the last 20 years; while Organization for Economic Co-operation and Development (OECD) countries reported unprecedented growth (despite the dot.com bubble) for the two decades preceding the crisis, CEECs experienced a huge downturn in the early to mid 1990s. In other words, there had already been a steep learning curve for those countries, and most of them passed the 'transformation lessons' with medium to high grades. The CEECs were distinguished from some other members of the EU by their previous 'training' in overcoming several economic and political difficulties; thus they seem to have passed through the crisis with the necessary courage and ability to sacrifice. This cannot be said about Greece, for example, nor many other nations and societies in Europe, who rather prefer to defend the status quo, and not pay too much attention to future difficulties that may stem from an attachment to an already attained – often too high – standard of living.

Acknowledgement

We are grateful to the Social Science Research Council for permission to include the chapter in this book.

Notes

1. This chapter analyses 13 countries of CEE including Belarus, Bulgaria, Czech Republic, Estonia, Hungary, Latvia, Lithuania, Poland, Romania, Russia, Slovakia, Slovenia, and Ukraine.
2. For CEECs for five decades and post-Soviet countries for almost 75 years.
3. Official statistics do not take into account the 'grey' or 'underground' economy. This unofficial sector has flourished after the beginning of transition, and its growth has definitely cushioned the overall economic recession.
4. A good account of this process appears in Derluguian (2001), p. 26.
5. It is not clear whether the output of the Belarusian economy is of a structure and quality that can be compared to those of the open economies, so the 'pure' quantitative data – even if correct – can be misleading. Also, the Russian subsidies in the form of oil prices well below the world level distort the objective evaluation of the potential and performance of the Belarusian economy.
6. This is the figure from official national statistics. However, the World Bank source indicated in Table 10.2 shows 1.6 per cent.
7. According to the Bank of Latvia, consumer prices, underpinned by lower personal income and contracting business costs, declined further in December, recording 0.5 and 1.2 per cent drops month-on-month and year-on-year, respectively. Annual consumer price core inflation slid down to –2.0 per cent. While annual deflation was recorded for the third consecutive month, the 2009 average annual inflation remained positive at 3.5 per cent.
8. The Parex Bank restructuring component required large funding as the Parex Bank (assets equivalent to more than 20 per cent of GDP) was taken over by the government following a run on deposits and the consequent need to avoid default on the 775 million EUR ($1 billion) of syndicated credits due in 2009. The problems at Parex Bank were one of the main reasons for Latvia to apply to the IMF and the EU for financial assistance.
9. On 17 September 2009, the World Bank approved a loan for Ukraine in the amount of $400 million (IMF, 2008).

10. This should not be read to mean that Slovakia's adoption of the euro in 2009 was a mistake, though the crisis in Slovakia could have been less grave had it remained with the koruna. In the short term, Slovakia may have lost some of its competitiveness, but in the long run the euro definitely has a positive stabilizing role for its economy.

Bibliography

Berend, I.T. (2003) *History Derailed: Central and Eastern Europe in the Long Nineteenth Century* (Berkeley: University of California Press).

Bradshaw, M. and A. Stenning (2000) 'The Progress of Transition in East Central Europe', in J. Bachtler, R. Downes and G. Gorzelak (eds) *Transition, Cohesion and Regional Policy in Central and Eastern Europe* (Aldershot: Ashgate), 11–32.

Braudel, F. and P. Gourou (1982) *L'Europe* (Paris: Arts et metiers graphiques).

Buckley, R.M. and F. Mini (2000) *From Commissars to Mayors: Cities in the Transition Economies* (Washington: The World Bank).

Chirot, D. (ed.) (1989) *The Origins of Backwardness in Eastern Europe: Economics and Politics from the Middle Ages until the early Twentieth Century* (Berkeley: University of California Press).

Davies, N. (1997) *Europe: A History* (Oxford: Oxford University Press).

Derluguian, G. (2001) 'Recasting Russia', *New Left Review*, 12, November–December, 5–31.

Dutkiewicz, P. and V. Popov (2009) 'Russia and the West: Linking Economic and Foreign Policy', in J.L. Black and M. Johns (eds), *From Putin to Medvedev: Continuity or Change?* (Manotick: Penumbra Press), 148–63.

European Commission (2009) 'Economic Forecast Spring 2009: Forecasts for Latvia', Brussels, 4 May, http://ec.europa.eu/economy_finance/pdf/2009/springforecasts/lv.html, accessed 4 May 2009.

Fazekas, K. and E. Ozsvald (2010) 'The Geography of the 2008–2009 Crisis – The Case of Hungary', in G. Gorzelak and C. Goh (eds) *The Geography of the Financial Crisis in Central and Eastern Europe and Policy Responses* (Warsaw: Wydawnictwo Naukowe Scholar), 2009,91–105.

Gaidar, I. (2007) *Collapse of an Empire: Lessons for Modern Russia* (Washington: The Brookings Institution).

Gorzelak, G. (1996) *The Regional Dimension of Transformation in Central Europe* (London: Jessica Kingsley Publishers).

Gorzelak, G. (2010) 'The (non-existing?) Polish Crisis', in G. Gorzelak and C. Goh (eds) *The Geography of the Financial Crisis in Central and Eastern Europe and Policy Responses* (Warsaw: Wydawnictwo Naukowe Scholar), 139–49.

Gorzelak, G. and J. Bachtler (2009) *The Financial and Economic Crisis in Europe, Its Regional Dimensions and Policy Responses* (Briefing Paper to DG Regio).

Gorzelak, G. and C. Goh (eds) (2010) *Financial Crisis in Central and Eastern Europe: From Similarity to Diversity* (Warsaw: Wydawnictwo Naukowe Scholar).

Gorzelak, G. and M. Smętkowski (2010) 'Regional Development Dynamics in Central and Eastern European Countries', in G. Gorzelak, J. Bachtler and M.Smętkowski (eds) *Regional Development in Central and Eastern Europe: Development Processes and Policy Challenges* (New York: Routledge), 34–58.

Goschin, Z. and D.L. Constantin (2010) 'Geography of the Financial Crisis and Policy Response in Romania', in G. Gorzelak and C. Goh (eds) *The Geography of the Financial Crisis in Central and Eastern Europe an Policy Responses* (Warsaw: Wydawnictwo Naukowe Scholar), 161–89.

Hellman, J., G. Jones and D. Kaufmann (2000, April, 5–8) 'How Profitable Is Buying the State Officials in Transition Economies?', *Transition, the Newsletter about Reforming Economies.*

Ioffe, G. (2004) 'Understanding Belarus: Economic and Political Landscape', *Europe-Asia Studies*, 56(1), 85–118.

Inotai, A. (2000) 'Core or Periphery? Economic Factors', in C. Lord (ed.) *Central Europe: Core or Periphery?* (Copenhagen: Copenhagen Business School Press), 12–34.

International Monetary Fund (IMF) (2008) *IMF Approves US$16.4 Billion Stand-By Arrangement for Ukraine*, http://www.imf.org/external/np/sec/pr/2008/pr08271.htm, accessed 28 November 2012.

Kolodko, G. (2000) *From Shock to Therapy: The Political Economy of Postsocialist Transformation* (Oxford: Oxford University Press), accessed 28 November 2012.

Krugman, P. (2009) *The Return of Depression Economics and the Crisis of 2008* (New York: W.W. Norton & Co.).

Muravska, T. (2010) *Crisis in Latvia: Economic Transformation, Regional Dimension and Developmental Constraints.* Paper prepared for Adaptability and Change – The National and Regional Dimensions in Central and Eastern Europe, A World Bank – EUROREG – Institute of Economics (Hungarian Academic of Sciences) International Seminar, Budapest, 14–17 October, 106–25.

Orłowski, W. (2010) 'The Puzzles of Convergence: Europe's Economic History in the 20th Century', in G. Gorzelak, J. Bachtler and M. Smętkowski (eds) *Regional Development in Central and Eastern Europe: Development Processes and Policy Challenges* (New York: Routledge), 7–18.

Pipes, R. (1999) *Property and Freedom* (New York: Alfred A. Kopf).

Polterovich, V. and V. Popov (2007) *Democratization, Quality of Institutions and Economic Growth* (TIGER Working Paper, No.102) (Warsaw: TIGER).

Popov, V. (2007) 'Shock Therapy versus Gradualism Reconsidered: Lessons from Transition Economies after 15 Years of Reform', *Comparative Economic Studies*, 49, 1–31.

Popov, V. (2009) 'Lessons from the Transition Economies', Research paper no. 2009/15 (Helsinki: UNU-WIDER).

Popov, V. (2011) 'The Long Road to Normalcy', in P. Dutkiewicz and D. Trenin (eds) *Russia: The Challenges of Transformation* (New York: New York University Press), 41–73.

Putnam, R. (1994) *Making Democracy Work: Civic Traditions in Modern Italy* (Princeton: Princeton University Press).

Slonimski, A. and M. Slonimska (2005) *Specyfika przedsiębiorczości mieszkańców zachodnich i wschodnich regionów Białorusi* (Entrepreneurship in Western and Eastern Regions of Belarus), *Studia Regionalne i Lokalne*, z. 1(19).

Stiglitz, J.E. (2003) *Globalization and Its Discontents* (New York: Norton).

Voinea, L. (2009) *Budget Deficits and Their Socioeconomic Consequences: The Economic and Fiscal Crisis in Romania.* Paper presented at The Global Financial and Economic Crisis: Challenges and Strategies in Southeast Europe, Berlin, 3 November.

World Bank (2010) *Country Brief 2010, Bulgaria*, http://www.worldbank.bg/WBSITE/EXTERNAL/COUNTRIES/ECAEXT/BULGARIAEXTN/0,,contentMDK:20149551~menuPK:305446~pagePK:141137~piPK:141127~theSitePK:305439,00.html, accessed on 11 January 2012.

Żuber, P. (2010) *The Need for Change – National and Regional Consequences of the Economic Crisis in Poland 2008–2010*. Paper prepared for Adaptability and Change – The National and Regional Dimensions in Central and Eastern Europe, A World Bank – EUROREG – Institute of Economics (Hungarian Academic of Sciences) International Seminar, Budapest, 15–16 October.

Conclusion

Joan DeBardeleben and Crina Viju

The three phases of the crisis that began in 2007 and erupted with full force in the Fall of 2008 had a multilevel character in Europe. At each level – the national level, the European (including the European Union [EU]) level, and the larger global context – different dynamics governed the impact of the crisis.

As noted in the Introduction and in several other chapters, the economic effects on individual countries in Europe varied considerably. One of the goals of this volume was to identify some of the key factors that explain these differential impacts. In the first phase of the crisis, a country's exposure to the international banking system and the strength of the national regulatory structures to protect from contagion were, as Inotai points out, of particular importance. Ironically, some countries that had experienced high growth rates in the period immediately prior to the crisis (the Baltic states, Ireland) were therefore among the hardest hit in the first phase of the crisis, in part because of their strong vulnerability to global contagion. The degree of export dependence was another economic factor that seemed to have had a particularly negative effect on those countries that did not enjoy a diversified range of trading partners, or whose goods were concentrated in particular sectors that were vulnerable to price fluctuations or depressed demand (e.g., for Russia, the particular dependence on energy and natural resource exports).

The first phase of the crisis spilled into a downturn in the real economy, with elevated unemployment and declining growth. But, in particular countries, there were also mitigating and aggravating effects. The degree of competitiveness of the country's production and service sectors was important both at this phase and later on; poor indicators on this measure particularly affected some of the Mediterranean countries that took a turn for the worse in this initial phase. Mitigating effects were, in some cases, contingent effects (e.g., as Inotai points out, the large-scale labour out-migration that helped to control the domestic unemployment rate in Poland). In other instances, policy choices may have made a real difference (e.g., Germany's decision to subsidize a part-time work scheme to reduce potential unemployment). While Inotai sees structural mismanagement and prior weak reform efforts as having a negative impact on the capacity of national governments to manage the crisis, Dutkiewicz and Gorzelak argue that deficient institutional development may have been an asset for some Central European countries in lending greater flexibility to their responses. This explanation would require further testing, as it would not adequately distinguish some of the more successful post-communist cases from others. An alternative view might be that although structural economic factors produced a particularly strong impact in some of the new Member States, their ability to manage the consequences more effectively than the Mediterranean countries was due to the fact that welfare structures and public finances had been reformed, in part as a result of the strong conditionality of the accession process, which had not been applied in the Greek, Spanish, or Portuguese cases. Another particularly intriguing possibility, as Dutkiewicz and Gorzelak suggest, is that the tolerance for austerity may have been higher in some of the new Members States, given past experience under communist rule and during the transitional recession of the 1990s. This factor may also affect Russia, but, as DeBardeleben and Zherebtsov point out, even more important was the availability of the Reserve and Prosperity Funds, which permitted the Russian leadership, for the most part, to maintain social entitlements throughout the course of the crisis and to avoid incurring high debt in the process.

Reasons for the particular vulnerability of Greece, Ireland, Spain, Portugal, and Italy to the third phase of the crisis (i.e., the Eurozone sovereign debt crisis), as Leblond documents, varied from case to case. For Greece and Italy, low competitiveness was at the root of the problem, whereas for Ireland high levels of bank exposure were most important, as they necessitated a particularly strong budgetary response from the government, thus feeding high debt levels. While the countries of Central and Eastern Europe for the most part escaped severe sovereign debt problems, this was usually because these countries started out with relatively low levels of public debt. In addition, most of these countries, as Inotai points out, were not hit as strongly by trade decline and showed above-average trade recovery by 2010, in part through a reorientation of trade to areas outside of the EU. Overall, as Viju and Kerr argue, protectionism was limited globally but especially within the EU; while this did not protect the EU from intra-Union trade declines, it led to a faster recovery than would have been the case if protectionist measures had been in place.

Inotai does not posit Eurozone membership as an important explanatory factor in either a positive or a negative direction, whereas Dutkiewicz and Gorzelak consider it a disadvantage in the short term by depriving countries of the devaluation tool. It is notable that Slovenia and Slovakia, the two new Member States to first adopt the euro, weathered the crisis more effectively than many other Central and East European countries (except Poland), meaning this factor requires further study. It seems likely that other factors may be more significant than Eurozone membership in explaining differential crisis outcomes, because many Eurozone countries performed well (e.g., Germany). Since all of the Mediterranean countries are Eurozone members, a comparative analysis cannot be undertaken there; had these countries had the option of devaluing their own currencies (if they had remained outside of the Eurozone), this would no doubt have produced its own extreme consequences.

At the national level, the short- and long-term impacts of the crisis still remain unclear. As discussed in the Introduction, both Gourevitch (1986) and analysts such as Drazen and Grilli (1993) suggest that previous economic crises of a similar scale have induced longer terms changes in terms of political alignments or policy approaches. It seems credible that the crisis that began in 2007 and continues until this writing may also have such effects, but it is too early to do more than speculate about their exact nature and direction. In terms of possible political realignments, in the first phase of the crisis no fundamental change was evident, even though incumbent governments generally faced an upward struggle in electoral competition during the first two phases of the crisis, as the analysis by LeDuc and Pammett demonstrates. This affected the performance of governing parties both in the European Parliament elections of 2009 and, moderately, in national elections held in the period from June 2008 to June 2010. In national elections, the negative impact on incumbent parties affected centre-right parties less than left or centre-left parties (exceptions being the parties on the left end of the political spectrum in Greece and Slovenia). This finding raises interesting questions about how voters understood both the nature of the crisis and the capacity of parties to respond. While *prima facie* one might have expected at least a substantial portion of voters to blame banks and the capitalist financial system for the problems, thereby bolstering support for left-leaning parties, in the first two phases of the crisis the trajectory seems to have worked in the other direction. LeDuc and Pammett speculate that when campaign talk turns to the need for increased trade and investment or focuses on the requirement for cutbacks in public services, then right-leaning parties may seem more credible to a worried public. What is clear from this analysis is that in the first phase there was no persuasive evidence of a critical electoral realignment as a result of the crisis. The shifts in electoral outcomes seem to have been within a 'normal' range of variation.

As the third phase of the crisis ensued, impacts on incumbent governments did, however, remain strongly evident, particularly in the hardest hit countries. Governments fell, one after the other, in the countries affected by the sovereign debt crisis (Greece, Spain, Portugal, Ireland, and Italy). With the prospect of severe austerity measures associated with the International Monetary Fund (IMF) and the EU bailouts and several ministerial resignations, the Irish government collapsed in January 2011, with new elections set for 25 February, which produced a clear defeat for Brian Cowen's Fianna Fail party (McKittrick, 2011). Similarly, in Portugal and Spain, in the legislative elections held on 5 June and 11 September 2011, respectively, the incumbent governments were swept from power, with dramatic declines in electoral support. The end of Silvio Berlusconi's term as prime minister of Italy came not as the result of an election but rather as a resignation in November 2011 in the face of a loss of the parliament's confidence; Berlusconi was then replaced by a government of technocrats headed by Mario Monti, a former European Commissioner (Pullella and Fonte, 2011). After months of government instability and mass protests against austerity measures in Greece, in November 2011 the socialist government of George Papandreou was replaced by a coalition of three political parties, with Loukas Papademos, a former vice-president of the European Central Bank (ECB), as prime minister; after some time new legislative elections were called for May 2012 (BBC News Europe, 2012). Those elections proved to be inconclusive, suggesting an increasingly disorderly electoral space, even though a repeat election in June 2012 allowed formation of a coalition government that was prepared to work within the framework of the austerity programmes required by the EU and the IMF.

Parliamentary elections took place in other EU countries in 2011 (Denmark, Estonia, Finland, Latvia, Poland, and Slovenia); they also generally showed reduced support for incumbent parties, the exception being Poland with its comparatively good economic performance. This did not mean, in every case, the replacement of the prime minister, due to complex coalition negotiations (as in Latvia), but the trend identified by LeDuc and Pammett seemed to continue. Nonetheless, over the course of the crisis, the political impact of the crisis seems to be strengthening, as reflected in electoral politics. Even in Russia as the chapter by DeBardeleben and Zherebtsov documents, the economic crisis may have had an indirect effect on the 2011–12 electoral outcomes and may have been a background factor stirring public activism against the government, although causes are variable.

As the French presidential and parliamentary elections of 2012 and the German regional (Land) election of 13 May 2012 in North Rhine-Westphalia suggest, political parties on the left end of the political spectrum may benefit as economic troubles continue and take on a more complex character. Of greater interest is whether the underlying structure of cleavages will be altered by the serial economic crises of recent years. A fundamental problem seems to be the difficulty that opposition forces face in fashioning a viable set of alternative responses to the economic downturn and the sovereign debt crisis. The position espoused by the newly elected French President François Hollande, that economic stimulus is needed rather than austerity, is hard to implement without aggravating worrisome levels of state debt, even in countries like France. Even more difficult is fashioning an adequate plan that reconciles the conflicting demands for austerity and growth-nurturing restructuring in countries faced with already paralyzing levels of national debt.

Attacks on collective bargaining rights and public sector unions in several American states (Greenhouse, 2011) and the highly polarizing impact of such measures may indeed suggest possibilities for new political alignments and intensified political polarization, in the face of a marked decrease in the influence of organized labour. The degree to which this trend, in some form, will affect Europe is still undetermined. New types of political coalitions may emerge that unite elements of the population disadvantaged by austerity measures, a public sector that is increasingly gutted by layoffs, and traditional elements of the political left. The rise of new, non-traditional parties, such as the Pirate parties, and the increasing difficulties that mainstream parties have in gaining adequate electoral support to form a government may intersect with these trajectories to challenge traditional patterns of party competition. These factors combined may make it even more difficult for the public to see a way to influence government policy through the ballot box.

In terms of policy change, Drazen and Grilli's (1993) suggestion that economic crises can stimulate policy change that would be difficult to achieve under 'normal' circumstances no doubt is relevant to the current context, nowhere more so than within the EU itself. Whether the crisis will ultimately facilitate the much-discussed shift from a monetary union to a fiscal one and to what degree and in what form is still undetermined, but the issue has certainly been placed squarely on the agenda. Such a shift would be of momentous political and economic significance not only for countries of the EU but also for the credibility of Europe's unique model of regional integration. The iterative interaction between political decisions and economic impacts is evident in the short-term reaction of markets to European decisions, which in turn press European leaders to respond; however, more fundamentally the sovereign debt crisis raises the issue, as Dorethee Bohle (2010, p. 10) has suggested, 'about how much [Europe] wants to allow markets to determine the fate of its citizens and countries'. Even if this more radical proposition does not make its way onto the EU's official agenda, framing the question in this way may awaken new foundations for political cleavage and coalitions and may lead to stronger public challenges to the EU's cardinal commitment to liberal economic principles.

At a minimum, as documented in the chapter by George Ross, at the EU level the crisis has indeed posed a major challenge to decision-making structures of the Union as well as eliciting broad-ranging reflection on how to reconcile a monetary union with a decentralized fiscal policy. As noted in the Introduction, the tortuous and extended negotiation process may have contributed to a significant drop in public confidence in the EU. Questions remain as to whether these skeptical public attitudes will be long lasting. Reduced confidence in both national governments and the EU itself could mark the beginning of a longer term trajectory or could be a temporary aberration. Due to the nature of challenges, the crisis may reinforce the distance between citizens, who are largely the recipients of policy decisions, and political leaders, who fashion these decisions in venues largely shielded from direct public input. This could reinforce the much-discussed 'democratic deficit' in the EU. On the other hand, the third phase of the crisis has elicited a Europe-wide discussion, which could, in an unexpected manner, serve to reinforce a consciousness of Europe's shared destiny and thus potentially contribute to a subtle and long-term process of creating a European identity.

In terms of its economic approach as well, the third phase of the economic crisis, in particular, represents the first important test for the Eurozone. According to the theory of optimum currency areas (OCAs) developed by Robert Mundell in 1961, which represented an inspiration for the formation of the Eurozone, the European countries that gave up their monetary independence to take on the single currency never formed an OCA. Mundell's paper *A Theory of Optimum Currency Areas* (1961) explains under what conditions groups of countries can maximize economic efficiency by the use of a common currency. He placed emphasis on two important criteria helping to identify an OCA: the mobility of factors of production (labour and capital) and the flexibility of prices and wages. Other factors were subsequently added to the list by a number of authors. To name a few, Ingram (1962) introduced the idea of financial market integration, McKinnon (1963) emphasized the importance of the degree of economic openness, Kenen (1969) concentrated on the importance of production and consumption diversification and fiscal integration, Fleming (1971) stressed the need for similar inflation rates, while Mintz (1970) and Haberler (1970) highlighted that the political will and a similarity of policy attitudes among the countries sharing the single currency as the most important criteria for a successful currency area. Thus, based on the previously outlined criteria, experts have intensively debated whether the Eurozone was/is an OCA. There are still various criteria that remain unfulfilled, the most important ones being labour mobility, labour market flexibility, and fiscal integration. The majority of economists have agreed that the group of 11 countries that originally formed the Eurozone do not represent an OCA and that the decision was mostly political. However, another hypothesis has been at the centre of attention in the late-1990s – early 2000s, namely the 'endogeneity of OCA'. Frankel and Rose (1997) showed that due to trade integration as a result of a currency union formation, the currency union may turn into an OCA even though countries do not fulfil the criteria before the monetary integration. Simply stated, the Eurozone can satisfy the OCA criteria post-monetary integration.

No doubt the successive phases of the economic crisis have brought this issue to the fore within the EU. Policy changes that were previously not considered, that might bring the monetary union closer to the criteria discussed above, are now on the table, and some have been adopted in principle. In particular, the economic challenges raised by the crisis in the Eurozone/EU were addressed through a package of crisis management measures and, most importantly, through permanent systemic responses set up and put in place by the EU Member States, together with the European Commission, the European Council, and the ECB, which would result in higher level of economic and political integration (European Commission, 2011).

The original EU response to the crisis was often criticized as hesitant and unable to respond to the crisis with a unified voice, allowing the Member States to adopt uncoordinated national solutions, which often resulted in 'financial protectionism' and beggar-thy-neighbour consequences (Taylor, 2010, p. 150). However, after a hesitant policy response, the EU has moved towards creating a strong institutional framework through systemic measures, which may result in a higher level of economic policy coordination at the EU level. One of the important initiatives is the strengthening of the surveillance framework expressed by the 'six-pack', which was adopted by the European Commission on 29 September 2010 and entered into force on 13 December 2011. The six-pack includes five regulations and one directive that cover both fiscal and macroeconomic surveillance and apply to all 27 Member States of the EU, with special provisions for the Eurozone countries. The six-pack reinforces the rules of the Stability and Growth Pact, which proved to be the weakest link of the Economic and Monetary Union (EMU) project, by defining strict fiscal rules and financial sanctions for the Eurozone member states that breach the rules. The economic governance, along with fiscal discipline and surveillance, is further strengthened by the Treaty on Stability, Coordination, and Governance, which was signed by 25 EU Member States (all but the United Kingdom and the Czech Republic) in March 2012. The Treaty includes the Fiscal Compact which will run in parallel with the six-pack.

The financial crisis revealed the need for a pan-European financial regulatory and supervisory system, which would impose strict regulations on cross-border banks and financial institutions. Despite the fact that the main responsibility for the banking and financial sectors remains in national hands, various EU bodies were created to increase the coordination between national regulations and supervision measures. Thus, the main goal of the new European Systemic Risk Board is to conduct macro-financial surveillance, while three European Supervisory Authorities were created for a better coordination of national regulations and supervision of the banking and financial sector. Aside from the new surveillance agencies created, various initiatives were implemented to improve the financial regulatory environment, including an increase in capital requirements for banks under Basel III,[1] which was further transposed into EU legislation.

With respect to fiscal and macroeconomic imbalances, in March 2011 the European Council established a permanent bailout mechanism for euro-area member states that are experiencing financial problems, with the main goal of safeguarding the whole Eurozone. The European Stability Mechanism will replace the European Financial Stability Facility and the European Stabilization Mechanism after their expiry date in June 2013. The financial assistance will be conditional on the implementation by the recipient countries of macroeconomic adjustment programmes and on a detailed analysis of the public debt sustainability conducted by the European Commission together with the IMF and ECB. However, the European Stability Mechanism will be an intergovernmental organization.

Last, but not least, one particularly important EU initiative is the adoption of the Euro Plus Pact (EPP) in March 2011, with the main goals of reinforcing the economic pillar of EMU, of deepening the economic coordination in EMU and of improving competitiveness. The Pact includes all EMU member states plus six non-euro area EU Member States. The members of EPP have the responsibility to specify and implement concrete measures that would eventually help them achieve the objectives outlined by the Pact (competitiveness, employment, sustainability of public finances, and financial stability). The EPP uses the EU open method of coordination, which is an intergovernmental governance system based on voluntary cooperation of the Member States.

Since the outbreak of the crisis, the EU has overhauled its economic governance through a comprehensive reform package, moving towards a higher level of economic integration. At the time of this writing (July 2012), it is too early to assess these initiatives and important questions still remain. These questions relate to how these initiatives will function as most of them are based on an intergovernmental logic. These questions concern whether they will be enforced, given that previous measures (Stability and Growth Pact) were never applied in practice and whether the EU institutions will be able to force the Member States to take appropriate measures against macro and fiscal imbalances, given the existence of a permanent bailout mechanism. However, these reforms demonstrate that the EU Member States are willing to move forward towards a more integrated Union. It seems likely that these actions will help the EU to at least partially regain its credibility at the international level. From a historical perspective, most of the major steps taken in the process of economic integration followed a certain situation of economic hardship. Thus, the global crisis of late 2000s, in revealing the weaknesses of the EU integration project, created a momentum for a further economic coordination and strengthening of EU economic governance.

It is less clear whether policy learning has occurred as a result of the crisis in Russia. In part in response to the economic crisis, Dmitry Medvedev put forth a modernization strategy which, as Kuznetsova and Inozemstev argue, was largely stillborn. As both they and DeBardeleben and Zherebstov maintain, the crisis does not appear to have produced the necessary impetus to promote effective liberalization in the political and economic spheres. The heavy reliance on energy exports, prices of which recovered fairly rapidly, has reduced pressure for reform, and the risk exists that under a new Putin presidency any lessons that might have been learned from the crisis will be forgotten. However, the crisis precipitated a monetary policy shift with the Central Bank of Russia transitioning from an exchange-rate-based monetary policy to one that is focused on inflation targeting, the final goal being the achievement of a floating exchange rate regime. If, after the 1998 financial crisis, Russia chose a monetary policy based on a currency-board with its currency pegged to a basket (US dollar and Euro), during the 2008 financial crisis a combination of factors (banks' unlimited access to the Central Bank's credit, falling oil prices, increased demand for foreign currency) resulted in the acceptance of a free-floating currency (Aleksashenko, 2011). So even in Russia, the crisis has induced policy change. Whether this would have occurred under other circumstances is more difficult to say.

The policy impacts of the crisis of 2008–09 were of course not limited to Europe and Russia. As analysed by Conway, the crisis created new mandates for some international organizations such as the IMF. Paterson argues that while the crisis did not undermine the EU's own climate change policy, its spinoff effects, to a degree, have lessened the effectiveness of the EU's global leadership role by challenging the legitimacy of its Emissions Trading System (ETS) due to a price collapse engendered by the crisis.

As discussed by Viju and Kerr, on a global scale trade protectionism was more limited than in previous crises of comparable scale. They argue that this was in part due to a process of learning that occurred in the wake of the Great Depression. Along with this came the gradual creation of a series of international institutions that would limit the ability of national governments to institute the type of protectionist trade policies that took hold in the 1930s. Governments also acquired other instruments to deal with economic crises, including fiscal policy, stimulus spending, and industrial policy. Viju and Kerr also argue that the EU itself may have had an impact on this process, not only by its example of breaking down barriers among its Member States but also through externalization of that model through participation in international organizations, such as the World Trade Organization, that have established institutional norms and procedures in part directed at limiting protectionism.

It appears that not only the EU but also other international actors face a sharp learning curve through the crisis. Here the EU has been an important actor in trying to influence the shape of global responses, including creation of a new global economic governance system that would set and enforce stricter regulations, with the goal of preventing a repeat of the late 2000s crash. In fact, President Sarkozy was the first national leader that pressed for a meeting of the Group of 20 (G20) in November of 2008 to discuss the necessary reforms for the international financial institutions and to set certain principles for new global financial governance. The EU has also pushed for the inclusion in the discussions of new emerging economic powers, with China, India, Brazil, and Saudi Arabia invited for the first time to meetings of the world's economic leaders. This showed a recognition of the changing international order and the increased economic role of emerging economies (Taylor, 2010, p. 154).

Ironically, the increased representation of emerging economies in international institutions such as the IMF and the World Bank has come to mean a proportionally reduced representation for European states. Russia, together with other emerging economies, is among the top ten IMF shareholders after the realignment of quota shares. However, Brazil, Russia, India and China (BRIC) demanded more decision-making power in exchange for additional financial contributions requested by the IMF. After a promise for a reform of voting power from Christine Lagarde, the managing director of the IMF, in June 2012 the BRIC countries boosted the IMF bailout fund with an additional of $430 billion for the European countries in need. From the total amount, Russia pledged $10 billion (The Voice of Russia, 2012).

There are many lessons that can, and hopefully will, be learned from this crisis, some that apply more generally and others that are important specifically for the EU and Russia, respectively. The broader conclusion is that we live in a world where the level of trade, finance, and labour integration is at its highest in history; thus, a crisis that affects even one large economy or a significant group of smaller ones will eventually spread to have a global impact. Hence, a global economic governance system that restricts risk taking and promotes strict regulations is in the common interest. For the EU specifically, an important lesson is that an integration project among 27+ countries that are at different levels of economic development cannot be successful without supervision and enforcement of rules. Within the EMU project, the non-enforcement of the Stability Growth Pact has resulted in unsustainable levels of public debt in various Eurozone member states. The EU should set the example it aspires to in other policy areas by creating effective mechanisms to assure compliance with the newly agreed rules and procedures; quite possibly this most recent experience in crisis management will instill this commitment. This would in turn be the foundation for restoring confidence in the EU as a model for other countries to emulate. For Russia, in particular, an important lesson is that dependency on oil and gas exports is not a recipe for economic stability and sustainability. The Russian economy will always depend on the resource prices. This is exactly what has happened during the latest economic crisis when the dip in oil/gas prices pushed Russia from having large budget surpluses to budget deficits. Thus, with a diversified economy, Russia would perform better in the long run and would be better protected against macroeconomic shocks transmitted to heavily resource-dependent countries, including those that might emanate from the EU.

Note

1. Basel III is a global regulatory standard on bank capital requirements, which was developed as a result of the late-2000s global crisis.

Bibliography

Aleksashenko, S. (2011) 'Russia's Currency Policy Struggles', *International Economic Bulletin*, Carnegie Endowment, http://carnegieendowment.org/2011/04/28/russia-s-currency-policy-struggles/1s8q, accessed on 27 June 2012.

BBC News Europe (2012, 11 April) 'Greece Election Announced for May 6', http://www.bbc.co.uk/news/world-europe-17673917, accessed on 14 April 2012.

Bohle, Dorothee (2010) 'The Crisis of the Eurozone', EUI Working Paper RSCAS 2010/77, European University Institute, Robert Schuman Centre for Advanced Studies, EUDO- European Union Democracy Observatory, Florence, http://cadmus.eui.eu/bitstream/handle/1814/14674/RSCAS_2010_77.pdf?sequence= 1, accessed on 10 July 2012.

Drazen, A. and V. Grilli (1993) 'The Benefit of Crises for Economic Reforms', *The American Economic Review* 83(3), 598–607.

European Commission (2011) 'Quarterly Report on the Euro Area', 10(1) (April), http://ec.europa.eu/economy_finance/publications/qr_euro_area/2011/qrea1_en.htm, accessed on 10 April 2012.

Fleming, J. M. (1971) 'On Exchange Rate Unification', *The Economic Journal* 81, 467–88.

Frankel, J. and A. Rose (1997) 'Is EMU More Justifiable Ex Post than Ex Ante', *European Economic Review* 41, 753–60.

Gourevitch, P. (1986) *Politics in Hard Times: Comparative Responses to International Economic Crises* (Ithaca and London: Cornell University Press).

Greenhouse, Steven (2011) 'Ohio's Anti-Union Law Is Tougher than Wisconsin's', *New York Times*, 11 March.

Haberler, G. (1970) 'The International Monetary System: Some Recent Developments and Discussions', in G. Halm (ed.), *Approaches to Greater Flexibility in Exchange Rates* (Princeton: Princeton University Press), 115–23.

Ingram, J.C. (1962) *Regional Payments Mechanisms: The Case of Puerto Rico* (North Carolina: University of North Carolina Press).

Kenen, P. (1969) 'The Optimum Currency Area: An Eclectic View', in R.A. Mundell and A.K. Swoboda (eds), *Monetary Problems of the International Economy* (Chicago: Chicago University Press), 41–60.

McKinnon, R. (1963) 'Optimum Currency Areas', *American Economic Review* 52, 717–25.

McKittrick, D. (2011, 21 January) 'Irish Government Falls and Calls 11 March Poll', *The Independent*, http://www.independent.co.uk/news/world/europe/irish-government-falls-and-calls-11-march-poll-2190335.html, accessed on 4 October 2012.

Mintz, N.N. (1970) *Monetary Union and Economic Integration* (New York: New York University Bulletin No. 64).

Mundell, R.A. (1961) 'A Theory of Optimum Currency Areas', *American Economic Review* 51, 657–65.

Pullella, P. and G. Fonte (2011) 'Berlusconi Resigns, Crowds in Rome Celebrate', Reuters, 12 November, http://www.reuters.com/article/2011/11/12/us-italy-idUSTRE7AA2GC20111112, accessed on 14 April 2011.

Taylor, P. (2010) 'Europe and Globalization' in R. Tiersky and J. Van Oudenaren (eds), *European Foreign Policies: Does Europe Still Matter?* (Lanham: Rowman & Littlefield Publishers, Inc.), 133–160.

The Voice of Russia (2012) 'Russia Pledges Additional $10 Billion to Boost an IMF Firewall', http://english.ruvr.ru/radio_broadcast/34718245/78704261.html, accessed on 20 June 2012.

Index

Notes: Locators followed by 'n' refer to note numbers

Printed and bound in Great Britain by
CPI Antony Rowe, Chippenham and Eastbourne

The manufacturer's authorised representative in the EU is Springer Nature Customer Service Centre GmbH, Europaplatz 3, 69115 Heidelberg, Germany. If you have any concerns regarding our products, please contact ProductSafety@springernature.com

Printed and bound by CPI Group (UK) Ltd, Croydon, CR0 4YY

14/10/2026

02233132-0011